Up From Excellence:

THE IMPACT OF THE

EXCELLENCE MOVEMENT

ON SCHOOLS

by
William W. Wayson
with
Brad Mitchell, Gay Su Pinnell, & David Landis

PHI DELTA KAPPA EDUCATIONAL FOUNDATION
Bloomington, Indiana

Cover design by Peg Caudell

Library of Congress Catalog Card Number 87-63159
ISBN 0-87367-435-9
Copyright © 1988 by the Phi Delta Kappa Educational Foundation
Bloomington, Indiana

TABLE OF CONTENTS

ACKNOWLEDGMENTS

Working on this study has been professionally rewarding. Dealing with the cutting edge of education reform and its accompanying policy changes generates an optimism that is contagious and intoxicating. So this has been an exciting work, but not without its frustration.

Like a soap opera not seen for several months, the rhetoric of education reform is familiar, as though we have seen it before and know that we are returning to some old events even as we are rushing into the new. Again, we have one more chance for reform.

I believe this study contributes something to the effort to improve schools. If it does, it will be due to the help we have received from many. The Phi Delta Kappa Headquarters staff, particularly Don Park and Lowell Rose, have shown remarkable faith and patience as they waited for this document to see printer's ink. Also, many Phi Delta Kappa chapters contributed to what is reported here, especially the Ohio State University Chapter, which gave its usual unstinting support to promote education research and leadership. Elsie Alberty gave unselfishly of her time and resources by sharing with us the literature she had painstakingly collected while teaching a course on the curricular impact of the reform reports. Joseph Davis, retired but untiring, sent us page after page of information pertinent to this study.

My dean, Donald Anderson, and my department chairperson, Charles Galloway, gave moral and material support without which this study could not have been completed and certainly would not have been as encompassing as it is. My teaching colleagues saw the need and picked up loose ends when I left them dangling. Joanne Little, Jan Dole, Kathy Shonkweiler, and Karen Kerr kept it all together and gave extra service, even when not required to do so.

Dedicated educators in state education departments, in school districts, and in individual schools gave thoughtful responses to our questionnaires when they had other things to do. Without their efforts, we would have nothing to report. Many graduate students preparing to become education leaders collected information and contributed ideas for this study.

David Landis tolerated my idiosyncratic style of operation. He kept the project in order and in motion at a time when I was not available to help, and he did it well. He prepared many background papers that do not appear in this document but have influenced most of it. He also provided analyses of, as well as significant insight into, the data we collected.

Brad Mitchell, who was a staff member of the National Commission on Excellence in Education, shared his insights and his materials. He added immensely to the quality of our study when he agreed to join in its authorship. His criticism and encouragement, complemented by his editing and polishing, helped us to finish the book.

My wife, Gay Su Pinnell, provided her usual keen insight into the issues covered in the study as well as generously contributing her typing abilities and her knowledge of *WordStar* to supplement my own keyboarding. It is another in a long series of productive professional collaborations we have shared.

My final and eternal appreciation goes to those wonderful people who never gave up while trying to educate me.

Without all those people, it could not have been done. The errors are mine. I trust that they are few enough and of small enough import to make the work truly useful to those who know how important educators are in a free society.

William W. Wayson
Department of Policy and Leadership
College of Education
Ohio State University
July 1987

CHAPTER ONE

What We Tried to Do and How We Did It

In a republic, the people constitute the government, and by wielding its powers in accordance with the dictates, either of their intelligence or their ignorance, of their judgment or their caprices, are the makers and the rulers of their own good and evil destiny. They frame the laws and create the institutions that promote their happiness or produce their destruction. If they be wise and intelligent, no laws but what are just and equal will receive their approbation, or be sustained by their suffrages. If they be ignorant and capricious, they will be deceived by mistaken or designing rulers, into the support of laws that are unequal or unjust.

— "Report of the Working-men's Committee of Philadelphia"
Working-man's Advocate, New York, 6 March 1830

On 26 April 1983, the U.S. Department of Education released *A Nation at Risk: The Imperative for Educational Reform,* a report by the National Commission on Excellence in Education. The 36-page report received extraordinary media coverage. Within the next few months educators were awash in studies, commission reports, and state-level actions, which had been fueled by growing public discontent with schools and schooling in America. As a group, these reports had created a new political agenda for U.S. education.

Late in 1983, the Phi Delta Kappa Educational Foundation decided to underwrite a study of the flood of reports that had come out with so much media fanfare during the year. Phi Delta Kappa's executive secretary, Lowell Rose, viewed the political and public interest created by the reports as a "window of opportunity," which had raised public consciousness of schools to a level that could be mobilized to support real improvements in the schools.

Because William Wayson was chairing the Phi Delta Kappa Commission for Developing Public Confidence in Schools, which was conducting a national survey of "excellent" schools and school districts, he was asked to submit a proposal for analyzing and interpreting the various reports and studies and then drawing some implications for the political climate for "excellence" that followed. Wayson had been a close observer of the Ford Foundation School Improvement Program and a participant in the War on Poverty, the Elementary and Secondary Education Act of 1965 (Wayson 1966, 1975), and other innovations of the 1960s (Wayson 1975). This gave him a perspective for examining the reports and their implementation.

Wayson's proposal was accepted. The intent was to produce something that added to the analyses, summaries, and continuing reports on state actions that already were available from other sources, such as the American Association of School Administrators, the Education Commission of the States, and the Northwest Educational Laboratory. Those sources provided excellent summaries and analyses, so Phi Delta Kappa did not want to repeat what they had done. Furthermore, by early 1984 redundancy already was blunting some of the initial interest in the reports.

We began by examining the literature. We located every possible report and a host of interpretive responses from local, state, and national sources. Both the popular and professional press delivered new material every week.

The reports yielded an unending list of recommendations, which were pared to a manageable set and compared with other analyses to ensure comprehensiveness. The literature also recounted, endlessly it seemed, state and federal actions that were taken or contemplated. More slowly and in fewer numbers, journals, as well as the popular press, revealed names of schools and school districts that had initiated programs or projects to pursue the "excellence" theme advocated by the reports. Descriptions of their programs were analyzed, and some were contacted to get additional information for this study.

The Good Schools listed in the report of the Phi Delta Kappa Commission on Discipline (1982) and those that had been identified by the Phi Delta Kappa Commission for Developing Public Confidence in Schools

4

(forthcoming) were carefully screened to identify any that specifically focused some part of their efforts on improved achievement or other outcomes related to education productivity. The information these schools already had provided was used in preparing this report. Readers may wish to consult the reports of those two Phi Delta Kappa commissions for models of excellence and for contacts with schools.

We generally looked for schools and districts that were reporting success in raising student achievement, because that seemed to be the focus of the Excellence Movement and because we had to narrow the scope of the study to keep it within our financial resources. Interestingly, our observations and interviews confirmed that cognitive outcomes cannot be achieved unless schools also have good social, physical, and affective environments.

In 1984 we asked each of the 50 state education departments to identify school districts that had instituted programs that reflected the recommendations from the reports. Those school districts were sent a questionnaire that listed the major recommendations and were asked to tell which ones they were addressing and when they had initiated them. They also were asked to identify specific schools in their districts whose programs best exemplified what they were doing. The principals of those schools were sent another questionnaire requesting data about the programs.

Beginning in 1984, the U.S. Department of Education periodically released a list of schools that were considered to be "excellent." Inasmuch as they were presented to the nation as exemplars of what the commission reports were seeking, we included them in our sample of schools.

Our purpose in identifying these various samples of schools was to collect information about features of their programs that were associated with their reputations for excellence and to describe those features as guides to actions that could be taken by other schools that wanted to improve their effectiveness. We also wanted to see how the Excellence Movement was affecting good schools and school districts and to report those effects in order to improve policy formulation and revision.

Additional data were collected in other ways. We attended the 1984 and 1985 conventions of the American Educational Research Association, where we participated in sessions dealing with the reports and their implementation and talked with scholars who were monitoring the reports. Wayson participated in the National Conference on Educational Excellence held in Houston in March 1984, and both Wayson and Landis attended the conference on excellence convened by the Ohio State Department of Public Instruction in May 1984. Both also participated in a conference sponsored by the consortium of colleges of education in western Wisconsin in September 1984.

From 1983 to 1986, Wayson, while performing other duties for Phi Delta Kappa, observed schools and interviewed school personnel in 65 regions of the United States and in Department of Defense schools in Italy, Belgium, and Germany. These educators were most generous in sharing their observations and analyses of what was occurring in their schools and districts as a result of the Excellence Movement.

Gay Su Pinnell's extensive experience in instructional processes, combined with her knowledge of state education policy formulation gained during her tenure in the Ohio State Department of Education, was most valuable in analyzing policy development and its effects on classrooms. Brad Mitchell brought to the study the insights of a scholar who had worked as assistant to the director of the National Commission on Excellence in Education, which produced *A Nation at Risk*. He has maintained his interest in state and national policy responses to the reports and brought a wealth of information to bear on what is reported in this study.

As the study progressed, it became clear that events were moving so fast that most of what we could say about the Excellence Movement would be outdated before it could be published. The first wave of response was a rash of reports and books, all rushed into print to take advantage of the popular interest and the well-orchestrated publicity barrage aroused by *A Nation at Risk*. In the election fervor of 1984, President Reagan and his administration used the report to pursue their own agenda. The President alone made 51 speeches on the topic of education reform during the campaign. He even published a piece under his name in the *Phi Delta Kappan* (September 1984). The fluff before the election hardly seemed substantial enough to support the assertion that a full-fledged movement was truly under way. The campaign strategy was to take advantage of popular unrest and general dissatisfaction with the schools in order to win votes rather than to support true reforms. The President's real agenda was more in keeping with the conservative policies of his administration than with any of the well-publicized recommendations from the reports. This present study was delayed to assess what substance would survive after the election.

Hindsight permits the observation that *A Nation at Risk* had been brilliantly, or at least cleverly, conceived by Secretary of Education Terrel Bell as a way of moving education into the spotlight and out of the shadows where it was in danger of quiet dismantling by forces historically opposed to public education (Bell 1986). These opponents, seizing the federal apparatus for controlling resources for education, have sought to promote tuition tax credits or voucher plans under the guise of giving parents a "choice" in the kinds of school their children can attend.

After the 1984 election, the Reagan Administration's conservative agenda moved rapidly as Secretary Bell was replaced by William Bennett. The Excellence Movement was taken up by states and local school districts, spurred by a steady stream of federally generated information showing weaknesses in the schools — information put forward in a manner that subtly undermines an institution, even if it confirms popular concerns.

Even casual observers could see that a flurry of activity was taking place in states where governors wanted to improve school systems in order to sustain economic growth and to satisfy demands of citizens with higher expectations for education. By the beginning of 1985, the federal initiatives and state mandates seemed repetitive and somewhat rhetorical. The movement had levered greater funding for schools in some states. Many had added new requirements and monitoring devices. But the effect on *children's* education has been mixed, unclear, and debated. Reactions from those closer to students gave little doubt that many educators were treating the movement as though it were another of the fads that had swept through U.S. education since 1955. The window of opportunity brought little light and less fresh air into the institutions that serve millions of students. One of those we interviewed put it bluntly:

> Just like the stuff that got all the hullabaloo in the Sixties, this is just whipped cream on mud — pretty on top but the same old thing underneath.

But such educators seemed to be missing a vital point: this new reform was driven by economic and political forces quite different from those that impelled earlier reforms. Previous reform efforts had been founded on moral and professional imperatives and were supported by minorities who traditionally had been neglected by the schools. Because of the political climate behind the movements of the late Fifties, the Sixties, and the early Seventies, school personnel tended to drag their feet or to settle for cosmetic changes. The education establishment did not have to move too far or too fast to teach black children, to educate former dropouts, to improve the status of women, to educate new immigrant populations, or to reverse the self-fulfilling prophecies of poverty. The economic system could support, and indeed seemed most satisfied with, education programs that could turn out a few well-educated leaders and many partially educated, obedient, and dependent workers.

The new 1980s-brand political climate had goals other than improving the schools, and it enjoyed a power base that reflected the heart of America's dominant core. Simply put, the excellence fad was a wedge for splitting the coalition that historically had supported the American concept of free, universal public education, thus opening the way for reducing the schools to a pauper status serving the poor with minimal education, while funneling public money and political support to those who aspire to a larger share of power and resources. With such a prevailing political climate and with professional laxity in attending to festering issues in our schools, the stage was set for the destruction of our free and universal school system.

Too few educators and too few would-be reformers fully realize that the economy no longer depends on workers educated with only lower-level skills. Yet the proportion of school-age children from historically neglected populations has grown to nearly three-fourths of the school population in some of our larger cities and will grow to three-fourths of all children by the next decade (Hodgkinson 1985; Lewis 1985). These demographic changes forecast a crisis for education that demands genuinely innovative approaches to provide higher quality education to greater numbers of students than ever before. The possibility of losing the free, universal school system in America and the need for educating more thoroughly than we have ever done are counterthemes, which make the Excellence Movement quite different from the reforms of the 1960s.

In December 1985 we asked many of our informants to describe current responses to, and effects of, the Excellence Movement. Throughout 1985 and through the first half of 1986, we asked knowledgeable observers to verify whether what was reported to us on questionnaires or in interviews and what has been reported in the literature is an accurate portrayal of what is occurring in school districts and school buildings in our sample. The report we have prepared presents an accurate view of the Excellence Movement as it stood at the beginning of the 1986 school year. We are confident that the material it contains can serve as the basis for effective reform when applied by knowledgeable and dedicated educators and citizens.

What follows, then, is not only a review of the major recommendations from the reports and studies that propelled the Excellence Movement but also a summary of what has been done at state and federal levels, thus serving as a status report on the movement itself. But this report goes beyond summarizing the reports and the responses to them; it presents several features that were developed specifically to be useful to educators who want to go beyond rhetoric. Among those features are:

1. An analysis of why the reforms of the Fifties and Sixties failed in their objectives, with implications for the present movement (Chapter Two).

8

2. Tables listing expected gains and enduring concerns inherent in the major recommendations from the reports and studies that initiated the Excellence Movement and from several more recent reports that represent the second stage of the movement (Chapter Three).
3. An analysis of the education philosophy and recommendations from a conservative report that has had more influence on federal initiatives than any of the reports and studies about which so much has been written (Chapter Four).
4. A summary of criticisms of the reports (Chapter Five).
5. A list of basic issues that help to explain why these reports received so much public attention and support and that provide guidance for long-range improvements (Chapter Six).
6. An analysis of the impact of the reports on local schools and districts (Chapter Seven).
7. Descriptions of what excellent schools do that can be done in any school setting (Chapters Eight and Nine).
8. A set of practical guidelines for effecting improvements in school productivity (Chapter Ten).

Our goal has been to present this report in language grounded in the real life of schools. We owe it to busy educators to present models that they can readily envision in their own schools and communities — models that promote excellent education in free schools serving all children.

We believe that fundamental changes in our school system are necessary. The original "window of opportunity," in our judgment, already is closed; and the clamor that accompanied the initial release of the reports already is fading. But a new generation of reports is raising new issues. The report released by the Carnegie Task Force on Teaching as a Profession in May 1986, *A Nation Prepared: Teachers for the 21st Century,* is both powerful and thoughtful. Some of its proposals seem naive, and it undoubtedly will encounter resistance from both educators and non-educators; but it presents the issues in unmistakable terms.

Ultimately, improvement in education must depend on the commitment, creativity, and staying power of personnel in individual schools. True educators in those schools will rise above superficial actions that have been touted as responses to the call for excellence. Many of the schools we have seen have done just that. They have exercised professional responsibility to mobilize what resources they have to do an extraordinary job that must, and can, become standard practice. They have accepted the challenge of providing every child in America with a school setting that promotes feelings of worth and accomplishment, with teachers who believe that their

9

students deserve their best effort, with an administrative structure that supports excellent work, and with community support that insists on, and rewards, efforts to surmount issues that have frustrated true educational excellence for generations.

References

Bell, Terrel H. "Education Policy Development in the Reagan Administration." *Phi Delta Kappan* 67 (March 1986): 487-93.

Hodgkinson, Harold L. *All One System: Demographics of Education, Kindergarten Through Graduate School.* Washington, D.C.: Institute for Educational Leadership, 1985.

Lewis, Anne. "Young and Poor in America." *Phi Delta Kappan* 67 (December 1985): 251-52.

Phi Delta Kappa Commission on Discipline. *Handbook for Developing Schools with Good Discipline.* Bloomington, Ind.: Phi Delta Kappa, 1982.

Reagan, Ronald. "Excellence and Opportunity: A Program of Support for American Education." *Phi Delta Kappan* 66 (September 1984): 13-15.

Wayson, William W. "ESEA: Decennial Views of the Revolution. The Negative Side." *Phi Delta Kappan* 57 (November 1975): 151-56.

Wayson, William W. "Organizing Urban Schools for Responsible Education." *Phi Delta Kappan* 52 (February 1971): 344-47.

Wayson, William W. "The New Breed of Principal." *National Elementary Principal* 50 (February 1971): 8-19.

Wayson, William W. "The Political Revolution in Education, 1965." *Phi Delta Kappan* 47 (March 1966): 333-39.

Wayson, William W.; Achilles, Charles; Pinnell, Gay Su; Cunningham, Luvern; Carol, Lila; and Lintz, Nan. *Handbook for Developing Public Confidence in Schools.* Bloomington, Ind.: Phi Delta Kappa Educational Foundation, forthcoming.

CHAPTER TWO

Changing Our Education System: Perspectives on the Problem

They dream of systems so perfect
that no one will have to be good
— W.H. Auden

Education in the United States has experienced an ebb and flow of school improvement efforts throughout its history, but particularly since the middle 1950s. Each effort has left its mark, or scars; but few survive and most have left a patchwork of programs, a host of disillusioned and jaded teachers and administrators, and a cynical and distrusting public cautious about investing in new educational ventures.

Much of the reform activity associated with the launching of Sputnik, the Ford Foundation Improvement programs, the War on Poverty, career education, some portions of the Elementary and Secondary Education Act of 1965, and other governmental and private endeavors, "blew in, blew off, and blew out," often leaving little more than a flurry of fancy pamphlets and pseudoscientific evaluations to protect or extend the reputations of those who created or supported them. The more things changed, the more they remained the same, except for a few notable exceptions. For example, ESEA Title I (now Chapter 1), though sometimes poorly implemented, and Head Start have proven to have positive results and have gained strong support, especially after parent advisory groups were mandated to ensure proper use of the resources.

Blame for the failures touched everyone except manipulative and fast-moving "innovators" and "consultants" who moved on to new ventures. Principals and teachers were blamed for being too uncooperative and resistant; central office administrators were seen as too authoritarian; school boards were viewed as too parochial and stingy; and teacher training programs were considered too insular and intractable to prepare teachers to support reforms. Inside the schools, the staff blamed the home, the peer group, and television. Of course, all the complaints were (and are) grounded in some truth; but blaming limits productive discourse on how reform can be accomplished.

Now the Excellence Movement has created a flurry of activity reminiscent of the earlier movements, and it seems to be making the same mistakes. The federal government and some state education departments continue the search to make schools "educator-proof." All early signs point to another round of hype and hoopla about changes that seem more likely to be mere "whipped cream on mud."

Improvement by Divine Right

The Excellence Movement is plagued by many of the same mistakes that were made in the reforms between 1957 and 1980. A fundamental mistake made in the War on Poverty and in implementation of the Elementary and Secondary Education Act of 1965 was the assumption that massive reform could be effected from the top down. The Excellence Movement seems to be following the same top-down, quick-fix strategy. Almost all proponents of top-down reform efforts assume that improvement by "divine right" is the way the education bureaucracy works and that each participant, from students to superintendents, should give allegiance to it and be governed by it.

The top-down, hierarchical model is characterized by a straight-line delegation of authority. Children are to be obedient to their teachers, who get their authority from the principal, whose power has been endowed by the superintendent, whose power emanates from the school board, whose members have been anointed by the state legislature, which is presumed to have gained its authority from divine sources.

The 1960s federal strategy was to use money and status to impress and to gain cooperation from school superintendents. In the 1980s that error has been recognized, so reformers have turned to higher authority – state governors, state legislatures, state boards of education, and state departments of education. Reliance on such an ill-conceived assumption hindered earlier attempts to improve education in this country and will continue to do so, even though experience and research on educational change provide ample evidence that the assumption is wrong.

12

The Ford Foundation recognized the naiveté of a top-down approach after its efforts to effect change in the late Fifties and Sixties (Ford Foundation 1972). The Rand Corporation has analyzed the characteristics of successful programs that survived from numerous federal attempts to improve schools (Berman and McLaughlin 1978). Both studies argue that policy mandates must enlist local teachers and principals or little change will take place. Unfortunately, policy makers who do not want real improvement, or who want it cheap, or who have extraordinary conceit about their powers of persuasion, or who believe so completely in the concept of divine right, will deny or ignore the evidence derived from experience and discover once again that digging in the same hole in the same way merely creates a larger hole.

Of course, it all would work that way if people were trained to jump when the master commands or if they were sufficiently concerned about the loss of job security to cause them to accept unquestioningly any mandates from higher-level policy makers. But they are not. Apathy, cynicism, alienation, stubbornness, or ineptitude may individually or in combination make top-down changes ineffective or short-lived.

How Schools Respond to Demands for Change

The top-down approach to change is based on the faulty premise that the school system is a monolithic structure. The system is seen as a box in which pressures coming from the outside are transformed into decisions and actions (see Figure 1). Pressures come in the form of demands and supports from sources outside the system. Decisions and actions are made in response to those demands and supports, which then feed back to the source of demands and supports. The process is cyclical.

Figure 1
A Simplified Model of Educational Reform

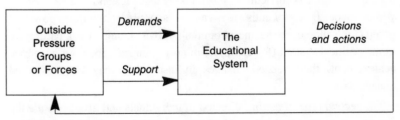

Adapted from *A Systems Analysis of Political Life* by David Easton, University of Chicago Press, 1965.

Serious students of educational change seldom see the system in the simple terms suggested by Figure 1. The box is more complex; the demands and supports are never as distinct as the arrows indicate; and the decisions and actions often are not direct responses to the demands. Reformers from the outside may believe the system to be hierarchically controlled, but they are not aware of the decision-making processes that occur in the box. Effective reform requires a better understanding of what happens in the box.

Within every decision-making unit, there is an authority or set of authorities that has the legal right and responsibility to make decisions. In complex decision-making units, these formal authorities generally are buffered by people, communication channels, and operating procedures that keep them from having direct contact with the sources of demands and supports. The buffer may be as simple as a time limit on the length of presentations at a board meeting or as complex as having to get through the superintendent's secretary. In large city school systems, one may never get to the authorities, let alone find out who makes a decision.

The transmitters, translators, and gatekeepers who buffer the authorities often distort or deflect the demands that come into the system. Outsiders should recognize that the demands they are making may never reach the authority or that they may be distorted when the authority does receive them. Formal action will not be taken until demands from outside the decision-making unit reach the attention of the authorities. Once pressures for change do reach the authorities and are strong enough to threaten normal operations, then decisions and actions usually will follow.

Once moved to decision, authorities may respond with two quite different types of actions. One type, directed to individuals or groups *outside* the system, is designed to reduce the demands for change or to increase support for the authorities. For example, if a speech by the superintendent to the PTA will reduce demands for a new homework policy, it is unlikely that changes in homework policy will occur. If an easily effected reform such as adding seven minutes to the school day appeases parental pressures for a more rigorous curriculum, it is unlikely that substantive improvement will be made. If school authorities can win support from a more powerful group (for example, the business community) by blaming a weak participant in the political system (for example, minority parents) for poor academic achievement, then needed changes in instruction may be considered unnecessary.

The second type of action, directed to individuals and groups *inside* the school system, is intended to produce changes. Of course, decisions directed inside also may affect outside pressures; and decisions made for outside

14

consumption often affect inside relationships or actions. Whatever decisions or actions the authoritative body takes, they will be designed to: 1) reduce the demands for change, 2) increase the level of support for the authorities, and 3) make as little change as possible in standard operating procedures. Decisions seldom emerge from the system without being distorted or deflected by translators, communicators, and implementers.

Obstacles to Change: Lessons in Systemic Resistance

School systems contain many decision units. True, the units are interrelated enough that we can call them a system; but each is a separate and distinct decision system with its own constituencies, its own processes, and its own goals. Relationships can be tense because goals differ and the units often are in competition with one another. As a teacher in a small city school district said:

> The district sees the school as the "armpit" of the district. When I was first hired and staff members from the district found I was coming here, they commented, "You are going to teach there? Boy, I feel sorry for you!" Another said, "Oh, you are teaching the animals," and another, "Good luck, no one likes that building." Still another asked, "Didn't they have anything else?" Our building is the last one notified about workshops, promotions, inservice, available money, or classes offered by other staff in the district. Central office people seldom come to our open house, and only the board members from our section of the district have ever set foot in the building. We are seen as having "little good" going on within our walls. Even in the district newsletter, we have one column compared to two or three for the other schools. We are considered and treated like second-class citizens.

Most school systems are composed of a loose coalition of several largely autonomous decision units that are jealous of their prerogatives, seldom see themselves as engaged in the same common enterprise, often work against each other, and simultaneously blame others for their problems while seeking protection by giving an appearance of solidarity. As an assistant principal of a school in a medium-sized city told us:

> Another advantage a new principal will have in this school is central office — not because central office will do anything and everything possible to help, I mean the opposite. Central office is much more concerned about the way the other high schools are run. It will be easier for the principal at our school to initiate change toward the effective school without a lot of interference or questioning from above. The central office looks at this school as being a low-achieving area;

thus, they will not be concerned if we do things differently. So the new principal can run the building the way he wants, where other principals will have to answer to the board for any changes they want to make. One disadvantage, though, is the central office's desire to have all the schools similar.

Like other organizations, school systems tend to resist fundamental change and to protect themselves from disruption. The resistance is compounded because a school system is a loosely coupled set of sovereign systems; therefore, reform efforts must pass through several separate buffers and authorities before they touch the students (Hawley 1984).

The concept of loosely coupled systems (Weick 1982) helps us to understand that top-down reform, particularly to achieve positive outcomes for students, is very difficult in school systems. Of course, built-in resistance to change has advantages if the costs and consequences of changing the system outweigh the benefits. Nevertheless, political and bureaucratic inertia may shield incompetence, hurt students, or make schools impervious to necessary improvements. For good or ill, inertia generally exists and must be accounted for in any reform effort, especially if massive change is desired.

Our education system can be thought of as four decision units: the state education department, the local district office, the school building, and the classroom. Each decision unit responds to outside pressures and demands as well as to pressures on each other. But they also may function as a buffer for one another. For example, the district office may protect teachers from angry taxpayer groups, or building principals may look to district administrators to protect them from state education department mandates to improve teacher performance. The principal of a school in a small suburban district told us:

> We had much discontent aroused when our program for high achievers was implemented several years ago. We are used to participating in decisions and curriculum planning; however, the district's programs for "gifted" students were not what some other surrounding schools were offering and not what parents wanted them to be. Our teachers were told, with little notice, that they were to teach "gifted" students in a pull-out program two days each week outside of regular teaching time. No training or preparation preceded this, and teachers were caught by surprise. The decisions came from central office, not from the principal. Since that time our staff has been very wary of and resistant to anything handed down. The gifted program has not run smoothly. Two building coordinators have come and gone. The position is presently open, and no one from within will take it.

16

The state education department usually is viewed as the top rung in a hierarchical decision-making model, but its ability to influence the local school system is much less than the hierarchical model would imply. Indeed, in many states the department may be viewed as an enemy and as a serious threat to local control. A teacher from a small rural school district said:

> Some recent mandates from the state department of education and the county board of education were implemented in the form of curriculum revisions. These changes were administered by the county board of education with guidance from the state department. The process of change was significantly hampered and sabotaged by the ambiguous nature of directives from the state department and by their frequent alterations in the original plan after implementation had begun. . . . Lack of foresight and thorough planning made the changes and the process less effective and more cumbersome than would seem necessary. Teachers lose faith in a plan that wastes their time and is poorly conceived.

The decision unit most crucial to authentic reform is the individual teacher in the classroom. Teachers may feel they have little power to implement changes beyond their own classrooms; yet it is this very power in the classroom that gives them virtual *veto power* over reforms initiated at other decision levels. While teachers cannot ensure that reforms will work, they can guarantee failure if they choose to do so. Moreover, teachers generally will oppose changes that appear to alter their work lives in ways that require more time and energy than they are willing to give. A teacher in a suburban district described another teacher's exercise of such power.

> The staff at my school includes a teacher who is strong-willed and outspoken. She is the informal power and leader of the teachers. She changed classes to avoid a new organization, and she is reluctant to use any new course of study and new textbooks. She freely admits that she does not want to take the time to acquaint herself with new materials. She actually cried when the psychologist reported that a low-achieving student did not test out of her class and into SLD [Severe Learning Disabled]. She then ignored the recommendations for giving individual help and assignments. Her dominance and power influenced the principal and molded his attitude toward students, parents, some staff, and discipline techniques. The staff has changed enough to reduce her power somewhat. Some of her friends have retired, while others have transferred. Still others have become disenchanted with her philosophies. New teachers have not shared her negative orientation toward children.

17

No policy changes will yield the desired improvements in student achievement unless they enlist teachers' commitment and support. The fatal flaw of top-down reform is the tendency to overlook the layers of decision involved in the daily enterprise of schooling. Failure to account for all those layers that lie between those who are demanding change and the teachers who actually carry out the change reduced the impact of reforms in the 1960s.

If the Excellence Movement reformers continue to act as though improvements in the U.S. education system can be mandated by higher authorities, they too will have little impact unless they take appropriate actions to ensure that teachers in classrooms recognize the need to change, feel that improvement is possible, have some sense of ownership in making improvements, and are committed to adapting their work lives to make change happen.

The Excellence Movement: Prospects for Change

When the federal government released *A Nation at Risk* in response to growing public dissatisfaction with the American educational product, it became one of the external pressures on state education departments and local school districts and set in motion some 225 commissions or task forces devoted to reform. Nearly every chief state school officer and many governors felt compelled to show an anxious public that something was being done. One year after publication of *A Nation at Risk,* the U.S. Department of Education released *The Nation Responds* and reported these actions:

> The number and quality of changes being publicized suggest a powerful and broad-based movement. Many local boards created their own local commissions and task forces . . . and rated their own schools against checklists of the findings and recommendations of the national reports. The National School Boards Association distributed about 100,000 checklists to local boards. (U.S. Department of Education, 1984, p. 16)

According to that report, states and local boards initiated "study groups on excellence," "joint statements," and "projects to enhance communication"; prepared "handbooks for implementation"; and presented "suggestions for action." Superintendents issued one, sometimes two, "reports" and distributed numerous "brochures." Numerous school boards developed five-year plans, and citizens' groups and blue-ribbon committees "assessed needs" and established "priorities." At conferences the word "excellence" appeared in most speeches made between 1982 and 1987.

Both state education agencies and local districts trotted out programs that had been under way before the Excellence Movement began in order to show how far ahead of the reform proposals they had been. Truly effective programs that had been under fire and poorly supported by higher authorities were brought into the spotlight and given somewhat longer and occasionally fuller lives. Pilot projects were created with vague directives and little connection to everyday activities in the schools. A flurry of activity was under way; but it hardly constituted a monumental movement, nor was it different from earlier movements.

While extolling the "comprehensive" changes that followed *A Nation at Risk,* the authors of *The Nation Responds* warned that:

> difficult, seemingly intractable problems of implementation and practicality remain to be understood and attacked. . . . It has always been clear that changes in one area of education, such as graduation requirements, immediately affect virtually all others, including the time available for instruction, the role and qualifications of teachers, fundamental questions about the purpose of American secondary schools, and local leadership and fiscal support. (p. 19)

This recognition of the systemic nature of the American school enterprise was not accompanied by any suggestions for systemic solutions.

The report goes on to praise citizens, educators, and leaders of business and government for "acting on the understanding that education is a seamless garment, and . . . proposing and supporting comprehensive solutions." Yet examination of the Excellence Movement indicates that it is piecemeal, top-down, and (except in a few states) almost oblivious to the true nature of the "seamless garment" that is the American school system. What seems likely is that the education system will produce more of the shallow cosmetics that it produced in the 1960s, while the search for solutions for truly difficult issues that plague the system is ignored.

Internal Barriers to School Reform

In the literature on school reform, little attention has been paid to what is commonly known inside the profession: the greatest barriers to school improvements are within the school system. True, some barriers may originate from outside; for example, real estate interests may not want schools desegregated. But those external groups depend on authorities inside the school system to take steps to ensure that their interests are served. Insiders are predisposed to defend the status quo either because they believe in it or because they have been trained in ways that blind them to other possibilities. Some few, of course, know on which side their bread is buttered and acquiesce when confronted with outside pressure. The pressure on the cen-

tral office is captured in the comment below from a secondary principal in a large school system in a Midwestern city.

> Every other thing in the world matters except the kids. The blacks and the Catholics are fighting over who will get the jobs, and quality be damned. The mainstream white Protestants, who used to control the system, have given up and moved to the suburbs. Fundamentalists want to keep the blacks out of *their* schools — and they are convinced that they are "theirs." The union wants to protect its membership. No one in the central office has thought about kids in years. We just stay in our school, keep our noses clean, and try to keep education going.

Most central office insiders know about "turf" battles in school systems, although little has been published about these internecine wars that on occasion rival any contest for the English throne. A researcher in a Midwestern city described the origin of one such battle:

> The school was among the best schools we have seen. Achievement was unbelievably high, staff morale unparalleled. Student deportment and morale was reflected in easy relationships with the staff combined with politeness and eager participation. And the evaluations on every dimension indicated high levels of production. Most all of it was due to the principal's unrelenting commitment to high expectations and his ability to win enough trust and commitment from the teachers to make it happen. Unfortunately, he had been a rival candidate for the superintendency and the new superintendent is easily threatened.

An assistant principal in the same city added:

> Now, the new superintendent is killing the program with apparent kindness. The principal has been "promoted" into a central office staff job with a charge to extend the program into all the schools. He even got a raise. Everyone who understands city districts can see what really has happened. The change agent has lost all line authority, and the subtle message now out to the staff is: "You don't have to do all of that hard work anymore." They also sense that what they have done is not really going to win any points. A few years from now there won't be a sign of what has been accomplished here.

Knowing about power contests in the central office, and realizing that extra efforts may not be rewarded and, indeed, may be punished, principals may become cautious about change and watch from the sidelines to see which direction to take. An assistant superintendent in an Eastern seaboard city described the caution practiced by principals:

School principals are survivors. They are adept at seeing how the wind is blowing, and they know how to play whatever game is in vogue. They watch the signs carefully to see what is getting support and what is not. They can tell who will be "in" for a while and who will not. They know who has real authority and who does not. And they know that survival comes to those who play on the winning side.

Many an innovative superintendent will attest that resistance from principals can sound a death knell to the chief executive's fondest hopes for improving a school system. One of our researchers gave this account of a large Midwestern city:

> The city was sponsoring one of the largest teacher inservice programs it had had in a long time: two weeks of Ron Edmonds and Wilbur Brookover and effective schools. It really was a play into the hands of the feds because 200 schools were still all black or all Hispanic, and the Justice Department wanted to "prove" that those "desegregated" schools would work. Now, when you call those schools "desegregated," that sends a message throughout the district anyway — and that one is from Washington. The message is, "No change is wanted, but make it look good." The people in those schools have been getting that same message since 1960, so they know nothing will happen. I stopped three separate people in the first floor lobby of the central office and asked them what they thought of the effective schools program. All of them were principals in schools in the city, but none of them had heard of it. That told me something right away, but I explained what it was and that the superintendent was sponsoring it. All three gave me the same answer, "Oh, you mean those people upstairs; they will be gone in three years."

Knowledgeable school administrators know that their formal authority is limited, but they amplify it by winning support from important constituent groups both inside and outside the system; and they utilize whatever authority and status they can muster to bolster the chances for an innovation to succeed. A principal in a Midwestern city described how the superintendent won support in the schools:

> The superintendent asks people to do what they are hired to do. He also attends all of the staff development meetings and shows by his presence and participation that it is considered important.

An assistant superintendent in a Southeastern city described the superintendent in that school system as follows:

> I can't tell you any better thing about [the superintendent] than that he can do what he says he can do, and he does what he says he will

21

do. You can trust him all the way. He also has a way of convincing us that we can do whatever we set out to do, and he does all he can to make it true. He is the best thing that ever happened to this city, and lots of us would go many extra miles for him.

There are many programs that serve a local community or neighborhood very well; but their life-span is confined to the tenure of the innovator, and they do not necessarily spread to other schools in the district. A principal in a highly effective school serving a population of children almost totally on the free-lunch program reported her frustration:

> When you keep poor kids under control, the world will praise you highly. But if you dare teach them too well, you will have to struggle to keep the school alive. It isn't only the community; the school system is full of teachers and principals who "paid their dues" down here and *know* these kids can't learn. They get very fidgety when someone raises test scores; we have been accused every year of cheating.

No one group holds a franchise on resistance. School principals can prevent teachers from solving problems and improving schools just as teachers can refuse to take any responsibility. A teacher in a Western middle school reported:

> I went to the principal and said I would chair the committee to develop the school's philosophy and goals if the staff members would be involved. Receiving an affirmative answer, I wrote up a timeline that included many staff meetings with small-group discussion. I provided handouts on the important reasons why we had to have a philosophy with input from all people in the building and recommended he read several chapters from two books on the subject. In the end, we had one staff meeting for informational reasons, but no discussions. All staff members were to write up several statements as to what they felt was their philosophy. That was the extent of "whole staff involvement." A philosophy committee of five synthesized the statements and wrote the school philosophy. It was approved by the staff in 30 minutes at a teachers' meeting.

A teacher in a Southern high school described the resistance to change by the principal in that school:

> The annual fights have started this month as the principal begins to formulate next year's schedule. As usual, there is little participation from the staff. Department heads, who have basically been conditioned to agree with the principal, give little representation to everyone's view. As one teacher put it, "Remember, we don't discuss things around here." The informal leaders of the school have tried to persuade the principal

that we want a schedule in which a group of 125 students would be shared by four or five teachers with a common planning period. Teachers could develop strategies for dealing with certain students. Consistency among those teachers and shared, coordinated lessons and units would benefit the children's overall education. Such a schedule would help students see how all subjects interrelate while teachers can work together rather than isolate themselves in a classroom. We won't get it this year.

The foregoing discussion does not exhaust the internal barriers to good education. Others include jealousies among school buildings and neighborhoods, distrust among staff in a building, and organizational structures that erode loyalty and responsibility among personnel at all levels. Rather, our purpose is simply to illustrate the many human forces that govern whether a reform will be successfully implemented.

Real Success or Pretense

Experience with past reforms suggests that if the following conditions exist, it is likely that the program will have a short life, and little genuine improvement will occur:

1. If the person put in charge is one who had a lot to do with creating the problem and never did anything to solve it, the program will be unlikely to get anywhere.

2. If the person responsible for implementing the reform is a political appointee or a friend of someone in authority and has no demonstrable credentials, the project is unlikely to gain the staff's commitment.

3. If the director has no ties to the informal power structure and has no track record that has earned respect and prestige, the project is not likely to succeed.

4. If the program is seen as the property of only one or a few people and is referred to as "John's program" or "their" program, the program will die as soon as the "owner" loses official power and can no longer offer rewards to buy participation.

5. If the people who must carry it out cannot describe the project and its objectives, the project has not penetrated enough decision levels to be successful.

6. If the program has been given a name with an acronym and a lot of publicity, and if it is separated from the normal functioning of the school, it usually will have a short and shallow life. Giving the program a name also gives the opposition a label to attack.

7. If a program's alleged successes are vague, difficult to ascertain, and poorly documented, it most likely will die the death of most education fads.

8. If the informal power structure attributes the program's successes to extra money, resources, and personnel, it probably will not be implemented elsewhere in the system. Such "extras" serve as excuses for others not to try the program.

9. If only line-authority personnel are committed to the program but are unwilling to defend and support it, it usually will be unsuccessful.

10. If the proposal requires expensive materials, outside consultants, packaged programs, or other extra-cost factors, it is highly unlikely to survive.

11. If teachers are not involved in creating the program or are recruited into it reluctantly, it will face stiff opposition and is unlikely to succeed.

12. If the program deviates dramatically from normal operating procedures in the school or district, or if personnel working with students can not convey the program's objectives to them and their parents, the program is not likely to survive unless some advocate has considerable influence with parents.

13. If the principal in the school where the project is implemented is not committed to it or feels unable to control it, the project will survive only by extraordinary effort from project personnel.

14. If the innovation requires personnel to perform functions that they are unable to perform or that they think they should not perform, then they must have intensive training and continuous support or the innovation will not survive.

Politics and Change in Bureaucracies

The politics of reform and the needs of education bureaucracies frequently are not compatible. Politics is a process of managing scarcity and conflict among diverse interests in unstable environments. Bureaucracies are concerned with the use of resources in a controlled and routinized setting that creates its own sense of stability. The mix of politics and bureaucracies during an era of reform can produce responses ranging from strategic resistance to creative insubordination. Anyone truly committed to systemic improvements must accept the tedious and long-range task of dealing with the internal decision systems that directly affect student outcomes. Anything less will be "ex" before it is excellent.

References

Barr, Rebecca, and Dreeben, Robert. *How Schools Work.* Chicago: University of Chicago Press, 1983.

Berman, Paul, and McLaughlin, Milbray. *Federal Programs Supporting Educational Change, Volume III: Implementing and Sustaining Innovations.* Santa Monica, Calif.: Rand Corporation, 1978.

Blumberg, Arthur. *Supervisors and Teachers: A Private Cold War.* Berkeley, Calif.: McCutchan, 1980.

Brown, Rexford. "Reform by Fiat Will Not Work." *State Education Leader* 3 (Winter 1984): 13.

Cuban, Larry. "Persistent Instruction: Another Look at Constancy in the Classroom." *Phi Delta Kappan* 68 (September 1986): 7-11.

Easton, David. *A Systems Analysis of Political Life.* New York: Wiley, 1965.

Easton, David. *A Framework for Political Analysis.* Englewood Cliffs, N.J.: Prentice-Hall, 1965.

Ford Foundation. *A Foundation Goes to School: The Ford Foundation Comprehensive School Improvement Program, 1960-1970.* New York, 1972.

Guthrie, James W., and Timar, Thomas B. "Public Values and Public School Policy in the 1980's." *Educational Leadership* (November 1980): 112-16.

Hawley, Willis D. "Improving Schools by Ending Poverty." *Education Digest* 49 (April 1984): 20-22.

Lortie, Dan C. "Teacher Status in Dade County: A Case of Structural Strain?" *Phi Delta Kappan* 67 (April 1986): 568-75.

Lortie, Dan C. *Schoolteacher: A Sociological Study.* Chicago: University of Chicago Press, 1975.

Mitchell, Douglas E. "Six Criteria for Evaluating State-Level Education Policies." *Educational Leadership* 44 (September 1986): 14-16.

Sarason, Seymour. *The Culture of the School and the Nature of Change.* Boston: Allyn and Bacon, 1971.

Smith, Louis, et al. *Kensington Revisited: Two Key Years of Context from the Milford Chronicle.* St. Louis, Mo.: Washington University, 1982.

Terkel, Studs. *Working: People Talk About What They Do All Day and How They Feel About What They Do.* New York: Ballantine, 1985.

U.S. Department of Education. *The Nation Responds: Recent Efforts to Improve Education.* Washington, D.C.: U.S. Government Printing Office, May 1984.

Walter, L.J., and Glenn, C.L. "Centralized Decision-Making Threatens Teacher Autonomy." *Educational Horizons* 64, no. 2 (1986): 101-103.

Weick, Karl E. "Administering Education in Loosely Coupled Schools." *Phi Delta Kappan* 63 (June 1982): 673-76.

Wirt, Frederick M., and Kirst, Michael W. *The Politics of Education: Schools in Conflict.* Berkeley, Calif.: McCutchan, 1982.

Wise, Arthur. "Why Educational Policies Often Fail: The Hyperrationalization Hypothesis." In *The Dynamics of Organizational Change in Education*, edited by James Baldridge and Terrence Deal. Berkeley, Calif.: McCutchan, 1983.

CHAPTER THREE

The Call to Excellence:
Early Promises and Enduring Concerns

Periodically, people discover with alarm problems that have been with us for decades. . . . Specific solutions are proposed. . .yet often these are recycled solutions from earlier eras: accountability and business efficiency, the career motive in education, or teaching the whole child.
        —H. Thomas James
        The New Cult of Efficiency, 1969

In May 1983 the National Commission on Excellence in Education, appointed by then Secretary of Education Terrel Bell, released its brief but provocative report, *A Nation at Risk*. Since that time dozens of reports have been released; and in 1986 there was a new wave of reform reports, which might be considered either a second-stage of the reform movement or an attempt to revive it.

None of these reports cornered the market on the "truth" about American education. However, all were more or less sincere attempts to gather accurate information to support the need for significant educational reform. Most of the reports tried to integrate facts with expert judgment or with informed opinion in order to make recommendations about the future purpose, nature, and scope of the nation's education system. Clearly, the majority of reports were intended to influence education policy or practice, even though most of them overlooked, oversimplified, or obfuscated basic issues in educational processes.

Two different types of reports emerged during the first year of the Excellence Movement, which defined the issues and set the stage for current efforts to extend education reform. Their essential differences pervade the discussions that follow and illuminate the contradictions in the movement. In Table 3.1 we compare some general differences between the two types. The first type is represented by such reports as *A Nation at Risk* and *America's Competitive Challenge*. The second type is the lengthier studies represented by Ernest Boyer's *High School,* Theodore Sizer's *Horace's Compromise,* and John Goodlad's *A Place Called School.* Familiarity with the differences between these two types will enable the reader to understand better the issues and trends in the Excellence Movement. In this chapter we shall consider recommendations from the two types of reports and the promises they hold for education. We then discuss some enduring concerns we have about the recommendations.

Table 3.1
Comparison of Emphases in Reports and Studies

Reports	Studies
Purpose. Arouse public action, motivate state legislatures to enact policies to improve education at local level.	Influence procedures and policies affecting individual schools and those involved directly with individual schools.
Belief guiding policy recommendations. Reform can be legislated or mandated from higher levels of the education hierarchy, particularly from state authorities.	Reform can and must occur in individual schools and districts based on local initiatives by staff, faculty, and community.
Method of research. Summaries of large-scale reports, polls, and studies; testimony from leaders and experts in education, politics, and business.	On-site observations and data collection from many schools of different types and situations.
Method for documenting decline in education. Focus attention on such quantitative measurements as declining SAT scores, declining enrollments in math and science courses, and poor reading skills.	Focus on qualitative observations that indicate problems in school settings, such as apathy, lack of intellectual stimulation, lowered expectations, lack of experimentation.
Basis for calling for reform. Deductive conclusion drawn from information indicating declines in economic competitiveness and standardized test scores; need for the nation to be more competitive in the world market.	Inductive inferences drawn from educated observations and large data bases accumulated in the field; need to produce better-educated individuals.

Role of school. Supply an intelligent and disciplined labor force; increase cognitive achievement and enforce standards for those who "want to learn."	Develop educated citizens; encourage cognitive, affective, and motor growth among all students, including those who do not seem to profit from traditional schooling.
Proposals for enhancing instructional quality. Use "carrot and stick"; initiate technical rather than structural changes; use "get tough" policies including raising standards, initiating merit pay, and establishing stiffer graduation requirements.	Implement structural approaches requiring greater variety of instructional techniques adapted to particular environments.
Style of presentation. Often hyperbolic in tone with emotional appeals about threats to the nation's well-being.	Descriptive analysis of conditions in schools based on interactions among teachers, students, and administrators.
Dissemination and form. Unabashedly written for media consumption in brief, simple form that avoids details. Follow-up publications cite local and statewide policy initiatives.	Books and lectures offering detailed, descriptive examples for spreading good practice attracted the attention of professional audiences.

Reform groups often make recommendations with little regard for their research bases, their feasibility, or their political consequences (Peterson 1983). They assume that their recommendations will yield *predicted gains*; but, when implemented, a number of problems arise, which we have called *enduring concerns*. When mandated to implement these recommendations, policy makers — legislators, administrators, school board members, and teachers — must try to maximize the predicted gains while minimizing the problems.

The set of tables in this chapter are designed to serve as a basis for policy choices. They illustrate the complexity of reform recommendations and alert policy makers to the need for anticipating and thus reducing negative outcomes. The recommendations we have chosen to analyze come from almost two dozen reports released in 1983 and 1984 and from three reports released in 1985. The source of the recommendations are marked with an asterisk in the references at the end of this chapter.

In reviewing each table, the reader must keep in mind that if predicted gains are to be maximized and concerns minimized, then the recommendations must be implemented by competent and sensitive people who have a comprehensive vision of what a fully educated person is and a clear understanding of the painstaking processes required to develop fully functioning citizens. A major criticism of the reports is that they were not inspired by such a vision or understanding; hence, our focus on enduring concerns.

Recommendations About Basic Skills

Table 3.2 lists predicted gains and enduring concerns associated with recommendations about teaching the basics, curriculum structure, and instructional practices. The predictive gains assumed in the recommendations are that they will clarify the purposes of education, increase student learning, improve curriculum content and organization, and enhance teaching effectiveness. However, implementing these recommendations raises concerns that educational purposes will be narrowed, learning will be retarded, individual students will be unduly discouraged or even punished, teachers and local boards will be constrained, and achievement actually will be lessened in the long run.

Table 3.2
The Issue of Basics

Recommendation: Redefining the "Basics"

Predicted Gains	Enduring Concerns
1. Upgrading minimum competency exams.	
Clarifies objectives for teachers, students, policy makers, administrators, and the public.	Extra instruction and assessment add costs.
Clearly states school's responsibility to the graduate.	Dropout rate may increase.
"Teaching to the test" enhances learning if the test tests what you want students to learn.	May lead to "teaching to the test."
	May limit curriculum by reducing content to the easily measurable.
Shows employers the basic skills they can expect from graduates of a given school.	Emphasizes lower-order thinking skills and de-emphasizes higher-order thinking skills.
Assures next year's teachers of a minimal level of performance on which they can build.	May lead to decrease in student motivation once the minimum is met.
Demonstrates faith that the students can learn and gives them an incentive for learning.	Difficult to find measures on which people can agree.
	Can lead to "second class" citizens who never get a diploma.
Could build student confidence when they achieve the suggested level.	Does not address the problems of students who cannot reach the minimum.
Could identify problems and deficiencies early enough to design programs for remediation and enrichment.	Could lead to lawsuits.
	Standards that are too high may discourage students from trying.
Could lead to reduction of remedial courses at higher grade levels.	Could force district to provide extra years of free schooling for those who need it before entering the work force.
Could prevent students from going on to the next level without necessary background.	Often punishes students without providing remediation or help.
	Difficult to develop tests free of cultural bias.

Could lead to more individualization as students who complete minimums early go on to more advanced programs instead of repetition of already mastered knowledge and skills.	May not have secondary teachers who can teach basic skills. May cause loss of most creative teachers and discourage new recruits to the profession. Causes schools to discontinue the most interesting (and most effective) instructional practices. Causes districts to rely on commercially prepared, programmed materials, particularly for students in lower socioeconomic schools.

2. Upgrade achievement in basic skills.

Predicted Gains	Enduring Concerns
Focuses attention on developing the skills children need to be independent, productive learners. Tries to ensure a "floor" of learning for next year's teachers and for employers. Communicates basic expectations for learning. Improves self-esteem because the student can do these things. Communicates the expectation that the school's responsibility is to develop basic skills. Assures minorities and poor children that they will receive instruction in these areas. Could focus resources in early grades for higher pay-off.	Often concentrates attention on low-level skills in reading and writing. Can lead to repetitive drill on reading, writing, and math without application to real-life situations. May cause schools to buy expensive "packaged" curricular programs that have no relevance for teachers or students and that may not be based on appropriate theory and research. May lead schools to increase time on activities that were not effective in the first place. Science, social studies, and other "non-basics" become less important and receive less attention. Can lower achievement among top students.

3. Increase requirements for high school graduation.

Predicted Gains	Enduring Concerns
Gives students a greater opportunity for in-depth knowledge of some content areas. Redefines the student's diploma in terms of the achievement it represents. Provides access to college and jobs for all students. Gives teachers greater influence over student's program. Could provide incentive for students to take more academic courses. Could better prepare students for the demands of the technological world.	May increase dropout rate. Could focus on archaic or useless content. Could rigidify instruction. Could further isolate schooling from life. Could disenchant teachers who find it difficult to teach less-able learners. Equates increased academic achievement with expansion of course requirements. May cause diversion of funds from early grades, reducing early instruction in basic skills.

Focuses instruction and resources on those academic subjects felt to be essential.

Communicates to colleges and employers that high school graduates have greater academic knowledge.

May increase community support.

Schools may not have teachers qualified to teach the requirements.

May increase stress for students.

May create a large group of seniors who have not completed requirements.

Increases the cost of education for expanded curriculum.

De-emphasizes extracurricular activities.

4. Redefine the traditional concept of basics to include modern requirements.

Predicted Gains	Enduring Concerns
Recognizes that modern society requires a higher level of basic skills.	Requires higher levels of instructional skills, which some teachers may not understand nor possess.
Improves employability of students in the workplace by emphasizing skills employers desire.	May add subjects with only short-term relevance or popularity.
Assures society of citizens instructed in skills for modern living.	Glorifies computers before people have thought about what they want to do with them.
Elevates speaking and listening to proper importance.	Difficult for people to agree on what and how "basics" should be redefined.
Broadens traditionally narrow role of school to meet new demands.	Some skills, such as speaking and listening, could be difficult to measure.
May facilitate a more effective integration of subjects.	
Prevents curriculum having a narrow focus.	
Develops a sense of purpose and direction.	

5. Organize and present the core curriculum to enhance interdisciplinary understanding.

Predicted Gains	Enduring Concerns
Takes advantage of natural human learning processes.	Difficult to organize properly.
Keeps students in touch with "real-life situations" and enhances their understanding of those situations.	Difficult to implement and maintain on schoolwide basis.
Allows practice of such skills as reading, writing, and math while learning interesting content.	Can lead to gaps in instruction.
	Can result in trivialization of content.
	Higher costs for planning instruction.
Could promote more cooperation and understanding among faculty.	Most teachers, administrators, and curriculum specialists lack training in interdisciplinary instruction.
Allows for social skills to develop as students work together.	Makes assessment of progress in specific content areas more difficult.
Should enliven academic instruction by allowing teachers to pursue their interests.	May be threatening to those who do not expect schools to teach higher thinking skills.
Should make subjects less elitist and more attractive for more students.	Some teachers do not have broad educational and cultural interests.

Could promote more interaction among students of differing ages and abilities.

Recommendation: Countering the Encroachment of Electives and Extracurriculars

6. Reduce electives to no more than one-third or one-fifth of the curriculum.

Predicted Gains	Enduring Concerns
Saves money and personnel time. Saves space. Rids the curriculum of faddish and trivial courses. Forces students to focus on a specific set of needed academic skills. Removes the school's capacity to "steer" poor students into trivial courses that they can pass without learning the basics. Prevents a tendency to create "easy" academic tracks for students. Forces teachers to grapple with better ways of teaching the basic curriculum rather than spending energy on new or marginal courses.	Takes away some of the experiences that add excitement and personal satisfaction in school. Takes away some courses needed by students whose parents are unable to provide life-survival skills. Impedes the teacher's creativity and decision-making power. Forces students who least use them into more study halls or other experiences that waste time. Takes away some of the student's opportunity to practice decision-making. Limits capacity to introduce innovations in the curriculum. Reduces student participation in the arts and vocational programs. Can increase dropouts and pushouts. Assumes everyone can and should learn the same things. May be too narrow for a pluralistic society.

Recommendation: The Case for Electives

7. Design elective clusters that allow for further academic inquiry or the exploration of career options.

Predicted Gains	Enduring Concerns
Allows students to experience in-depth study in an area of interest. Helps students make better decisions about their future careers. Encourages students to use higher-level thinking skills. Permits students to make choices about their own learning. Helps students to recognize the relationships among different subjects.	Makes class scheduling more difficult. Requires time and resources for special courses. Requires staff members with special areas of expertise. Takes away time that should be spent on core subjects. Narrows the student's school experience. May force students into career decisions too early.

8. Special arrangements for gifted students (independent study, credit by examination, special courses for gifted, mentorships).

Predicted Gains	Enduring Concerns
Ensures that talents are utilized and pushed to maximum capacity.	Promotes elitism in student relationships and in teacher assignments.
Relieves teachers of having wide ability ranges in classrooms.	Can remove talented students from classes in which they have been positive forces for learning.
Relieves gifted students of activities they find boring and unchallenging.	Removes the pressure to demand excellence from all students.
Ensures that talented students are not held to "minimum" levels.	Criteria for selecting gifted students are imperfect.
Relieves able students from anti-school peer pressures and anti-intellectual staff pressures.	Increases parental pressures on class and teacher assignments.
May increase feelings of belonging to a unit.	Promotes labeling and sorting students.
Reinforces gifted students' beliefs in their abilities.	May promote too much competition among students.
Provides outlets for gifted students with physical handicaps.	Takes funds from general program.
	May fail to consider student as a whole, over-emphasizes academics.

9. Teach a broad set of manual training skills rather than a narrow set of skills for specific job training.

Predicted Gains	Enduring Concerns
Provides broader, more adaptive set of skills to ensure greater employability for students.	Can result in trivial instruction and diminution of the value of the skills.
Teaches useful skills for hobbies, home repair, etc., thereby improving use of leisure time and building economic independence as well as higher self-confidence for living.	Requires more staff resources with specialized skills.
	Could turn vocational classes into time wasters.
Provides opportunity to apply such academic skills as mathematics and reading to the needs of everyday life.	Could enhance elitist divisions among departments.
Reduces job obsolescence.	Could diminish concept of vocational education.

Recommendations About Curricular and Instructional Changes

The recommendations listed in Table 3.3 deal mostly with competency examinations, tracking and ability grouping, and time allotments for instruction. A few deal with textbooks, instructional methods, and computers.

The predicted gains focus on accountability, more measured outcomes, use of comparative achievement results, more specific curriculum goals, narrower roles for schooling, making instruction easier for the teacher, and making the educational process more comprehensible for the public. The concerns are that accountability measures are inadequate and constraining, that measured outcomes usually emphasize minimum competencies that are less than what society needs or requires, that achievement comparisons will be unfair for many students who require more from school than the recommendations acknowledge, and that schools will fall short of what both individuals and communities need.

Table 3.3
Curricular and Instructional Changes

Recommendation: Assessment of Learning and Promotion Policies

10. Minimum competency examinations with well-designed remedial programs.

Predicted Gains	Enduring Concerns
Establishes clear set of expectations for staff, students, and parents. Provides remediation for students who need help. Ensures a level of competency that teachers, parents, and students can expect from a school program. Limits the tendency to promote ill-prepared students.	Reduces the curriculum to the lowest levels of accomplishment, the easily measurable outcomes. Reduces motivation of some students to achieve beyond the minimum. May pull students out of regular interaction with other students. May divert funds from early grades, thus increasing problem over time.

11. Promotion based on performance rather than on age grading.

Predicted Gains	Enduring Concerns
Helps ensure proper instruction for more students. Motivates some students. Forces a clarification of academic expectations. Allows students to proceed at a rate comfortable for them. Encourages articulation between and among grade levels.	Often punishes students for bad instruction. Can increase dropout rate. Supports staff prejudices about ability to learn. Forces students to repeat entire grade experience rather than areas in which they are deficient. Puts wider age range of students together, which may cause social problems. May track students.

12. Monitoring instruction and learning with periodic testing of general achievement and specific skills.

Predicted Gains	Enduring Concerns
Provides information about learning problems to guide instruction. Increases sense of personal responsibility on part of staff. Provides incentive to improve instruction.	Causes staff to revert to least-interesting styles of instruction. Reduces curriculum to tested and testable material. May cause teachers to compete for the "best" students rather than trying to teach all students.

Predicted Gains	Enduring Concerns
Gives students a sense of how well they are doing.	Can impose authoritarian control over the professional judgment of teachers and reduce their morale.
Helps parents and community to see how well students perform.	Can ignore affective factors relevant for learning.
Causes teachers to follow a well-defined course of study.	Increases standardization.
Forces teachers to articulate the curriculum on a K-12 basis.	Lessens attention to decision-making, self-esteem, higher-level thinking, and aesthetics.
	Can encourage widespread cheating.

13. Emphasize proficiency rather than minimum competency.

Predicted Gains	Enduring Concerns
Prevents minimal academic standards from dominating the curriculum.	May set unrealistic and arbitrary levels of proficiency that some students cannot attain.
Presses each student to use talents.	
Encourages higher levels of performance from students.	There is lack of agreement on what the proficiency levels should be.
Raises student expectations.	Difficult to assess proficiency, particularly in higher-level skills.
Challenges staff to improve instruction.	
Increases individualization of instruction.	

14. Assessment based on a variety of measures beyond pencil-and-paper tests.

Predicted Gains	Enduring Concerns
Promotes higher levels of learning and integration of subject matter using problem-solving and real-life situations.	Opens door for social promotions on criteria other than tested and comparable achievement.
Allows assessment of knowledge and skill in the real-life situations in which they will have to be applied.	Makes assessment more time-consuming.
Encourages more individualized ways of assessing knowledge and skill.	May lead to less objectivity in measurement.
Encourages in-depth assessment, which can be used to guide instruction.	May lead to such a range of measures that it is difficult to assess the quality of instruction being offered students.
Reduces student's perception that schooling is merely to pass tests or get grades.	Makes it difficult to communicate expectations to students and parents clearly.
Allows parents, community, teachers, students, and others, to see learning reflected in everyday actions.	

Recommendation: Reorganizing to Enhance Achievement and Eliminate Tracking

15. Eliminate tracking.

Predicted Gains	Enduring Concerns
Forces closer attention to educational purposes.	Removes some options to keep some students in school.

Gives every student a common core of learnings.

Takes away structural support for beliefs that some students cannot learn academic subjects.

Opens way for having all types of students grouped together for instruction.

Prepares students for living with people from different backgrounds and with different abilities.

Simplifies school organization and staffing.

Ensures access to a full curriculum for vocational students.

Could increase students' self-esteem.

Allows students to explore more career options.

Requires students and teachers to be more creative.

May facilitate mastery of basic skills.

Reinforces an elitist concept of curriculum.

Reduces positive feelings about work and vocational-technical activities.

Narrows the curriculum.

Teachers may not be prepared to teach outside existing tracks.

Students' skills may be poorly developed for some classes.

Student needs may not be met.

16. Organize units or "houses" that contain students of similar ability rather than similar age.

Predicted Gains

Allows students to work at the maximum of their ability.

Makes planning easier.

Permits students to work at a pace comfortable for them.

Allows students to compete with those similar in ability and removes unfair competition.

Could increase student's self-esteem.

Instruction may be easier.

Enduring Concerns

Makes scheduling difficult.

Results in tracking with all its disadvantages.

Locks students into a curriculum that makes it hard to change groups.

May result in wide age ranges within ability groups.

Deprives students of learning from a full range of peers.

Community may not accept the plan.

May decrease students' self-esteem.

Instruction may fail to meet individual needs.

17. Create multiple tracks so that students can progress at their own rate.

Predicted Gains

Allows students to move at a pace commensurate with their ability.

Removes unfair competition.

Allows setting realistic goals for students.

Makes planning and instruction easier for teachers.

Allows students to experience academic success more often.

Enduring Concerns

May unduly increase competitive pressures on students.

Makes scheduling more difficult.

Creates problems for standardized curriculum.

Promotes student stereotyping.

May result in categorizing students incorrectly.

Keeps some students in school to get at least a basic education.

Decreases gap between aptitude and achievement.

Enhances chance that peers will communicate.

Reduces frustration.

May create elitism among students and in teacher assignments.

May lock students into a curriculum, making it difficult to change tracks.

Prevents students from learning from a full range of peers.

Precludes equal access to knowledge, especially for poor, minority, and vocational students.

Recommendation: Classroom Management and Conditions

18. Improve instructional techniques.

Predicted Gains

Enduring Concerns

Makes better learning environments.

Increases student motivation and achievement.

Increases teachers' feeling of success.

Increases students' feelings of self-worth.

Creates a sense of classroom community.

Facilitates higher-level thinking skills.

Enhances student creativity.

Focuses reform where it is most beneficial for students.

Improves such conditions for learning as use of time, student engagement, and instructional feedback.

Will have limited success if the whole school environment is not also improved.

Requires time and resources for effective staff development.

Could conflict with goals and latent social roles that schools serve.

Could increase teaching duties and responsibilities.

Requires radical changes in preservice and inservice programs.

19. Reduce class sizes.

Predicted Gains

Enduring Concerns

Removes one of the most common excuses for poor instruction.

Allows greater attention to individual students.

Allows more flexibility in planning and a richer curriculum.

Reduces the number of management tasks teachers have to do.

Provides more time to communicate with parents and contact community resources.

Gives more opportunity to use specialized equipment (computers, physical education equipment, home economics equipment).

Provides opportunity for small-group instruction and student interaction.

May result in higher costs but no achievement gains.

May not result in real differences in instruction or curriculum, just more of the same with smaller numbers.

Requires more space (rooms, laboratories, staff offices) and more staff.

Administrators may be tempted to use teachers in non-instructional capacities.

20. Make time periods more flexible.

Predicted Gains	Enduring Concerns
Cuts down on wasted time.	Makes planning and scheduling more difficult.
Makes in-depth learning possible for subjects that need longer periods.	May result in many short courses that cover subjects superficially.
Encourages creativity in planning.	Increases possibility for unbalanced curriculum.
Encourages use of long-term student assignments or projects.	Teacher responsibility could become lax.
Allows for differences in learning and teaching styles.	Opposition from parents and teachers may arise if it requires significant modifications of time allotments.
Allows for variety of teaching styles.	

21. Extend the school day and year.

Predicted Gains	Enduring Concerns
Permits more time for teaching and learning.	Requires more staff and other resources to implement.
Provides less time off in which students may forget knowledge or skills.	Could result in less efficiency, same coverage in more time.
Allows more time for creative programs in the school.	Removes opportunity for students to get work experience and earn money during school vacations.
Permits use of school buildings for a longer time.	Reduces time youth can contribute to the family.
Satisfies those in power who equate time with quality.	Could decrease parental role in child's total development.
Provides educational environment for children whose homes do not provide such an environment.	Not as cost effective as peer tutoring, smaller class sizes, or computer-assisted instruction.
May give more opportunity for individual attention.	
Could increase teachers' attention to higher-level skills, social and emotional growth.	

22. More time on task in the classroom.

Predicted Gains	Enduring Concerns
Communicates that the top priority of the school is learning.	Doesn't judge the quality of tasks, just "more is better."
Encourages better use of time in class.	May spend too much time on drill or tasks that are too easy or too hard for students.
May increase student achievement.	May result in too much time spent on basic skills and meaningless drill and not enough time on applying them or understanding them.
Encourages serious efforts on the part of students and teachers.	Often substitutes teacher talk or paperwork for student engagement.
Requires more instructional planning.	
Reduces interruptions in instruction.	

Often adds to the tedium of school work, inhibits the more interesting parts of the curriculum.

Often increases reliance on consumable materials.

Often decreases creativity.

Can cause the skills essential for good teaching to atrophy.

Does not adapt to individual learning patterns.

23. Reduce interruptions in class.

Predicted Gains

Reduces distractions.

Increases likelihood of more time on task.

Communicates that learning and teaching are the most important activities in school.

Reduces tension for teachers and students.

May improve morale among conscientious teachers.

Enduring Concerns

Makes it more difficult to carry out routine communication tasks in the school.

Can be used as excuse for eliminating valuable experiences that occur outside the classrooms.

24. Ensure that teachers teach only the subjects they know well.

Predicted Gains

Makes teachers more satisfied and comfortable with their jobs.

Raises the school's credibility among parents and the public.

May increase teachers' interest in their work.

May increase creativity in teaching because teachers are more secure with the subject.

Enduring Concerns

May increase barriers between departments.

May lead to some subjects not being offered because of lack of credentialed teachers.

Demands more staff in particular areas.

Reduces flexibility for staff.

Assumes that "teaching" is conveying only subject matter.

Recommendation: Textbooks and New Technology

25. Increase difficulty and quality of textbooks.

Predicted Gains

Makes it easier to treat complex subjects with more depth.

Offers a challenge to gifted or serious students.

Increases students' ability to deal with more complicated texts.

Reduces superficial treatment of academic subjects.

Enduring Concerns

May force students to try to read material that is too difficult for them, thus discouraging them because they cannot understand.

Makes teaching more difficult when students cannot understand reading materials.

May increase dropout rate.

Reinforces textbook dominance over instruction.

26. Have more teachers write textbooks.

Predicted Gains

Ensures that textbook authors know the realities of the classroom.

May result in more readable texts that are easier to use.

Enduring Concerns

May be based on dated material rather than on new research.

May over-emphasize activities or drill rather than higher-level thinking skills.

27. Initiate large-scale curriculum projects to improve textbooks and instructional techniques.

Predicted Gains

Involves teachers in planning the curriculum, thus increasing their commitment to its goals.

Provides a comprehensive approach to instruction.

Improves the overall program for students.

Enhances instruction by providing new ideas to teachers.

Enduring Concerns

Requires long-term effort and resources.

May be accomplished by a small elitist group who are not the ones who must implement the changes.

Requires high level of knowledge and skill to link curriculum to instruction in meaningful ways.

Reduces local planning and increases reliance on commercial packages.

May make teachers too dependent on curriculum materials.

28. Use primary source material rather than summarized or abridged material.

Predicted Gains

Puts students in the role of investigator or historian so that they can make their own conclusions.

Makes subjects more interesting and challenging for teachers and students.

Involves students in higher levels of analysis and interpretation.

Enduring Concerns

Reading may be too difficult for some students.

Requires a high level of skill and knowledge on the part of both the teacher and student.

Makes planning more time-consuming because teachers do not have the teacher's manual that comes with standard textbooks.

Some schools may not have access to material.

29. Use more videotape and other media.

Predicted Gains

Makes instruction more interesting.

Provides information beyond that which can be expected from individual teachers.

Provides another avenue of learning for students who have difficulty reading.

Provides a way to make study of a subject more realistic and true to life.

Enduring Concerns

Requires equipment and extra materials.

May detract from the students' own study of a subject by putting them too often in a passive role.

May seem like "frills" to outsiders.

Mechanizes curriculum and reduces creativity.

Materials become dated quickly.

May encourage use of untrained teachers.

30. Use computers and computer-assisted instruction.

Predicted Gains	Enduring Concerns
Provides ways to individualize learning. Increases student motivation, at least temporarily. Reduces the amount of teacher time needed for drill and practice. Increases skills that students can use in a high technology society. Links schooling with technological world of work.	Requires funds to acquire and update computers and software. Unavailability of good software that goes beyond skills and drill. Requires teacher skill in using the new technology. May become tedious as the "newness" wears off. Depersonalizes instruction if used as a substitute for good teaching. May reduce learning to lower-level skills if used as electronic workbooks.

Recommendations About Developing Teacher Effectiveness

Table 3.4 lists predicted gains and enduring concerns of recommendations for making teachers more effective by instituting more rigorous staff evaluation and staff development procedures. These recommendations, of course, have implications for preservice teacher education as well. The need for improvement in teacher education already has spawned a second generation of reform reports on teacher and administrator preparation and certification (Holmes Group 1986; Carnegie 1986; NCEEA 1987; and Feistritzer 1984). Attempts to implement any of the proposed recommendations in colleges of education should take into account the gains and concerns listed in Table 3.4. The predicted gains are that we will have more qualified teachers; we will hold them longer; and they will have greater influence on students, especially in terms of cognitive outcomes.

The concerns raised by the recommendations are that they will divide professionals into competitive camps; they will result in arbitrary and narrow evaluation procedures; they will leave the majority of teachers with inadequate salaries and low status; they will confine teaching to inculcating lower-level skills to the neglect of creative and affective outcomes; they will discriminate against ethnic and racial minority candidates; they will not provide sufficient funds for the training needed to carry out effective evaluation or to pay salaries commensurate with training and experience; they will fail to attract enough new teachers into the profession; they will not get sufficient support from local school boards; and they will drive some competent teachers from the profession.

Table 3.4
Developing Teacher Effectiveness

Recommendation: Incentive Plans and Salaries

31. Initiate career ladders with commensurate salaries.

Predicted Gains	Enduring Concerns
Motivates talented individuals to enter and remain in teaching. Permits selected teachers to engage in professionally rewarding activities. Provides a way of monitoring the profession, which may enhance public confidence. May enhance teachers' effectiveness. Permits raising salary schedules to higher levels. Involves teachers in important instructional decisions. Could encourage collegial interactions.	Changes traditional roles of teachers. Assessment of teachers, even by peer review, leads to resentment. May link rewards with measures not related to effective instruction. Pay differential may not be sufficient to attract teachers to advance up the ladder system. May make parents dissatisfied if their children are placed in classes with teachers at the bottom of the ladder. Political factors may detract from promoting the most able. May foster competition and conflict among staff members. Will increase personnel costs. If funded by the state, it may increase existing inequalities among districts. Ignores research indicating that pay alone does not induce higher performance. May add a new layer of "superiors" who lose touch with teaching.

32. Establish merit pay programs.

Predicted Gains	Enduring Concerns
Motivates teachers to go beyond required duties. Eliminates restrictions imposed by single salary schedule. Establishes mechanisms to recognize superior teacher performance. Could help establish a superior evaluation system. May motivate teachers to promote individual student achievement. Could attract superior teachers to work with difficult-to-teach students. Could be incentive for talented teachers to remain in profession. Salary increases would be based on teacher performance rather than degrees, courses, years of service.	Reduces incentives to monetary rewards. Increases costs of education. Requires closer attention to which outcomes are attributable to teaching. Identifying and measuring criteria for merit is difficult. Requires staff development to help all teachers reach merit levels. May lead to rejection by parents of "non-meritorious" teachers. Plan may violate state laws or union agreements. Could restrict the definition of "teaching" to narrow concepts. Merit criteria could vary widely from school to school, resulting in loss of confidence in the plan.

42

Could give teachers a financial stake in improving student performance.

Pits teachers against one another, leading to dissension.

Could deepen division between staff and administrators.

Would likely be subjective or political.

Differential pay may not be enough to justify the trouble.

Measures for merit may not be related to quality performance.

Quotas for merit pay shut some people out, reduce confidence in the system.

33. Establish the position of "head teachers" or "master teachers," granting them more responsibilities and more authority.

Predicted Gains	Enduring Concerns
Could provide greater involvement for qualified teachers in developing the curriculum.	May create an authoritarian structure of decision-making in the school leading to resentment, lack of creativity, and lack of commitment.
Provides a way of coaching younger, inexperienced teachers.	Could serve as negative role models for younger teachers.
Less threatening to teachers than rigid career ladder or merit pay schemes.	Current system of appointing department heads often doesn't reward best teachers.
Could serve as positive role models for younger teachers.	Adds a new level of authority.
Establishes a path for career and salary advancement while continuing to teach.	

34. Establish a National Master Teacher's program.

Predicted Gains	Enduring Concerns
Provides an incentive for talented individuals to enter and remain in the profession.	Creates an elite corps of teachers causing dissension and resentment within the ranks of average teachers.
Provides a structure for sharing instructional innovations and sound practices.	May lead to the kind of bureaucratic relationships and practices that stifle innovation.
Provides role models on a nationwide scale.	Difficult to achieve national consensus on what a good teacher is.

35. Increase teachers' salaries to be competitive with other professions.

Predicted Gains	Enduring Concerns
Provides an incentive for talented individuals to enter and remain in the profession.	Perhaps the most costly of all the recommendations.
May decrease teacher burnout by reducing the need to find a second, part-time job.	Does not provide incentives once the teacher has entered the profession.
Increases public expectation for performance and respect.	Does little to improve teacher preparation or performance.
	Ignores quality of worklife for teachers.

43

May improve teachers' attitude toward work.	Does not attract people to subject areas experiencing shortages.
May be incentive to improve quality of performance.	Might attract people who work only for extrinsic rewards.
May increase supply of teachers and permit more selectivity.	May increase public's demands on education.
May increase enrollments in teacher education institutions.	Public may not support it unless perceived quality increases.

36. Establish a future teacher club or other program for high school students who show potential.

Predicted Gains	Enduring Concerns
Encourages students to enter the teaching profession.	High school may be too early to identify potential for teaching.
May enhance rapport between teachers and students in the school.	May not develop into a meaningful experience if students are given trivial or uninteresting work.
Enables students to get more accurate perception of teaching as a profession.	Difficult to develop a program that provides direct experiences.
Club could increase a feeling of community between students and teachers.	May require a faculty sponsor or other adult supervision.
	May encounter parent resistance.

37. Provide loans or full scholarships to qualified students who want to become teachers, especially in shortage areas.

Predicted Gains	Enduring Concerns
Creates incentives for talented individuals to enter the profession.	Increases costs.
Attracts people into teaching profession when there is a shortage.	May attract people who enter for money only, without commitment to the profession.
Strengthens college programs in shortage areas.	Many recipients may not ever enter teaching.
May focus recruitment where need is.	Creates wild swings in supply and demand.
	Creates problems in teacher education as need changes but professors are tenured.

38. Make provisions for qualified, non-certified individuals to teach where shortages exist.

Predicted Gains	Enduring Concerns
Ensures that all general and basic courses will be offered.	May result in assigning the least prepared to classes of difficult-to-teach children.
Allows greater variety in the curriculum.	Paves way for school boards to employ substandard personnel, reducing educational opportunity for some students.
Permits talented individuals to teach.	
May serve as incentive to improve teacher education.	
Enables persons with applied knowledge to complement certified teachers.	Having a particular skill may not qualify one to teach.

May provide fresh approaches to instruction.	Non-certified teachers may be viewed as second-class by other teachers, or by students and parents. Provokes tensions within school over who is in charge of curriculum development, discipline, etc.

39. Initiate a more general, liberal, and humanistic training program for teacher education.

Predicted Gains	Enduring Concerns
Provides teachers with background necessary for understanding the interrelatedness of the curriculum. Provides students with teachers who are models of well-educated citizens. Enhances teachers' self-confidence among other professional groups. Raises public respect for teachers. Allows teachers to understand personality and cultural differences.	If not organized and taught properly, teachers may receive only a potpourri of shallow courses. May decrease time spent on instructional techniques and theories of pedagogy. May discourage some candidates from entering profession. May add to costs for preparing teachers. Does not prepare students for specific job skills.

40. Require more concentration in academic majors in teacher training programs.

Predicted Gains	Enduring Concerns
May give teachers more confidence and knowledge in their chosen subject field. Involves more departments in colleges and universities in preparing teachers. Raises enrollments in liberal arts colleges. May enhance public image of teachers and teachers colleges.	Emphasis on subject matter may detract from time for developing pedagogical abilities. Reinforces idea that subject matter is education. Confuses governance and mission of teacher preparation programs.

41. Require that teachers demonstrate competence in their academic majors by taking a written examination administered by a Board of Examiners.

Predicted Gains	Enduring Concerns
Ensures that teachers know the basics of their chosen subject field. Could raise teachers' self-confidence. Could raise public regard for teachers and for teacher education. Provides incentive for learning during preservice program. May attract more people into teaching. Will force revision in teacher education programs.	May inhibit good teachers who are weak scholars from entering the profession. Examination may be culturally biased or unrelated to teaching performance. May reduce number of candidates for teaching. Does not ensure that teachers who pass will keep up in the academic field. Might reduce number of minority-group teachers.

May attract more students into education.

May reduce enrollments in teachers colleges.

42. Require all teachers to pass a basic skills competency examination.

Predicted Gains

Ensures that teachers have at least minimal basic skills.

Builds public confidence in teachers' abilities.

Provides data for improving or dismissing teachers with low academic skills.

May attract more capable people into teaching.

Identifies needs for teacher induction and training.

May prevent school boards from employing unqualified teachers.

Forces profession to specify basic competencies.

Enduring Concerns

May not be related to competence in teaching.

May lower public image of teachers if scores are low.

Difficult to measure many competencies easily.

May make more capable college students resentful.

May distract attention from poor working conditions that affect teaching performance.

May do little to improve poor teacher preparation.

Can lead to corrupt practices such as cheating.

May cause a shortage of teacher candidates.

43. Help teachers learn a repertoire of better instructional techniques.

Predicted Gains

Provides a means for teaching higher-order skills.

Provides a means for serving gifted students rather than creating special courses or tracking students.

Should promote better study habits by students.

Should increase teachers' confidence.

May help teachers reach difficult-to-reach students.

Should help teachers meet individual differences.

May strengthen college training.

Enduring Concerns

Requires retraining many teachers already in the field, who may be reluctant to change.

May make teachers feel insecure if not properly trained in appropriate methods for various types of learners.

Preservice teachers may not see the value of, or need for, techniques they have not experienced.

Effective techniques may not be known

44. Design better field experiences before certification.

Predicted Gains

Could give beginning teachers more confidence before entering the classroom.

Could assure school districts of more competent new teachers.

Could strengthen college/school relationships.

Adds more teaching personnel to the school's resources.

Enduring Concerns

May extend teacher training programs, thus exacerbating shortage problems and raising costs to students.

Unexamined or poorly examined experience may be worse than no experience.

Will require either increased staff at colleges of education or increased load for existing staff.

Challenges norms in higher education.

46

Permits coaching as beginner engages in real teaching activities.	If training time is not extended, practical experience requirements will detract from the acquisition of academic knowledge.
Raises status of those supervising student teachers or interns.	Students may learn the negative norms of the profession too early in their careers.
Gives prospective teachers better basis on which to make decisions.	
May help to discourage weak candidates from entering teaching.	Good teacher models may not be available.
	Teachers may feel supervising student teachers interferes too much with their classroom work.

45. Remove credentialing of teachers from colleges of education.

Predicted Gains	Enduring Concerns
May provide more centralized control of teacher quality in each state, assuring school districts of competent teachers.	May fail to link education research with teacher training requirements.
	May reduce value of credentialing.
May allow qualified students to enter teaching, even though they lack pedagogical training in colleges of education.	Credentialing process may become unwieldly and too costly.
	Lowers enrollment in colleges.
May link credentialing more closely to performance.	
May raise teachers' status.	

46. Provide better professional development programs.

Predicted Gains	Enduring Concerns
Provides professional help and support to teachers.	Adds additional demands on teachers' limited time.
Enhances professional solidarity and provides links between colleges of education and schools.	May create resentment in teachers when presented in a condescending manner by consultants or college professors.
Acquaints experienced teachers with current research and trends in education.	May perpetuate ineffective practices currently used in staff development.
May enhance teachers' commitment to change.	
May foster broader roles necessary for effective instruction.	
Reinforces concept of continuing, lifelong learning.	

47. Lessen bureaucratic control over teachers.

Predicted Gains	Enduring Concerns
Requires more professional responsibility from teachers.	Could make teacher assessment more subjective and political.
May improve teachers' working conditions.	Could fragment school programs still further.

Eliminates common excuse for poor instruction. Could enhance self-confidence among teachers. Creates an atmosphere of trust within the profession. Encourages innovative practices to emerge. May raise teachers' status.	Requires staff development to change teachers accustomed to dependent role. Could promote laissez-faire instruction in the absence of clear goals.

48. Exempt teachers from noninstructional duties that can be done by noncertified staff.

Predicted Gains	Enduring Concerns
Allows teachers more time to plan for instruction. Increases time teachers have to help individual students. Makes teaching more desirable as a profession.	Decreases informal contacts with students. Lowers expectation for teachers to perform informal, out-of-class functions vital for teaching. Narrows definition of teachers' role.

49. Assign teachers no more than five presentations a day.

Predicted Gains	Enduring Concerns
Decreases the number of students the teacher must work with. May raise the quality of lessons the teacher prepares. Gives teachers more time during the day for planning or helping students. Could increase individual tutoring, more interaction with individual students.	Requires more staff and space. Reduced work load may not result in better teaching. Assumes that teaching is "lecturing" or "presenting."

Recommendations About Changing School Governance and Decentralizing Reform

Table 3.5 lists predicted gains and enduring concerns of recommendations for changing the governance or structure of schools. Predicted gains revolve around the issue of centralization versus decentralization. Depending on one's point of view, the schools might expect to gain by having decisions made from one central source that prescribes teacher roles, curriculum organization, and instructional practices. Efficiency is presumed to be maximized by central planning and coordination. Many of the commission reports and the federal and state policy initiatives associated with the Excellence Movement reflect a bias for centralization and efficiency. Goodlad, Boyer, and Sizer all suggest that both effectiveness and efficiency would be enhanced by more decentralization; and they point to the failure of most top-down attempts at reform. Their concerns are with the dysfunctions of bureaucracy and hierarchical decision-making systems. Advocates of centralization, on the other hand, are concerned about the loss of central purpose, the inefficiencies of decision-making in many localities, the lack of standardized procedures for implementing change, and the loss of control over outcomes.

Proponents of both centralization and decentralization acknowledge the primary role of the principal in implementing reforms. Decentralizers especially acknowledge the principal's role, because of their belief that essential reforms first have to be devised and then implemented at the school building level. Nevertheless, concerns are expressed because there are not enough competent leaders in the position, or because building administrators may act autocratically and arbitrarily, thus undermining the initiative and creativity of the teaching staff.

Table 3.5
Changing Schools and Decentralizing Reform

Recommendation: Organizing the School for Effectiveness

50. Establish a policy group to do long-range planning that affects the whole school.

Predicted Gains	Enduring Concerns
Group could engage in long-range planning without having to deal with immediate problems.	Policy planning might become so long-range that implementation becomes impractical.
Group could have a more wholistic view of policy-making.	May result in lack of staff understanding and commitment.
Planning could give schools a long-range view, reduce faddism.	Has potential for conflict between this group and formal control structures (e.g., school board).
	Such a group could become highly political.

51. Create fundamental structural changes in the way schools operate.

Predicted Gains	Enduring Concerns
Removes excuses for not changing, which usually are linked to logistical problems (scheduling, hall traffic, etc.)	Will not result in improvement if not related to other changes taking place.
Allows planners to operate with less constraints and more creativity.	May be too much of a change for parents and the community.
May be the only way to make real change happen.	May produce only cosmetic change, such as a change in scheduling.
Has potential for promoting new roles for schools and new conceptualizations of the role of education in society.	May raise staff resistance.
May remove obstacles to students achieving.	

Recommendation: Role of the Principal

52. Principal exercises strong leadership in reform efforts as well as daily management.

Predicted Gains

Provides building-level leadership needed for change to be successful and to continue.

Puts decision-making closer to the problem.

Builds expectation that school administrators can make a difference in educational achievement.

Promotes selection of administrators who have both vision and management skills.

Promotes changes in administrator preparation programs.

Enduring Concerns

Could be a lack of principals and other administrators trained to provide leadership for reform.

Puts pressure to preserve administrative training programs on status-quo management rather than on change and innovation.

May reduce teacher role and commitment.

Encourages martinets.

53. Principal becomes the leader in instructional quality and curriculum development.

Predicted Gains

Reinforces the idea that instruction is central concern in schools.

Prevents administrative actions that inhibit improved student outcomes.

Brings the whole staff together to focus on the most important mission of the school.

Removes the focus from management to the important issues of student learning.

Enduring Concerns

Could be a lack of instructional leadership training for administrators.

May result in lack of attention to management details in operating.

Might be implemented in authoritarian manner, which undermines educational outcomes.

Principals may have little control over key variables affecting learning.

Current school structures and the nature of the job may inhibit instructional leadership roles and activities.

54. The principal should monitor instructional quality in the school.

Predicted Gains

Reinforces student achievement as the major goal of the school.

Identifies factors that inhibit learning.

Helps to build a sense of purpose.

Enduring Concerns

Can perpetuate ineffective instruction through authoritarian control.

Can be very time-consuming and without positive results.

May put the administrator in the position of being "policeman."

Reduces the curriculum to behaviors that can be measured easily.

55. The principal should create an orderly learning environment.

Predicted Gains

Creates conditions that are essential for learning.

Enduring Concerns

Can lead to rigid systems simply to keep children quiet.

Can have "spin off" effects since orderly environments contribute to higher
achievement.
Reduces causes for teacher stress.
Improves parental support.
Supports staff collegiality and teacher
productivity.

Can contribute to a punitive, exclusionary climate that worsens problems
and deprives poor, minority, or other underserved students of appropriate instruction.
Seldom deals with institutional causes
for discipline problems.

56. The principal should act as a staff developer.

Predicted Gains	Enduring Concerns
Builds a sense of mutual purpose. Builds the administrator's awareness of staff members' knowledge and skills. Enriches the administrator's role.	May not have administrators who are qualified to become staff de-velopers. Mixes roles of supervisor/evaluator and staff developer.

Recommendations for School/University/Business Partnerships

Inasmuch as the reports were propelled by doubts about America's ability
to compete with foreign business and industry and have been implemented
in a climate of returning governmental functions to state and local governments and to private institutions, it is not surprising that many recommendations call on schools to enter into close alliances with local universities
and businesses. Table 3.6 contains an analysis of predicted gains and enduring concerns arising from those recommendations.

Gains are expected to arise from blending the resources presumed to be
in each locale. Schools should get greater financial and material resources
as well as expertise from the university or the business with which they
affiliate. In turn, communities should gain understanding about the school
system, its problems, and processes for educating children. Both schools
and businesses are presumed to gain better control over the interchange
of resources and services between schools and the communities they serve.

Concerns arise from the possibility of equating business interests with
the larger community interest, having business dominate educational processes and outcomes, giving some schools greater access to resources than
others, and diluting (or polluting) the distinct functions of each partner.

Table 3.6
School/University/Business Partnerships

Recommendation: What Business and Industry Can Do

**57. Adopt-a-school, financial assistance for equipment, endowed chairs, sum-
mer institutes, enrichment programs for gifted students.**

Predicted Gains	Enduring Concerns
Offers incentives to teachers and stu-dents to learn and excell.	Could be a waste of time and money if efforts are not taken seriously or if funds are spent unwisely.

Increases experiential opportunities, thus making school more exciting for both teachers and students.
Adds prestige to the teacher's role.
By involving businesses, they understand school's role better.
Increases available funds and other resources.

Could make schools "tools" of business.
Could become discriminatory if support goes to schools that already have a lot of resources.

58. Share effective management techniques with educators.

Predicted Gains

Can broaden educators' awareness of better ways to manage organizations.
Can make management more efficient, thus leaving more time for instruction.
Could add educational perspectives to local business management.

Enduring Concerns

May not be appropriate techniques for educational organization, which has different clients and goals than industry.
May lead to overreliance on a business model, rather than creating a unique education management model.
Adopting techniques without appropriate technical and material supports might lead to frustration among school administrators.

59. Enhance knowledge about careers and career requirements through visits and internships.

Predicted Gains

Helps students learn about potential careers so that they can make better decisions.
Links students' future more closely with their current work in school.
May help to motivate some students to do better work.

Enduring Concerns

May be a meaningless exercise for students who are not ready to make career decisions.
May lead to businesses using schools for recruiting workers.

60. Have business staff provide tutoring or teach courses.

Predicted Gains

Provides variety for students.
Provides expertise for courses that might not be available from regular staff.
Involvement helps business people learn more about the schools.

Enduring Concerns

May involve people who know subject matter but are poor teachers.
May encourage school boards to use substandard staff.

Recommendation: Universities as Partners

61. Offer courses to gifted students.

Predicted Gains

Allows students to work in challenging academic situations.

Enduring Concerns

May set up an elite system in which talented students are separated from the rest.

Helps students become more knowledgeable about college life.

May challenge universities to improve instructional practices.

May increase college enrollment.

May cause schools to shift their responsibility for offering challenging, high-level courses to the university.

Reduces schools' and teachers' status if colleges "skim off" talent.

62. University involvement in local staff development.

Predicted Gains

Enhances teachers' professional status by involving them with university personnel and programs.

Improves skills and raises level of teachers' knowledge.

Reduces "town-gown" stereotypes.

Adds life to university courses, improving instruction and programs for developing better educators.

Enduring Concerns

Does not guarantee that the staff development will be well designed or effective.

Requires new models for staff development if this is to help teachers.

Threatens professors' status at university if they spend too much time with schools and neglect research and publications.

Recommendation: Community and Family Ties

63. Programs for training parents to help children at home.

Predicted Gains

Provides a more comprehensive approach for developing children's knowledge and skills.

Enhances collaboration between home and school.

Helps whole families get more education.

Strengthens family as a social unit.

Reduces staff fears of working with parents and other family members.

Makes parents aware of what good (and poor) schooling is.

Enduring Concerns

School may abdicate its responsibility by expecting parents to do the educating.

Does not address the problems of children whose families cannot help them.

Schools may assume some roles more suited to the family.

64. Give a new Carnegie Unit for public service to the community.

Predicted Gains

Communicates to students their obligation to serve the community in which they live.

Increases students' sense of self-worth.

Gives students practical work experience to learn both skills and responsibility.

Broadens students' view of the world beyond the narrow perspectives of home and neighborhood.

Provides real-life experiences that integrate knowledge.

Adds manpower to perform community activities for which resources are not available.

Enduring Concerns

Can detract from study of academic subjects.

If not planned carefully, can result in superficial experience with students just putting in time.

If expectations are unclear and supervision ineffective, students will not learn to be responsible.

Improves chances that social problems
will be resolved.

65. Volunteer programs to bring community members into the school.

Predicted Gains	Enduring Concerns
Increases the number of adults who have contact with students.	Volunteers may not understand children and therefore are not very helpful.
Brings adults with special skills into the school.	Puts teachers and the school on display at all times.
Shares teacher's work load.	Takes time and resources to organize program and keep it going.
Helps students make contacts with adults outside the school.	
Can improve the quality of instruction.	

Recommendations for Promoting Equity

Table 3.7 analyzes recommendations from a second-stage report issued under the title, *Our Children at Risk*. The coalition of organizations that issued the report are concerned primarily about promoting equity and equal educational opportunity for children who historically have been neglected or discriminated against in the education system.

Of course, the expected gains are those associated with equity and equal educational opportunity. The recommendations are designed to protect children, regardless of their race, ethnicity, national origin, political power, or socioeconomic status, from being neglected or from being adversely affected by the reform movement. Obviously, achievement scores would rise if lower-achieving students were better educated. These reformers hope that discriminatory or disciplinary instructional practices would be minimized or eliminated, and fewer children would drop out of school.

Concerns arise from doubts that schools can educate everyone or that all students can profit from schools. Educators may not have the will or skill to promote equity. Communities — indeed, state and local governments — may be less inclined than ever to enforce or support equity and equal opportunity in a political climate emphasizing excellence and elitism. Sufficient resources or personnel may not be available or may not be provided even if available.

Table 3.7
Gains and Concerns from *Our Children at Risk*

66. Continued attention to rights of the disadvantaged and those discriminated against because of race, language, sex, or handicap.

Predicted Gains	Enduring Concerns
Protects children from local traditions of discrimination.	Requires special efforts to motivate students and parents to participate.

Reduces societal problems that will arise later if these groups are neglected in schooling.	School people may be poorly prepared to work with these children.
Assures that "excellence" will be achieved with equity.	Many encounter much local resistance to special programs for these students.

67. Restore and expand support for programs serving economically disadvantaged students.

Predicted Gains	Enduring Concerns
Counteracts previous neglect of these students in local schools.	May restore programs that were ineffective to begin with.
Communicates that it is false economy to cut programs that help children escape poverty.	May make teachers dependent on "extra" or outside programs to help poor children, while they are neglected in the regular classroom.
Helps teachers do their job better.	
Continues programs that have improved achievement.	May create resentment if disadvantaged students receive special resources not available for all students.
	May separate disadvantaged students from other groups.
	Increases costs of education, sometimes without tangible results.

68. Eliminate or alter school practices that result in minority children dropping out or being "pushed out."

Predicted Gains	Enduring Concerns
Improves educational services and outcomes for racial minorities.	Requires special programs to be designed to keep students in school.
Best investment for meeting many social and economic needs.	Requires extra effort from school personnel.
Reduces discipline problems stemming from racial prejudice.	May face opposition because of tradition.
Reduces failure rate for minority students.	Many school people are unprepared to serve diverse populations.
Reduces social problems that derive from segregation and educational neglect.	

69. Ensure that female students have an opportunity to develop fully their talents and skills.

Predicted Gains	Enduring Concerns
Reduces the loss of female talents to society.	Requires more funds, especially for athletics.
Communicates to female students they are important and are expected to achieve.	May create strained relationships with some staff.
Reduces discipline problems related to sex-role stereotyping.	May require change in traditional community and school practices.
	Many school people are unprepared to provide equitable practices.

70. Improve services to children with moderate and severe handicaps and develop regular-education options for children with milder handicaps.

Predicted Gains

Maximizes the chances for self-sufficiency for children with moderate handicaps.

Helps families to deal with their exceptional children.

Enduring Concerns

Many teachers are unprepared to handle children with special needs.

May increase the funding needed for special education.

71. Change the focus of vocational education away from a narrow range of job skills and toward preparing students for a changing world of work.

Predicted Gains

Provides employers with workers with higher-level skills.

Recognizes that new skills are needed for changing technology.

Provides individuals more flexibility when seeking jobs.

Provides youth a broader, more useful education.

Can help students escape the poverty cycle by increasing their chances for employment.

Enduring Concerns

Requires continuous updating of teacher skills, equipment, and procedures.

Requires new conceptualization of the vocational curriculum.

May not be practical without participation of business and industry.

May increase dropout rate.

72. Create opportunities for parental involvement in staffing, programming, discipline, and resource allocation.

Predicted Gains

Could increase parental support for education.

Could provide more personnel for the school at no cost.

Could result in more student participation.

Could help to create a sense of community in the school.

Could increase resources allocated to the school.

Could help staff overcome fear of working with community.

Could improve discipline and student achievement.

Enduring Concerns

Could create stress for teachers.

Could reduce teachers' autonomy.

Only some parents may be willing to participate.

Might involve parents in making decisions they are not qualified to make.

73. Make students aware of their due-process rights in such matters as school suspension and expulsion.

Predicted Gains

Communicates to students that they belong in the school, which is there to serve them.

Enduring Concerns

Requires better understanding of due process by administrators and teachers.

Teaches students the rights of individuals in a democratic society.

Reduces unfair treatment by administrators and teachers.

Creates stimulus for staff to learn more educational approaches for teaching self-discipline.

May pose a threat to insecure teachers and administrators.

Takes more time to handle discipline problems properly.

Permits some students to "play lawyer."

74. Strengthen counseling services for non-college-bound youth, and develop job-placement services in high school.

Predicted Gains

Communicates to non-college-bound students that they are important part of the school.

Reduces unemployment and lack of direction.

Provides motivation for mid-range students.

Reduces dropout rate and discipline problems.

Could strengthen school/community relations.

Demonstrates respect for a wide range of occupations that do not require college degree.

Should generate greater public support from a corps of loyal alumni.

Enduring Concerns

Requires change of counselors' responsibilities from scheduling and college placement.

May require greater cooperation from business and industry.

Recommendations for Making Children Better Readers

Table 3.8 shows the analysis for recommendations from a report titled, *Becoming a Nation of Readers*, another second-stage report, which focuses on reading instruction, probably the most basic of "basics" for nearly all the reports.

As the title suggests, recommendations from the reading report are expected to improve reading ability among the nation's youth. The gains they hope to achieve are to eradicate poor instruction and ineffective practices from reading classrooms. They hope especially to stem the widespread use of dull lessons; to abate the focus on letters and words at the expense of meaning and interest; to break instructors' dependence on workbooks and other ineffective materials that have characterized local responses to the pressures for excellence; to have children value reading in their personal lives and to see its value for economic and civic competence; and to promote learning to read as a basis for improving the other communication skills of writing, speaking, and listening. They aspire to produce a fully literate society as a basis for economic and political competence.

Concerns aroused by these recommendations are: they may produce some of the very problems they propose to eradicate; school personnel do not possess the expertise necessary for implementation; school organization precludes the cooperation necessary for implementing some of the recommendations; the costs for material and personnel will be too great; and the curriculum will become too rigid for some children.

Table 3.8
Gains and Concerns from *Becoming a Nation of Readers*

75. Preschool and kindergarten reading readiness programs should focus on reading, writing, and oral language.

Predicted Gains	Enduring Concerns
Eliminates "reading" exercises that do not teach reading.	Could eliminate such important activities as art and field trips, which may not teach reading but which have educational value.
Avoids wasting children's and teachers' time on meaningless activities.	
Could result in more challenging curriculum in early grades.	Runs the risk of a narrow focus on reading alone and ignoring problem-solving.
	Could lead to widespread use of commercial packaged programs that may not be appropriate.

76. Teachers of beginning reading should present well-designed phonics instruction, which is kept simple and completed by the end of the second grade.

Predicted Gains	Enduring Concerns
May lead to new and better ways of teaching children sound-letter relationships.	Could lead to continued use of poorly designed phonics lessons.
May improve general methods of teaching phonics.	Could lead to overuse of phonics to the neglect of other beginning reading strategies.
	May de-emphasize comprehension in learning to read.
	May lead to blind following of commercial phonics materials.
	Could involve staff in endless debate over methods and materials.

77. Reading primers should have complete stories that are interesting and comprehensible.

Predicted Gains	Enduring Concerns
Helps children develop a "sense of story," which is needed for independent reading.	Requires wide knowledge of basal series to select the ones that are appropriate.
Develops higher-level reading processes.	Stories selected may be too difficult for some readers.

58

Increases students' motivation because reading is meaningful.
Provides practice in the whole act of reading.
Provides story selections that are closer to natural language.

78. Teachers should devote more time to teaching comprehension.

Predicted Gains	Enduring Concerns
May increase teachers' strategies for teaching comprehension.	Difficult to teach such a complex cognitive process as comprehension.
Helps children focus on meaning in reading.	Need for better understanding of how to teach comprehension by teachers, textbook writers, and reading experts.
Promotes reading as a whole process.	May lead to use of exercises that have very little to do with comprehension.

79. Children should be asked to complete fewer workbooks and skill sheets.

Predicted Gains	Enduring Concerns
Prevents wasting time on activities that are not related to reading.	Poses a management problem for teachers who are used to keeping children quiet and busy with workbook exercises.
Decreases cost for consumable materials.	Difficult for teachers to think of alternatives to workbooks and skill sheets.
Requires children to use higher-order skills.	Needs intensive staff development to provide alternatives to workbooks and skill sheets.
Decreases paper load for teachers.	
Prevents equating reading with doing workbook exercises.	

80. Children should spend more time on independent reading.

Predicted Gains	Enduring Concerns
Provides practice in reading whole selections rather than isolated paragraphs.	Requires a reallocation of time in the curriculum.
Requires school districts and teachers to provide more books for independent reading.	Requires relinquishing some time for direct instruction.
Could result in widening children's background in many subjects.	May be difficult to accomplish with poor readers.
Provides opportunity for reading that may not occur at home.	Requires time to help children select appropriate books.
Contributes to improved writing.	
Teaches children to take responsibility for their own learning.	
Helps children connect reading with other subjects.	
Can substitute for seatwork.	

81. Children should spend more time writing.

Predicted Gains

Provides guided practice in the process of writing.

Improves children's performance in all subjects.

Builds children's confidence in composing increasingly complex pieces.

Helps children make connections between talking, thinking, reading, and writing.

Improves reading.

Enduring Concerns

It takes more time for teachers to respond to each child's writing.

Requires staff development to help teachers understand the stages of the writing process.

Requires reallocation of time in the curriculum.

82. Schools should cultivate a climate that supports reading.

Predicted Gains

A positive climate for reading gives a clear sense of purpose to everyone in the school.

Supports instruction in other content areas.

Has immediate lifelong educational benefits beyond reading outcomes.

Enduring Concerns

May require changes in way teachers are accustomed to organizing their reading program.

Could be structured so rigidly that children turn off to reading.

83. Schools should maintain well-stocked and well-managed libraries.

Predicted Gains

Provides greater access to books.

Stimulates interest in reading.

Communicates the importance of reading.

Offers support to all content areas.

Offers support for writing activities.

Enduring Concerns

Requires trained personnel to make library function successfully.

Requires adequate funding to keep collection up to date.

Requires cooperation between teachers and library personnel if library is to be fully utilized.

84. Schools should supplement standardized tests with more comprehensive assessments of reading and writing.

Predicted Gains

Overcomes some of the limitations of standardized testing.

Should provide more meaningful assessments of students' reading and writing.

Increases awareness of teachers, administrators, and evaluation personnel concerning alternative ways of assessing reading and writing * achievement.

Helps teachers in diagnosing students' problems.

Enduring Concerns

Increases time needed to carry out more comprehensive assessments.

Requires retraining staff so that they can administer other forms of assessment and interpret results.

Recommendations to Enhance Early Education and Fund Research to Reach Difficult Learners

Table 3.9 shows gains and concerns related to several selected recommendations from a second-stage report issued in 1985 by the Committee for Economic Development under the title, *Investing in Our Children*. Many of the committee's recommendations have been discussed in other tables above. Some others referred to reforms in higher education and are outside the scope of our analysis.

The recommendations chosen for this analysis relate to putting greater attention and resources into education during the early years in the hope that doing so will eliminate some of the problems that are more difficult to solve in the later years. The CED Committee also recommends allocating resources for research to find more effective ways to promote learning among those youth who are not reached by the methods currently known or used. The expected gains are more cost-effective investments in early childhood education, reaching more youth in the groups who have been least educated by current methods but will constitute a large proportion of school populations and the labor force in the next decade, and expanding the meager knowledge available for reaching those youth or for more effectively educating children in the early years – particularly in view of demographic and sociological changes in communities and families.

Concerns associated with these recommendations relate to the availability of funds and the willingness to allocate them in the recommended ways, to the present structure of schools and organizational behavior of school personnel, to whether genuine commitment exists to educate all children, to whether researchers are able to produce the desired information, and to the willingness and ability in schools and colleges to implement findings that require changes in current practice.

Table 3.9
Gains and Concerns from *Investing in Our Children*

85. Devote more resources and attention to preschool programs.

Predicted Gains	Enduring Concerns
Invests educational funds in most cost-effective ways, that is, with preventive programs rather than high-cost remedial programs.	May foster rigid, authoritarian practices destructive to child development.
Uses research on child development gained in past 20 years.	Could be accused of undermining family.
	Will require new staff and special facilities.

Permits interventions for bilingual children at most effective time in their development.

Meets the needs of single-parent, working-mother families.

Should reduce dropout rates.

Should result in upgraded academic content in later years.

Funding program may be burden on already depressed school district budgets.

May encounter opposition from parts of the system that compete for funds.

86. Devote more resources and attention to the early elementary grades.

Predicted Gains

Permits smaller class size in early years for concentration on basic skills.

Reduces costs for remedial work in upper grades.

Should reduce dropout rates.

Enduring Concerns

Will take a long time for positive effects to be felt.

May focus too much on drill and skill rather than critical thinking or comprehension.

Requires new approaches to instruction if positive effects are to be achieved.

Must be accompanied by long-term teacher inservice programs.

May encounter opposition from parts of the system that compete for funds.

87. Devote more resources to "at-risk" junior high school students.

Predicted Gains

Addresses the most crucial years for developing academic and civic competence and interests.

Helps prevent academic and social adjustment problems in high schools.

Should prevent dropouts.

Should enhance transition from elementary to high school.

Should strengthen instruction for all early adolescents.

Enduring Concerns

May drain resources from regular program serving the majority of students.

Junior high may be too late to deal with "at-risk" children.

Does not address the organizational causes for problems at this level.

88. Fund education research that facilitates greater student learning.

Predicted Gains

May enhance overall quality of education research.

May yield breakthroughs for solving chronic instructional problems.

May attract researchers to focus on problems that have been neglected.

Enduring Concerns

May not overcome traditional antipathy between practitioners and researchers.

Assumes that research can affect practice, which frequently has not been the case.

May result in misapplications of spurious or inappropriate research.

May attract researchers to engage in projects that will be funded rather than what is needed.

References

*Adler, Mortimer J. *The Paideia Proposal: An Educational Manifesto*. New York: Macmillan, 1982.

Alexander, Karl L., and Pallas, Aaron M. "Curriculum Reform and School Performance: An Evaluation of the 'New Basics'." *American Journal of Education* 92 (1984): 391-420.

Alexander, Lamar. *Time for Results: The Governors' 1991 Report on Education*. Washington, D.C.: National Governors' Association, 1986.

Alexander, Lamar. "Time for Results: An Overview." *Phi Delta Kappan* 68 (November 1986): 202-204.

Anderson, Beverly, and Pipho, Chris. "State-Mandated Testing and the Fate of Local Control." *Phi Delta Kappan* 66 (November 1984): 209-12.

*Anderson, Richard C., et al. *Becoming a Nation of Readers: The Report of the Commission on Reading*. Champaign, Ill.: University of Illinois Center for the Study of Reading, 1985.

Association for Supervision and Curriculum Development. "Taking Charge of School Reform." *Educational Leadership* 44 (September 1986): 1-96.

*Boyer, Ernest. *High School: A Report on Secondary Education in America*. New York: Harper & Row, 1983.

*Carnegie Forum on Education and the Economy. *A Nation Prepared: Teachers for the 21st Century*. Washington, D.C.: Carnegie Forum, 1986.

Cameron, Don. "An Idea that Merits Consideration." *Phi Delta Kappan* 67 (October 1985): 110-12.

Cohn, Marilyn M., and DiStefano, Anna. "The Recommendations of the National Commission on Excellence in Education: A Case Study of Their Value." *Issues in Education* 2 (Winter 1984): 204-20.

*College Board Educational Equality Project. *Academic Preparation for College: What Students Need to Know and Be Able to Do*. New York: College Board, 1983.

*Committee for Economic Development. *Investing in Our Children: Business and the Public Schools*. Washington, D.C., 1985.

Cross, K. Patricia. "The Rising Tide of School Reform Reports." *Phi Delta Kappan* 66 (November 1984): 167-72.

Doyle, Denis P., and Levine, Marsha. "Business and the Public Schools: Observations on the Policy Statement of the Committee for Economic Development." *Phi Delta Kappan* 67 (October 1985): 113-18.

Earley, Penelope M. *A Summary of Twelve National Reports on Education and Their Implications for Teacher Education*. Washington, D.C.: American Association of Colleges for Teacher Education, 1984.

Education Commission of the States. *Action for Excellence*. Denver, 1983.

Education Commission of the States. *Report of the Task Force on Education for Economic Growth*. Denver: ECS Distribution Center, May 1983.

Educational Research Service. *Merit Pay for Teachers*. Arlington, Va., 1979.

Educational Research Service. *Merit Pay Plans for Teachers: Status and Descriptions.* Arlington, Va., 1979.

English, Fenwick; Clark, David; French, Russell; Rauth, Marilyn; Schlechty, Phillip. "Incentives for Excellence in American Schools: the ASCD Task Force on Merit Pay and Career Ladders." *National Forum of Educational Administration and Supervision* 2, no. 3 (1985-86): 1-17.

*Feistritzer, Emily C. "Cheating Our Children." In *Why We Need School Reform,* edited by Warren Rogers and Lawrence M. O'Rourke. Washington, D.C.: National Center for Education Information, 1985.

*Feistritzer, Emily C. *The Making of a Teacher: A Report on Teacher Education and Certification.* Washington, D.C.: National Center for Education Information, 1984.

Feistritzer, Emily C. *The Condition of Teaching: A State by State Analysis.* Princeton, N.J.: The Carnegie Foundation for the Advancement of Teaching, 1983.

*Frymier, Jack; Cornbleth, Catherine; Donmoyer, Robert; Gansneder, Bruce; Jeter, Jan; Klein, Frances; Schwab, Marian; and Alexander, William. *One Hundred Good Schools.* West Lafayette, Ind.: Kappa Delta Pi, 1984.

Furtwengler, Carol. "Tennessee Career Ladder Plan: They Said It Couldn't Be Done." *Educational Leadership* (November 1985): 55.

*Goodlad, John I. *A Place Called School: Prospects for the Future.* New York: McGraw-Hill, 1983.

Gray, William A. *Challenging the Gifted and Talented Through Mentor-Assisted Enrichment Projects.* Fastback 189. Bloomington, Ind.: Phi Delta Kappa Educational Foundation, 1983.

Griesemer, J.L., and Butler, C. *Education Under Study.* Chelmsford, Mass.: North-East Regional Exchange, September 1983.

Gross, Jacqueline. *Make Your Child a Lifelong Reader.* Los Angeles: Jeremy P. Tarcher, 1986.

Haberman, Martin. "Licensing Teachers: Lessons from Other Professions." *Phi Delta Kappan* 67 (June 1986): 719-22.

The Holmes Group. *Tomorrow's Teachers: A Report of the Holmes Group.* East Lansing, Mich.: Michigan State University, April 1986.

Hoogeveen, Kim, and Gutkin, Terry B. "Collegial Ratings Among School Personnel: An Empirical Examination of the Merit Pay Concept." *American Educational Research Journal* 23 (Fall 1986): 375-81.

Johnson, Susan Moore. "Merit Pay for Teachers: A Poor Prescription for Reform." *Harvard Educational Review* 54 (May 1984): 175-85.

Kauchak, Donald. "Testing Teachers in Louisiana: A Closer Look." *Phi Delta Kappan* 65 (May 1984): 626-28.

Lieberman, Myron. "Educational Specialty Boards: A Way Out of the Merit Pay Morass?" *Phi Delta Kappan* 67 (October 1985): 103-107.

Lowney, Roger G. *Mentor Teachers: The California Model.* Fastback 247. Bloomington, Ind.: Phi Delta Kappa Educational Foundation, 1986.

McDonald, Alice. "Solving Educational Problems Through Partnerships." *Phi Delta Kappan* 67 (June 1986): 752-53.

Miller, Richard D. "An Alternative Proposal." *Phi Delta Kappan* 67 (October 1985): 112.

Morrow, Lesley Mandel. *Promoting Voluntary Reading in School and Home.* Fastback 255. Bloomington, Ind.: Phi Delta Kappa Educational Foundation, 1985.

Murnane, Richard, and Cohen, David. "Merit Pay and the Evaluation Problem: Why Most Merit Pay Plans Fail and a Few Survive." *Harvard Educational Review* 56 (February 1986): 1-17.

Murray, Frank B. "Goals for the Reform of Teacher Education: An Executive Summary of the Holmes Group Report." *Phi Delta Kappan* 68 (September 1986): 28-32.

Nathan, Joe. "Implications for Educators of *Time for Results.*" *Phi Delta Kappan* 68 (November 1986): 197-201.

*National Coalition of Advocates for Students. *Barriers to Excellence: Our Children at Risk.* Boston, 1985.

*National Commission on Excellence in Education. *A Nation at Risk: The Imperative for Educational Reform.* Washington, D.C.: U.S. Government Printing Office, 1983.

National Commission on Excellence in Educational Administration (NCEEA). *Leaders for America's Schools.* Tempe, Ariz.: University Council for Educational Administration, 1987.

National Governors' Association. *Time for Results: The Governors' 1991 Report on Education.* Washington, D.C.: National Governors' Association, 1986.

*National Science Board Commission on Precollege Education in Mathematics, Science, and Technology. *Educating Americans for the 21st Century.* Washington, D.C.: National Science Foundation, 1983.

O'Connell, Carol. *How to Start a School/Business Partnership.* Fastback 226. Bloomington, Ind.: Phi Delta Kappa Educational Foundation, 1985.

Parkay, Forrest W. "A School/University Partnership that Fosters Inquiry-Oriented Staff Development." *Phi Delta Kappan* 67 (January 1986): 386-89.

Passow, Harry A. *Reforming Schools in the 1980's: A Critical Review of the National Reports.* New York: ERIC Clearinghouse on Urban Education, 1984.

Peters, T.J., and Waterman, R.H. *In Search of Excellence: Lessons from America's Best-Run Companies.* New York: Harper & Row, 1982.

Peterson, Paul E. "Did the Education Commissions Say Anything?" *Brookings Review* (Winter 1983): 3-11.

Schlechty, Phillip C. "Evaluation Procedures in the Charlotte-Mecklenburg Career Ladder Plan." *Educational Leadership* (November 1985): 14.

Shanker, Albert. "Separating Wheat from Chaff." *Phi Delta Kappan* 67 (October 1965): 108-109.

Seeley, David S. "Educational Partnership and the Dilemmas of School Reform." *Phi Delta Kappan* 65 (February 1984): 383-88.

*Sizer, Theodore R. *Horace's Compromise: The Dilemma of the American High School.* Boston: Houghton Mifflin, 1984.

*Task Force of the Business-Higher Education Forum. *America's Competitive Challenge: The Need for a National Response.* Washington, D.C.: Business-Higher Education Forum, 1983.

Tom, Alan R. *How Should Teachers Be Educated? An Assessment of Three Reform Reports.* Fastback 255. Bloomington, Ind.: Phi Delta Kappa Educational Foundation, 1987.

Tomlinson, Tommy M., and Walberg, Herbert J. *Academic Work and Educational Excellence: Raising Student Productivity.* Berkeley, Calif.: McCutchan, 1986.

Tucker, Marc, and Mandel, David. "The Carnegie Report: A Call for Redesigning the Schools." *Phi Delta Kappan* 68 (September 1986): 24-27.

Twentieth Century Fund Task Force on Federal Elementary and Secondary Education Policy. *Making the Grade.* New York: Twentieth Century Fund, May 1983.

CHAPTER FOUR

The Federal Agenda for Excellence: Practicing the Politics of 'Equitable' Neglect

Inequalities of mind and body are so established by God Almighty, in His constitution of human nature, that no art or policy can ever plane them down to a level. I have never read reasoning more absurd, sophistry more gross. . . than the subtle labors of Helvetius and Rousseau, to demonstrate the natural equality of mankind. . . . The golden rule, do as you would be done by, is all the equality that can be supported or defended by reason or reconciled to common sense.

—John Adams writing to Jefferson, 13 July 1813

The slogan of "Excellence," stimulated by the Peters and Waterman book, *In Search of Excellence,* which so lifted American businessmen's sagging spirits in 1982, now has become a tired cliché; but it remains a catchphrase for education policy makers. Most observers concede that the initial impetus for the Excellence Movement was the publication of *A Nation at Risk* in 1983. Since then reporters, columnists, and college professors have tried to enhance the movement by linking excellence to every line of educational prose they write. Without that 36-page report, the others that came soon after would have died of neglect, the fate that usually befalls such commission reports. Many observers credit its widespread influence to its brevity, to its crisis tone, and even to its exaggerations of problems and its simplistic recommendations. Its endorsement by the President and the Department of Education during the 1984 election campaign also attracted considerable support for the report.

At first, the President did not seem to recognize the political value of *A Nation at Risk*. When he did acknowledge the report after questioning from the media, he spoke of the need for tuition vouchers, prayer in the schools, and reduced school busing (none of which were mentioned in the report). He made no reference to the call for a greater federal role, which the report recommended. It seems clear, in view of the President's education agenda, that federal initiatives will not be drawn from *A Nation at Risk* or any of the other reports, despite the widespread attention they have received.

Instead, federal policy relative to education is being drawn from another document, one that has been neither widely studied by educators nor analyzed by the popular media. The tone of this influential document is admittedly conservative, and its commitment to the public schools — or to their improvement — is slight.

This document is in two parts that must be considered together. The first part, *Mandate for Leadership* (Heatherly), was issued in 1981 and the second, *Mandate for Leadership II* (Butler et al.), was issued in 1984, both under the auspices of the Heritage Foundation, a conservative policy studies group. Several contributors to the document have been given powerful positions in the Department of Education, the Department of Justice, and other federal agencies. Some have been reprimanded, transferred, or fired for making public statements that made their respective departments appear to be insensitive to social issues or to such groups as handicapped persons.

The Agenda

Before 1980, the Heritage Foundation was a little-known source of publications for conservative activists. It gained respectability and power after it became known that President Reagan relied heavily on it to develop his executive and legislative agenda. The foundation claims that of its 1981 recommendations, "nearly two-thirds had been or were being transformed into policy" by the end of the President's first year in office. The cover for *Mandate II* quotes U.S. Attorney General Edwin Meese as saying that President Reagan "personally will use *Mandate II*, and . . . it will be an important contribution to what happens in this country in the years ahead." Educators would do well, then, to know what *Mandate for Leadership* I and II recommend for education.

In 1981, *Mandate for Leadership I* called on the federal government to:

- Provide tuition tax credits and vouchers to give parents greater control over their children's education and to stimulate competition for an ailing education monopoly;
- Allow school districts to convert Chapter One aid into vouchers, so that the disadvantaged could purchase educational services in either public or private schools;
- Pass a school prayer constitutional amendment to remove any suggestion that the Constitution prohibits prayer in schools, requires participation in prayer, or prohibits composed prayer;
- Abolish the Department of Education to break the stranglehold of centralized special-interest control over education policy and to return responsibility for education to its rightful place, the states and local communities;
- Adopt educational block grants to free state and local levels of crippling regulatory burdens and high administrative costs and to end the preemption of the education process by the federal government;
- Limit federal funding for higher education to help for those individuals truly needing assistance, to reduce federal subsidization of interest rates, and to require students receiving grants to pay for a larger portion of their expenses;
- Clarify the interpretation of the term "recipient" as applied to Title IX, so that it means only the program or activity receiving direct or indirect federal funds, thus curtailing federal regulation and protecting the integrity of private schools; and
- Redefine the federal role as one of leadership; that is, "defining and encouraging excellence," making available the most up-to-date and well-proven methods of its attainment and recognizing people and programs that exemplify excellence in education with Presidential Excellence Awards.

One needs to read the *Mandate* documents carefully to find what the real agenda is. The 1981 *Mandate* that calls for giving vouchers to the disadvantaged was designed to avoid accusations that tuition tax credits would benefit only the middle class and, at the same time, to lay the groundwork for reducing aid to disadvantaged students (a long-time target of conservative groups). According to *Mandate*, the intent is to:

> Keep Title I separate from all the other programs, and retain its character as aid specifically targeted for the disadvantaged; but transform it into a voucher system. . . . the aid itself would go . . . directly to the parents of disadvantaged children in the form of vouchers which could be used for either public or private education.

Even if it did not pass, this proposal would make it impossible for anyone to accuse the Administration of "middle class bias" in its advocacy of private-school tuition tax credits. (It would also lay the rhetorical groundwork for fighting for cuts in Title I appropriations under the existing structure). (P. 177)

The 1984 *Mandate For Leadership II* reported that the 1981 initiatives "were successfully realized in direct proportion to the degree to which the Administration had control of decision making." It lauded *A Nation at Risk* as evidence that the foundation's objectives can be achieved through presidential and federal intervention:

> The greatest success was at the executive level. The bipartisan Commission on Excellence in Education['s] . . . timely analysis in 1983 of the education malaise and its prescription for cure triggered widespread affirmative response: a national consensus on certain education principles emerged — core competencies for all students, higher standards, better teacher preparedness. . . . The Education Department's January 1984 State Education Statistics report . . . shattered some long held illusions (such as that more money automatically improves academic performance) and laid the groundwork for additional analysis. Finally, the Department's Secondary School Recognition Program . . . and the President's Academic Fitness Awards Program . . . have proven to be effective stimulants of educational excellence. (p. 52)
>
> Another "success" resulted from folding 42 narrow, categorical education programs into the Chapter 2 Block Grant. It "has given state and local agencies greater discretion over the application of federal funds and has saved them an estimated $1.8 million in administrative costs and 191,000 man-hours in paper work. In addition, case studies indicate that state agencies have been careful and responsible in applying the grants."* (p.53)

Mandate II deplored lack of success at judicial and legislative levels. Although applauding a "major victory" in the Grove City decision, which permitted sexual discrimination in a private university, the report warned that "congressional liberals" may be expected to renew efforts to pass new versions of the "so-called Civil Rights Act of 1984, which would mandate unprecedented and devastating intrusion by the federal government into the activities of the states and private institutions" (pp. 52-53).

Attempts to achieve conservative initiatives through legislative action failed almost completely. According to *Mandate II*, tuition tax-credits legis-

---

*Studies indicated that much of the money was being used to purchase computers and software for general use.

lation failed because of "the dilatory manner in which the Secretary of Education and the White House (with the notable exceptions of President Reagan and Counselor Edwin Meese) dealt with this proposal." No action was taken during the first term to use Chapter One funds for vouchers. The prayer amendment fell short of the two-thirds majority needed for passage. Efforts to abolish the Department of Education were abandoned: "Indeed," says the Heritage Foundation, "the procrastinating manner in which the Administration dealt with the proposal sent signals to the Hill that the Administration was less than serious about the venture."

> Several of the incomplete initiatives of the last four years might have succeeded if an early, unified effort had been focused on the task of winning congressional and public support. In some cases, factions within the Administration either failed to act at crucial points or acted counterproductively, thereby ensuring defeat of the effort. A carefully designed game plan and a Secretary dedicated to President Reagan's agenda and to working with the conservatives in the Department to implement it were often lacking. (p. 53)

The Heritage Foundation's proposed initiatives for 1985 pressed harder. On page 62 of *Mandate II* appears the following:

1) Appoint a national commission to examine the effectiveness of federal education programs.

2) Encourage state initiatives to establish tuition tax credits and education vouchers.

3) Publicize state efforts to allow prayer in school.

4) Obtain unitary declarations from school districts that can pass the two-part test on discrimination – do not harass such districts if they pass the test, even if they are composed of a majority of one race.

5) Review civil rights regulations affecting education, with the goal of eliminating the effects test wording.

6) Enact legislation that would require students receiving federal financial assistance to adhere to minimum academic standards.

7) Appoint a Presidential Commission on Higher Education to examine the purpose of higher education and to suggest ways of achieving that purpose.

8) Merge the Office of Management with the Office of Planning, Budget and Evaluation.

9) Merge the Office of Inter-Governmental/Inter-Agency Affairs with the Office of Legislation and Public Affairs.

10) Abolish or consolidate the Regional Offices.

11) Abolish the National Institute of Education, the National Center for Education Statistics, and the Office of Education Research and Im-

provement, and combine their functions into a new Office of the Assistant Secretary for Research.

Mandates for the Role of the Federal Government

The principal agenda item stated for the federal role in education, found in both *Mandates*, is to leave education decision making to state and local officials. According to *Mandate I,* the federal government "has absolutely no business dictating to local school districts how or what they must teach" (p. 185). The report says that federal education policy should "restore authority to the states and local communities, and increase their discretionary funding power" (p. 170).

> Local authority has always been one of the greatest strengths of our educational system. . . . Local school officials must certainly know the needs of their students better than the federal government. (p. 185)

The Heritage Foundation states that the federal government should become "supportive" of state and local school systems rather than "interventionist." The prescribed way to avoid an interventionist role is to eliminate regulation, cease all investigatory actions, initiate no advocacy for any groups or persons, and collect no information relative to compliance with court orders or legislative mandates. Indeed, the executive departments of federal government are expected to change judicial and legislative mandates, to blunt their administration, or to render them harmless through neglect.

The rhetoric about state and local control must be understood in terms of the long-range conservative agenda, which has not changed much since the early days of this nation's history. Since Andrew Jackson's election to the White House, American conservatives have been strong proponents of their brand of states' rights and local control. After Jackson's election, the Federalists believed that the devil (common people) had taken over the federal government; so they left Washington and returned home in order to use state and local agencies (churches, courts, and schools) to promote their philosophy of government (Schlesinger 1950).

The current call to return control to states and local agencies springs from a conviction that state and local officials may be more responsive than federal officials to conservative pressures to blunt or to reduce gains resulting from federal initiatives to open educational opportunity to Black-Americans (through desegregation, affirmative action, and college loans), to women (through Title IX, affirmative action, and college loans), to the handicapped (through P.L. 94-142 and Department of Education regulations), and to new immigrant populations (through bilingual education programs and re-

72

lated regulations). During the past two decades, federal court decisions, legislative actions, and supportive regulations have tended to support these groups while local and state traditions generally have not.

The Heritage Foundation does not wish to get the federal government out of education altogether. The reports recommend a "more genuinely 'federal' . . . program of federal and state cooperation." The federal role is to press for improved academic performance and traditional values as defined by conservatives.

> But this [reduced federal presence in our schools] need not mean that the federal role in education must be passive or that the government should abandon its legitimate concerns about the quality of American education. Rather, the federal government will be freed to pursue a far more effective role in helping our schools and colleges improve their performance. (*Mandate I*, p.164)
>
> The American people do not need Washington to run their schools. All they need is a sense that excellence is legitimate and achievable, some suggestions about what standards to set for their own schools, the relevant questions to ask their teachers and local administrators, and some information on how the schools are doing and what seems to work around the country. (*Mandate II*, p. 56)

A Shift in Thinking About the Department of Education

Mandate for Leadership II abandons the call for abolishing the Department of Education. Rather, it calls for controlling and using the agency to promote the conservative agenda.

> The question now becomes: How can it be turned into an agency of minimum nuisance, modest scope and yet *positive moral influence on the nature and quality of American education*. (p. 54, emphasis added)

Even the 1981 *Mandate* noted that "the status of the [Department of Education] as a Cabinet department is less critical . . . than the overhaul of federal education *policy*" (p. 166). In 1984, *Mandate II* recommended that the department should become a "three-room school house" with each room serving a different function:

> The first room would house a check-writing machine from which funds are disbursed to states and localities . . . [in] block grants. . . . [I]t will be the obligation of the recipients, not federal bureaucrats, to decide exactly how to spend the funds. (p. 54)
>
> The second room . . . would house a small but outstanding statistical bureau . . . to collect education data of high quality and reliability

and to issue reports on the condition and progress of American education at all levels . . . direct the administration of professionally designed
achievement tests, conducted under controlled conditions. . . . Honest
comparisons based on high standards could be obtained and promptly
publicized.

The third room . . . would house a "bully pulpit." From there the
Department's leaders and other Americans with sound ideas would assist
in the effort to improve schools and colleges. Ideas would issue forth,
with serious talk of values and curricular content, and "moral pressure" for school reform could be mobilized . . . projecting a vision
of what citizens might reasonably expect from their children's schools,
teachers, textbooks and colleges. (p. 55)

After commenting that "it is not necessary that the federal government
must be coercive to be effective in education," *Mandate II* states that the
federal level ought to establish a "comprehensive, timely and reliable information system," which is "necessary for the improvement of educational quality." Information gathering is to be bolstered by "consultation and
technical assistance . . . an area where the federal government is positioned
to attract the limited number of genuine experts who can offer advice." Controlled research and development projects, "if oriented toward practical
problem-solving, rather than 'values clarification,' can be worthwhile" to
lend credibility to the information that is disseminated.

Using the Department of Education to disseminate "credible" information seems a laudable objective, until one understands how much power
over state and local policy is gained by controlling what that information
will be, how it is gathered, and how and when and to whom it is disseminated. Indeed, the Heritage Foundation's traditional opposition to the Department of Education and to other information-gathering agencies stems from
their having collected and disseminated information that refuted the conservative position on civil rights, disciplinary practices, and instructional
techniques.

Mandate II concludes that it is "futile" to think of depoliticizing research
and data collection; so, steps need to be taken to link it with "larger policy
concerns" and the "political agenda" rather than leaving it "captive to educational data collection and research interest groups" (p. 62). Data collection
is to be reorganized and headed by a person "of distinction and demonstrated
accomplishment" (p. 62) who also has been appointed by a President who
knows that "every action, every activity is measured against how it advances
the accomplishment of the [political] agenda" (p. 511). Clearly, the Foundation feels that the federal role is to use information collection and dissemination as an instrument for promoting conservative political goals.

According to *Mandate II*, the federal government should stop regulating local and state governments as well as private agencies for compliance with civil rights mandates and other federal regulations odious to the foundation. Instead, "credible" people should collect and disseminate information favorable to conservative objectives. That information could be used by vocal interest groups that would put pressure on state legislatures, governors, and local officials to force them to implement programs that cannot be achieved through federal action.

> Given the resistance at the federal level to amending the U.S. Constitution, state referenda are central to maintaining the political momentum [for a prayer amendment]. To encourage this trend, state efforts should be publicized by the new administration. (p. 58)

Reshaping the Goals of Education

The Heritage Foundation is a voice for traditional conservative philosophy, which emphasizes basic academics and traditional values, neither of which is specifically defined. A "basic" education is defined as facts tested by achievement tests:

> A Secretary of Education should make it clear that he *does* have a clear objective against which all education programs will be evaluated: their contributions to the basic academic skills of reading, writing, and calculation, *as measured by standardized norm-referenced tests*. (*Mandate I*, p. 178, emphasis added)

The *Mandates* also set forth some broader educational functions: "the search for truth, the acquisition of academic skills, the development of a responsible citizenry" (*Mandate II*, p. 56). Education is expected to fulfill some quite utilitarian values: "still another opportunity to stress traditional values (employment, job preparation, productivity, etc.)" (*Mandate I*, p. 178).

According to the foundation, the traditional values are not humanistic, aesthetic, or affective. Such objectives are labeled "social engineering," "liberal-left," or "psycho-social" (*Mandate I*, pp. 187-88).

> Positions with the Department of Education . . . should be filled with individuals with strong commitment to the attainment and improvement of basic academic skills. Those individuals should also oppose any further Federal support for "humanistic" or psycho-social education activities, projects or programs.
>
> All personnel who indicate support of "humanistic" or psycho-social programs in the schools should be relocated to other agencies or moved to positions where they will have no authority. (p. 194)

The foundation certainly does not see education as a means for improving society, except as individuals are taught to conform to the American values as defined by conservative special-interest groups:

> Capitulating to the demands of special interest groups, the federal government has imposed upon the nation's schools false dogmas that have undermined the education process and distorted education's primary mission. (*Mandate II*, p. 56)

Mandates for the Future of Public Schools

Mandates I and II continue the American conservatives' historical opposition to public schools. The 1980s version of the opposition is to point to real deficiencies of the public schools, exaggerate them as needed, link the schools with unpopular court decisions or legislative actions, denounce school officials and their associations, and then appeal to an upwardly mobile middle class with expendable income and to the declining number of taxpayers with children in schools. *Mandate II* calls for government support for non-public schools, stressing tuition tax credits and vouchers. To secure such aid, federal officials should use their office as a "bully pulpit," from which pronouncements could be backed up by federal block grants, which would ensure state-level attention to the federal agenda:

> The Secretary of Education should travel widely, stressing the importance and necessity of parental choice, and indicating that credits and vouchers can facilitate choice for parents of all income levels. (p. 57)

Parents apparently should have choice only to attend schools that teach a set of acceptable norms:

> A system of alternate schooling will be preferable only to the degree that the guiding principles of the new schools are an improvement over those that have guided the old. No improvement will be made if, for example, the alternate schools pursue distorted or antisocial objectives. (p. 57)

Apparently, the foundation feels it has found a way to control schools more effectively. The 1981 *Mandate* castigated values clarification (a teaching technique actually used by very few schools) for dictating values (p. 188-89). But by 1984 *Mandate II* seemed to be proposing a national values clarification to control all schools.

> One option that should be considered is that of publicly debating the purpose of schooling in the United States, and the values this na-

tion represents, and the feasibility of instituting broad, reasonable agreed-upon guidelines at the state level. (p. 57)

Mandates Against "Special Interest Groups"

Mandate II continues the foundation's efforts to halt enforcement of affirmative action and other civil rights legislation, primarily through budgetary controls, restaffing, shifting responsibility to offices currently controlled by people the foundation trusts − all in an effort to undercut any action from the federal level:

> All civil rights enforcement activities . . . should be shifted to the Department of Justice. There, enforcement action should proceed only from private suits or suits filed by the Justice Department and not through compliance reviews. (p. 56)

Civil rights and school desegregation are old-time targets for conservatives; and the foundation thinks that the time is politically right to eradicate the gains made under administrations that, in its terms, "pandered to special interest groups."

> The administration should move to obtain unitary declarations from school districts that can pass the two-part test. Even if the districts are composed of a majority of one race, they should be free of harassment.
> [The school] should no longer be subject to remedial supervision by the courts. Neither should the school have to submit plans concerning the future administration of the school district. Control of the district should be left in the hands of the school board, parents and other local education agencies. (pp. 58-59)
> [R]eview . . . civil rights regulations with the goal of eliminating the effects-test wording. . . . enforcement proceedings should be limited to concrete, specific acts of discrimination; practices should not be considered discriminatory if they have the effect, but not the intent of leading to an imbalance of legally protected groups. (p. 60)
> Affirmative action and numerical quotas should not be considered acceptable methods of achieving parity. The schools should be free to do their job, which is to educate the nation's youth. (pp. 59-60)

Having fought desegregation in every possible way at state and local levels, the conservative coalition is now seeking ways to undermine desegregation by withholding budgets from or restaffing those that are charged with compliance reviews and investigations.

The *Mandates* are especially opposed to bilingual education, women's rights, handicapped aid, professional educators and their organizations, and federal grants for research and development. They particularly oppose those

77

curriculum projects that arouse emotional opposition. According to *Mandate I*:

> Women's Education Equity is . . . more in keeping with extreme feminist ideology than concern for the quality of education. . . . Its programs require immediate scrutiny and its budget should be drastically cut. (pp. 179-80)
>
> Teacher Corps should continue to receive continued support, but . . . support for Teacher Centers (which function as taxpayer financed union halls) should be cut. (p.180)
>
> [Bilingual programs] fail to equip students to advance and compete in the mainstream of American society. . . . In the eyes of many, it has become a means of cultural maintenance. There is nothing wrong with people trying to maintain their culture, but they should be in charge of doing it – not the federal government. . . . Our schools should concentrate on teaching English to these children. They are going to have to learn English sooner or later – so why not sooner? (pp. 186-87)

The Foundation's Strategy for Change

Mandate II presents a clear strategy for achieving recommended objectives. Indeed, the subtitle of the report, *Continuing the Conservative Revolution*, is supported throughout with specific ideas about how it can be achieved. Chapters 23 and 24 analyze the powers and constraints on presidential power; and Chapter 25, "Techniques for Managing Policy Change," presents a political agenda guiding all actions to circumvent or to subvert legislative and judicial mandates and prerogatives:

> If every . . . political executive controlled only ten percent of the bureaucratic discretion in his area of responsibility, the federal government could be turned upside down. Much of the President's conservative mandate could be implemented without legislative changes. (p. 560)

Federal agencies, such as the Departments of Justice and Education, are to be restaffed with new personnel who are "credible" to conservatives and who support conservative ideological views of what education is for and who should be educated. In managing tenured career civil service personnel, the President is to rely primarily on motivating staff members who are termed "*climbers*" because they are "purely self-interested and motivated by things . . . power, income and prestige . . . over which the political executive has some control" (p. 522). Both new appointees and the climbers are to control what gets attention and what gets funded. The President is to use appointments and budgetary controls to weaken programs that enjoy congressional or popular support. Part-time personnel or contracted consultants are to be used to meet this goal when full-time personnel cannot be co-opted or controlled.

Most educational programs, particularly those that have strong support in Congress, are to be given to state and local officials to administer with little oversight and few regulations. State officials are to be empowered to exercise more influence over local programs; they are to be the primary funnels for federal initiatives. Federal influence over state and local policies and practices is to be exercised by controlling information and by focusing public opinion on getting the desired action from state and local officials.

Information and influence are to be directed to create and sustain alternatives to public schools, to reduce government initiatives to provide services for historically neglected groups, to preserve conservative views of individual and institutional roles in society, to promote conservative values, and to strengthen and ensure the longevity of conservative influences and controls at all levels of government.

What We Can Expect to See from the Federal Government

Mandate I and II certainly will be influential in developing federal policy until at least 1988, and personnel appointments and actions stemming from that policy will be affecting education policy for a decade or more. The Heritage Foundation's role as advocate of conservative policy and practice in the United States leaves little doubt that federal policies will be designed to fulfill the traditional conservative agenda.

The foundation states that it is "dedicated to the principles of free competitive enterprise, limited government, individual liberty, and a strong national defense." But there are other, less accepted objectives that have been on the conservative agenda for decades; and those, too, may influence policy in order to make education serve that agenda. Such policies include initiatives that at root have the effect of: 1) indoctrinating children with conservative ideology and preventing schools from teaching anything contrary to this ideology; 2) weakening public support for public schools; 3) promoting the interests of private schools; 4) keeping black, immigrant, or other poor minority students out of neighborhood schools that conservatives feel are linked to their property values; and 5) laying the groundwork for long-range conservative influence in federal government, regardless of who is in the White House or Congress.

The Heritage Foundation *Mandates*, viewed in conjunction with traditional conservative goals and actions, presage the following initiatives from the federal level:

1. Consolidate control over federal education agencies.
2. Control the collection and dissemination of information about education.
3. Direct pressure on local boards and state legislatures to clarify and standardize educational expectations and to press for vouchers and prayer in the school.
4. Undermine confidence in public schools.
5. Reduce educational opportunity for historically neglected populations.

If the federal agenda does follow that set forth in the *Mandates*, the question becomes, "Who benefits and who loses from the Excellence Movement?" That question is now being debated in virtually every state legislature. While appearing to disassociate itself from education policy, the federal government perhaps is exercising greater influence over policy than it does in those areas in which it traditionally has provided funds.

References

Aquila, Frank D. *Title IX: Implications for Education of Women*. Fastback 156. Bloomington, Ind.: Phi Delta Kappa Educational Foundation, 1981.

Beauchamp, Edward R. *Bilingual Education Policy: An International Perspective*. Fastback 227. Bloomington, Ind.: Phi Delta Kappa Educational Foundation, 1985.

Bell, Terrel H. "Education Policy Development in the Reagan Administration." *Phi Delta Kappan* 67 (March 1986): 487-93.

Bennett, William J. *First Lessons: A Report on Elementary Education in America*. Washington, D.C.: U.S. Government Printing Office, 1986. Stock No. 065-000-00259-1

Bernstein, Harriet T. "The New Politics of Textbook Adoption." *Phi Delta Kappan* 66 (March 1985): 463-66.

Bordewyk, Gordon I. "You're in Good Hands." *School Administrator* 42, no. 2 (February 1985): 30. Reprinted from *Christian Home and School* (February 1984).

Bryant, Gene. *Profiles of a New Right Group*. Nashville: Tennessee Education Association, 1983. Contains profiles of Moral Majority, Heritage Foundation, Public Service Research Council, and Educational Research Analysts.

Butler, Stuart M.; Sanera, Michael; and Weinrod, W. Bruce. *Mandate for Leadership II: Continuing the Conservative Revolution*. Washington, D.C.: Heritage Foundation, 1984.

Catterall, James S. *Tuition Tax Credits: Fact and Fiction*. Fastback 188. Bloomington, Ind.: Phi Delta Kappa Educational Foundation, 1983.

Clark, David L., and Astuto, Terry A. *The Significance and Permanence of Changes in Federal Educational Policy 1980-1988*. Bloomington, Ind.: Policy Studies Center of the University Council for Educational Administration, Indiana University, 1986.

Copperman, Paul. *The Literacy Hoax: The Decline of Reading, Writing and Learning in the Public Schools and What We Can Do About It.* New York: Morrow, Quill, 1980.

Crawford, Alan. *Thunder on the Right: The New Right and the Politics of Resentment.* New York: Pantheon, 1980.

Crawford, James. "Conservative Groups Take Aim at Bilingual-Education Programs." *Education Week,* 19 March 1986, pp. 14-15.

Docksai, Ronald F. "Education." In *Mandate for Leadership: Policy Management in a Conservative Administration,* edited by Charles L. Heatherly. Washington, D.C.: Heritage Foundation, 1981.

Educational Research Service. "Coleman Report on Public and Private Schools." Draft summary and eight critiques. Arlington, Va., April 1981.

Farr, Roger, and Tulley, Michael A. "Do Adoption Committees Perpetuate Mediocre Textbooks?" *Phi Delta Kappan* 66 (March 1985): 467-71.

Finn, Chester E., Jr. "The Drive for Educational Excellence: Moving Toward a Public Consensus." *Change* 15 (1983): 14-22.

Gardner, Eileen. "The Department of Education." In *Mandate for Leadership II: Continuing the Conservative Revolution,* edited by Stuart M. Butler, Michael Sanera, and W. Bruce Weinrod. Washington, D.C.: Heritage Foundation, 1984.

Glenn, Charles L. "New Challenges: A Civil Rights Agenda for the Public Schools." *Phi Delta Kappan* 67 (May 1986): 653-56.

Greene, Bert I., and Pasch, Marvin. "Observing the Birth of the Hatch Amendment Regulations: Lessons for the Education Profession." *Educational Leadership* 43 (December 1985/January 1986): 42-48.

Heatherly, Charles L., ed. *Mandate for Leadership: Policy Management in a Conservative Administration. (Mandate I).* Washington, D.C.: Heritage Foundation, 1981.

Hermann, Margaret G. "Assessing Personality at a Distance: A Profile of Ronald Reagan." *Mershon Center Quarterly Report* 7, no. 6 (Spring 1983), Ohio State University.

Iannaccone, L. "Excellence: An Emergent Educational Issue." *Politics of Education Bulletin* 12, no. 3 (1985): 1, 3-8.

Jenkinson, Edward B. *The Schoolbook Protest Movement: 40 Questions and Answers.* Bloomington, Ind.: Phi Delta Kappa Educational Foundation, 1986.

Justiz, Manuel J., and Moorman, Hunter N. "New NIE Peer Review Procedures." *Educational Researcher* 14, no. 1 (January 1985): 5-11.

Keller, Edward. "Put the CHOICE Act in Layaway — And Leave It There." *Communicator: Newsletter of the National Association of Elementary School Principals* 10, no. 2 (October 1986): 7.

Kluger, Richard. *Simple Justice: The History of Brown v. Board of Education and Black America's Struggle for Equality.* London: André Deutsch, 1977.

Nathan, Joe. "The Rhetoric and the Reality of Expanding Educational Choices." *Phi Delta Kappan* 66 (March 1985): 476-81.

Pipho, Chris. "Student Choice: The Return of the Voucher." *Phi Delta Kappan* 66 (March 1985): 461-62.

Robertson, Wilmot. *The Dispossessed Majority*. Cape Canaveral, Fla.: Howard Allen Enterprises, 1981.

Ross, Doris. "Getting to a New Look for Textbooks." *State Education Leader* 3 (Winter 1984): 14.

Schlesinger, Arthur M., Jr. *The Age of Jackson*. Boston: Little, Brown, 1950.

Shakeshaft, Charol. "A Gender at Risk." *Phi Delta Kappan* 67 (March 1986): 499-503.

Shapiro, H. Svi. "Education, the Welfare State, and Reaganomics: The Limits of Conservative Reform." *Urban Education* 20 (January 1986): 443-72.

Stimson, Jim. "Will NIE Reform Create a Productive Unit or 'Federal Research Czar'?" *School Administrator* 43, no. 6 (June 1986): 21-24.

U.S. Department of Education. *What Works: Research About Teaching and Learning*. Washington, D.C.: U.S. Department of Education, 1986.

Tetreault, Mary Kay, and Schmuck, Patricia A. "Equity, Educational Reform, and Gender." *Issues in Education* 3 (Summer 1985): 45-67.

Thanksgiving Statement Group. "Developing Character, Transmitting Knowledge: Sustaining the Momentum for Reform in American Education." A Thanksgiving Day statement by a Group of 27 Americans. Thanksgiving Statement Group, c/o ARL, 2605 W. 147th St., Posen, IL 60649. 21 November 1984.

Turner, Donald G. *Legal Issues in Education of the Handicapped*. Fastback 186. Bloomington, Ind.: Phi Delta Kappa Educational Foundation, 1983.

Viguerie, Richard A. *The New Right: We're Ready to Lead*. Falls Church, Va.: Viguerie Company, 1981.

Warger, Cynthia L.; Aldinger, Loviah E.; and Okun, Kathy A. *Mainstreaming in the Secondary School: The Role of the Regular Teacher*. Fastback 187. Bloomington, Ind.: Phi Delta Kappa Educational Foundation, 1983.

Watrous, Mary Woodworth. "Excellence in Schools: A Matter of Who Is Taught." *Education Digest* 49, no. 8 (April 1984): 12-13.

CHAPTER FIVE

Implementing Excellence:
Some Cautionary Notes

The time has come when we owe it to our country and ourselves to speak the whole truth in this matter, even though it disturbs our self-satisfaction a bit.

—James Gordon Carter, 1824
Early Massachusetts Educator

In Chapter One reference was made to reformers who prostitute the pursuit of educational excellence by indiscriminately plopping "whipped cream on mud." The Excellence Movement has had its share of hucksters and mountebanks who exploit the call for reform by promoting ill-conceived and limited programs and policies. It probably is not surprising that some educators are attracted to the quick fix or high profile solutions, given the intense pressures for accountability and the precipitous decline in public confidence in the schools. However, superficial responses to complex educational problems actually may exacerbate the current troubles plaguing U. S. schools.

Successful implementation of reforms to achieve educational excellence must confront and resolve a wide range of philosophical, political, economic, and social issues. A short list of such issues would include: What is excellence? Can we provide excellence for all students? Who will pay for excellence? How will the pursuit of excellence affect extant social relationships? Will educational excellence promote economic prosperity and

83

social justice? Clearly, it is important that we focus on these questions as we consider the salient criticisms in the reform reports and their recommendations for change.

The reform reports have been criticized on many fronts. In some instances, these criticisms were defensive reactions from professional educators or other apologists for public schools. Various efforts at implementing excellence have been criticized for setting unrealistic performance expectations without providing adequate support and resources. Although some reactions have been defensive, even petty, many have come from thoughtful analysts whose criticisms have been useful for anyone genuinely trying to improve educational quality. Nevertheless, if educational quality is to improve, reformers need to know some of the shortcomings, inconsistencies, and unanticipated negative consequences of their recommendations and their implementation. Let us now look at some of the most frequent criticisms relative to the reform reports and their implementation in order to identify impediments to the improvement of educational quality and to overcome them by designing more successful efforts.

Tenuous Ties Between Education Research and Policy

Some of the reform reports did not purport to be based on education research; rather, they were written as political documents that would arouse public attention and move policy makers to action. Others claimed to have research to support their recommendations.

The research base used to justify the Excellence Movement in its early stages has been described as being "patchy, dated and not nearly as dramatic as the rhetoric" (Peterson 1983). For example, some of the state and federal reports since 1983 have called for more time in school, even though research has consistently demonstrated that the nature and quality of students' *engaged time* in learning tasks is more important than the amount of time spent in school (Karweit and Slavin 1982).

The reform reports have tended to emphasize evidence that the schools were failing, while overlooking or ignoring other evidence. Many reports failed to acknowledge that achievement had improved somewhat in basic skills in populations targeted by federal funding programs, while it had declined in populations neglected under federal funds (Lapointe 1984). Some reports exaggerated the need for more technological personnel and engineers (Rotberg 1984). They also underplayed the need for higher-level skills in problem-solving and failed to note that SAT scores had declined more in verbal skills than in math (Rotberg 1984).

Astute state and local politicians have used existing research to gain credibility in order to push their particular reform initiatives. Nevertheless, the use of education research as evidence to support one side or another of a political debate lessens its potential contributions to the improvement of practice. Unfortunately, those unsuspecting souls who implement policies on the persuasive power of research-based rhetoric must deal with the broken promises and unanticipated consequences when negative results are forthcoming.

While we do not now have, nor probably ever will have, an adequate research base to provide unequivocal guidance for policy and practice, it seems poor policy to overstate the problems in our schools and to exaggerate the outcomes of reform recommendations based on inaccurate or incomplete research data. Change should be based as much on informed, professional judgment as on the currently available research base. Research simply is too contradictory and too inadequate to provide the sole basis for making national education policy decisions.

Oversimplifications

Some reports have been criticized for making simplistic recommendations. For example, more instructional time does not necessarily result in greater productivity and achievement, particularly if the teacher makes the same pedagogical mistakes over and over again. More pay does not automatically make better teachers. Spending more time or more money as a way to achieve quality is a simplistic response to a very complex problem. This is a lesson that we should have learned from the mistakes of past faddish reforms.

Some reform reports seem to oversimplify research that purports to show a relationship between educational reform and the resolution of a social problem, such as unemployment, when actually little evidence exists to indicate that more and better education opens jobs for groups who are victims of job discrimination or for workers whose jobs have become obsolete because of technological advances in their occupations.

The reports also have been accused of oversimplifying how easy it is to get reforms enacted. Almost always they ignore the costs of implementation, and they suggest few ways to deal with the resistance and the inertia that makes change difficult.

Top-Down Reform

The most prevalent state and local responses to the reform reports assume that education can be improved by imposing authoritiy from the top down. The prevailing mood seems to be that moral leadership from national authorities and prescriptive leadership from state authorities can change the schools. The whole reform process seems to be a repetition of the fallacies that caused the Great Society and the War on Poverty reformers to believe that they could reform the schools by selling ideas and packages to state education agencies and superintendents. We failed miserably in those attempts because we did not reach the classroom; we did not reach into the everyday lives of students and teachers; we did not recognize that the schools function through a network of decision systems over which other higher authorities have limited control or impact. Too often, top-down reforms are proclaimed using slick, four-color brochures to convince the public that something is being done, when the real purpose is to maintain the status quo. Authentic educational reform requires fundamental changes at the building level and in each classroom (see Chapter Two).

When central office administration is isolated from classrooms, its impact on teaching and learning is small and may even be negative. Some school districts, in an effort to improve instruction, unleash a horde of authoritarian supervisors, who do little more than engender hostility and resistance from teachers.

The effective schools literature, which has influenced many local responses to the Excellence Movement, tends to emphasize strong administrative control, particularly by the building principal. Faulty interpretations of strong administrative control may lead to the single-minded pursuit of a narrow academic purpose while stifling teacher creativity (see Chapters Eight and Nine).

Inadequate Attention to Cost

Lack of attention to the costs of reform and to the federal role in implementing those reforms is a frequently mentioned criticism of the reports. Although many of the second-stage reform reports acknowledge that greater funding will be necessary, few of the early reports paid any attention to the costs of the reforms they proposed (some did call for more federal assistance). Adding time to the school day or year adds costs. Merit pay plans add costs. Adding graduation requirements adds costs. Reducing class size adds costs. Better evaluation systems or more staff development for staff members add costs. The American Association of School Administrators estimated that education would cost 28% more per year if recommendations from *A Nation at Risk* were fully implemented. The Carnegie report, *A Nation Prepared: Teachers for the 21st Century* (1986), estimates that needed reforms, including some extraordinary proposals for compensating teachers, will require "substantial" costs, which can be met only if the proportion of gross national product allocated to education is maintained rather than continually reduced.

While the essential reforms needed for true excellence are not ensured simply by adding more money to school budgets (many reforms truly do not require more money), the recommendations from the reports calling for more time, more supervision, more development, better materials, and technological assistance definitely will cost more money. The reports have been widely criticized by educators for failing to consider ways for schools to get additional money.

For many educators, one of the salutary effects of the reform movement has been increased expenditures at the state level, although in general these have not been sufficient to support widespread reform. Rather, they have resulted in small-scale pilot projects and showcase programs that have won media and public attention.

Overreliance on the Power of Computers

Many school districts across the country have responded to the perceived "computer illiteracy" crisis by purchasing computers and software with no clear plans for how to use them. The trend has been for school districts to buy computers when funds are available and sometimes when they are not. Block grant funds often are used for such purchases in some states. In the rush to look up-to-date, school districts showcase computers because they are highly visible evidence of reform in this era of rapid technological change. The rush for computer hardware is reminiscent of the purchase of language laboratory equipment in the late 1950s in response to the hysteria that surrounded the launching of Sputnik. A few years later, most of the sophisticated tape recorders, carrels, and headphones were catching dust in thousands of schools because teachers did not know how to use the equipment or competent foreign language teachers were not available to supplement electronic instruction.

Quite understandably, criticism has begun to emerge about the rush to implement reform recommendations for "computer literacy" with the purchase of thousands of computers. Apparently, schools are not the only institutions that have made foolish decisions about computer applications; one prominent investment newsletter reported such problems in business and industry:

> Will it save money? Teleconferencing does cut cost, true, . . . but equipment and transmission costs can easily exceed any savings.

Will it really save time? Electronic bulletin boards put information on display fast, but getting data takes longer; . . . In many cases an old fashioned bulletin board will work as well. Same thing holds for voicemail. It cuts back and forth calling, makes sure recorded messages get to the other person eventually. But in most cases dictating a quick memo will be just as effective.

Will it really boost business? Certainly not as much as fast-talking hardware salesmen claim. . . . [It will not provide] the "in person" touch that's so important in business agreements. (*Research Institute Recommendations*, 4 December 1984, p. 3)

Many observers have pointed out that computers and high technology will not open many jobs. Schools and colleges may be flooding the high-tech labor market and, as a result, reducing labor costs for that market. Meanwhile, students are not getting instruction and training that would be more appropriate for other types of employment.

There is little argument about the importance of computer literacy, but the lack of compatibility among the various types of hardware and software make it difficult to provide training that does not have to be undone or redone by employers. A related problem is that there is no consensus on what "computer literacy" means, so the public is confused when claims are made that the schools teach computer literacy in the curriculum.

Computer instruction seems to be most successful when the school has a teacher who has unusual interest and ability combined with the time and energy to design a program, recruit students into the program, secure the cooperation of other teachers and the principal, and generate continuing enthusiasm. The danger is that if this person leaves, the program might dry up or become so routine and mundane that student interest will wane. Then, protecting and maintaining the equipment becomes more important than student utilization.

Software seems to be another weakness in computer instruction. Much of what is available seems no better than the workbooks traditionally used to provide endless drill and practice. The initial motivation students might have to learn to use the computer dies quickly if all the computer program delivers is drivel.

Cost and maintenance present other problems. Even when the hardware is "donated" to the school, the costs for the software to use the computer may be more than what the "gift" is worth. Some have even suggested that the gift is merely a gimmick to get the school committed to a certain brand of computer, which then requires the purchase of expensive peripherals and software to make the computer operational. Maintenance costs to keep the equipment operating and in good repair is an important budgetary consideration. Failure to consider such factors has caused many other types of equipment to end up in school closets or storerooms. Finally, security is an increasing problem as both professional and amateur thieves find schools to be easy targets for stealing both equipment and software.

Staff resistance is another barrier to better and more widespread use of computers. Teachers in general have not taken well to instructional technology (textbooks and the chalkboard are notable exceptions). They show no more hospitality to computer keyboards and video monitors than they did to phonographs, film projectors, and tape recorders when those innovations first appeared on the scene. Certainly, there will be a need for extensive staff development and preservice training if computers are to be used effectively in the classroom.

None of these criticisms is to say that schools should not teach computer courses or use computer software to teach content or skills; but it does argue for clearer definition of purposes; better marshalling of personnel, equipment, and software; and long-range planning before rushing into poorly conceived programs. The public relations value of such purchases and programs will be shortlived and can backfire when malcontents in the community realize that mistakes have been made and begin to look for persons to blame. Recrimination and retribution are more likely than reform when educators hitch on to shortsighted bandwagons.

Elitism and Inequity

The reform reports with their focus on excellence carry a tone of elitism. Indeed, one definition of excellent (now archaic, according to *Webster's New Collegiate Dictionary*) is "superior, of higher rank or importance." Such a definition seems to be guiding some reform-minded policy makers. The dark side of elitism is captured by Kenneth Goodman (1984):

> Excellence as a goal is not itself incompatible with the goal of equity. But those who propose "Education for Excellence" argue that the attempts to produce educational equity have failed, that they have brought mediocrity and low standards, and that as a result a crisis exists in the school which is somehow related to a political, social and economic crisis in the society as a whole. They see the problems of education as flowing from this relaxation of standards and a lowering of expectations. So what they propose is that schools stop trying to serve all young people and concentrate on only those who can excel, who can achieve excellence.

Understandably, some educators resist the call for educational excellence because they consider such a stand elitist and a way of circumventing the need for expanded educational opportunity for all students. Equity has been a central goal of education policy during the last quarter century. Any actions that will diminish this goal should be scrutinized by educators. One of the reform reports addressing the issue of educational equity called it the "unfinished agenda." The National Coalition of Advocates for Students, in its report *Children at Risk*, argues:

> The United States cannot afford to leave under-developed the talents of millions of children who happen to be born different by virtue of race, language, sex or income status. Nor can it ignore, under the pretense of educational excellence, the unfinished national task of offering *every* child – Black, Hispanic, Native American, Asian and White – a fair chance to learn and become a self-sufficient citizen. The unique promise of this nation has been its commitment to extend opportunity to *all* – not just some – of its children.
>
> Policy makers at many different levels talk of bringing excellence to the schools and ignore the fact that hundreds of thousands of youngsters are not receiving even minimal educational opportunities guaranteed under law. In the current climate of educational reform, many observers have assumed that past legislative actions have achieved access and equity for students in our schools. With these matters taken care of, they believe, they can now turn attention to the distinct and separate issue of quality. (p. 4)

The *Children at Risk* report goes on to provide the following evidence to support the claim that "the income level of a child's family is a major determinant of the quality and quantity of education that a child receives":

> The average child from a family whose income is in the top quarter of the income range gets four years more schooling than the average child whose family income is in the bottom quarter.
>
> Many school districts allocate substantially fewer dollars to schools in poor and minority neighborhoods. The disparities among schools within a district are often just as great as the gap between low-income urban and rural districts and affluent suburban districts within the same state.
>
> Studies of classroom interactions reveal significant differences in teacher expectations and behavior towards students based on the social class of the students. Of the more than 40 million public school students, between 20 and 25 percent were eligible for Title I programs in 1980-81. Only about half of those eligible actually received services. . . . In 1980, Title I provided compensatory education services to over five million children, 70 percent of whom were in elementary schools. Over half of the students served were White, nearly a third Black, and the rest "Spanish surnamed," or other. (p. 8)

Since 1981, . . . in real dollars, the program has suffered a 20 percent reduction in funding. . . . This erosion has occurred despite research findings which indicate that the Title I Program contributed to the improvement of educational achievement for low-income students and reversed the impact of low expectations, inferior materials and resources, and overcrowded classes. . . . The National Assessment of Educational Progress in 1981 showed dramatic increases in reading scores for disadvantaged students over the past ten years. Most impressive were reading level gains among Black elementary school-age and 11-year-old students, which reduced the gap between Black and White students by 40 percent. Reading experts cited federal aid for reading instruction in elementary schools as a vital factor in these gains. Similar patterns were evident in mathematics. . . . However, . . . under the "new federalism," Title I was collapsed into Chapter I of the Education Consolidation and Improvement Act of 1981. Chapter I weakened targeting requirements, removed previously required parent advisory councils, eliminated many other accountability requirements, and substantially reduced federal monitoring and enforcement. (pp. 8-9)

Passow (1984), in a comprehensive analysis of the reform reports, criticizes them for providing little attention to and inadequate solutions for the problems of the urban poor. His criticism is based on intensive work with the problems of urban poor children since the beginning of the War on Poverty (another reform effort whose history the current reformers should heed). He writes:

The levels of literacy and numeracy among students in urban schools tend, for the most part, to fall below those of the nation's schools in general and probably account for a sizable share of the National Commission's perception of risk. Some urban schools are "effective," of course, but they are far too small in number to justify ignoring the needs of poor and minority students. (p. 680)

Inequities are increasing. For example, children in middle-class white schools are four times more likely to have a computer than children in lower-status black schools. They are more likely to have a teacher skilled in computer applications, who uses the computer to promote creativity and problem-solving, while the lower-status school uses it to monitor rote and drill exercises. These discrepant statistics occur in many other comparisons, reflecting the inequities of social class. The challenge before us is well expressed in the following quote from the report of the Carnegie Task Force on Teaching as a Profession, *A Nation Prepared: Teachers for the 21st Century*:

We do not believe the educational system needs repairing; we believe it must be rebuilt to match the drastic change needed in our economy if we are to prepare our children for productive lives in the 21st century. It is no exaggeration to suggest that America must now provide to the many the same quality of education presently reserved for the fortunate few. The cost of not doing so will be a steady erosion in the American standard of living. (pp. 3-4)

Narrow Curricular Focus

Increased graduation requirements and mandated time allocations for basic subjects have narrowed the high school curriculum. Enrollments in vocational schools and vocational classes have been curtailed. Teachers in the arts state that they have lost enrollments. The call for more time-on-task is used as an excuse for eliminating or reducing assemblies, field trips, educational games, extracurricular clubs, and informal times for teachers and students to interact.

> We are so busy preparing for time-on-task, marking the workbook pages, and keeping records of progress that we have no time left for educating. I try to get twenty minutes for it each day. I'm going to retire early. Not only is the fun gone for the kids, but it's gone for me, too. I won't be around to watch it. (a master elementary teacher in Texas)

With an increasing emphasis on testing achievement with standardized tests and focusing the curriculum exclusively on "cognitive" processes, there is less time and little inclination for teachers to deal with the affective, motor, and motivational facets of education.

All of these changes, with their emphasis on memorization and recall, leave little time for higher-level thinking. Students have little opportunity to perform the intellectual functions of analyzing and synthesizing demanded by adult life.

> Students need to learn how to learn. Instead, too often they learn how to satisfy the teacher. They need to learn to think and to develop skills of logic, analysis, and problem-solving. Instead, they learn to memorize sets of information. They need to learn to be adaptive, resourceful, and productive people who can thrive in a rapidly changing job market and society. Instead, they learn basic social habits and technical skills that help them enter the job market as it is and at the lowest levels. They need to learn to be democratic citizens, active agents in building a better society. Instead, they too often learn to accept limited rights and responsibilities and passive acceptance of the status quo. (*Children at Risk*, pp. 37-38)

Punitive Rigor

One of the outcomes of the Excellence Movement is an attempt to impose greater rigor in the curriculum. In practice, such efforts often are little more than punishment. A case in point is the widespread increase in the amount of homework required of students, often with the justification that it involves the family in the child's education. Homework may be assigned for two or three hours a night but with little direction for parents on how to help. Teachers then blame parents for not helping their children. Much homework becomes more punitive than instructional.

Furthermore, children whose families are ill-equipped to help them fall further behind and become more frustrated with their school work. Even families with the ability to help their child can find homework oppressive, particularly if the family is a two-career family with a working father and mother:

> Our daughter brought home five hours of homework on Labor Day. She brings home three to five hours of homework every night. I wonder how many adults bring that much home to do? My wife and I both work; so we don't want to spend every evening until eleven or twelve with the homework either. The worst part of it is that the school expects us to do the teaching; so we spend each night doing the school's work; we teach the number facts, the tropic zones and polar regions, the spelling words, and the metric system. Two different teachers told us they didn't have time to teach the number facts. We wonder what the teachers do. If we weren't working, we would take her out for home instruction, and let the school be damned. We really wonder what chance poor kids have when no one at home can help them with all that stuff. (a suburban parent)

> Our kindergarten child brought home a two-page list of things we were supposed to teach. The colors, the alphabet, the numbers, the days of the week. What does the teacher teach? (an urban parent)

> The homework situation just about destroyed our family life. It was a battle every night as we tried to teach the concepts she needed to do the assignment, which she should have learned in school. We ended up night after night yelling at one another and coming to hate being together — all three of us. I even grabbed her once, and we never do anything physical at our house. I just say that we don't want a kid who has to be hit before she does the right thing. But I grabbed her and left bruises. The teacher reported the bruise marks, and the county health woman came to investigate. I told her just what happened. She must have told the school people, because the homework assignments have been much more reasonable. And they even changed her

study hall from first period so she could do more work at school and get some help there. (a rural parent)

> Everything they are recommending is driving schools to take out all of the activities that make school enjoyable, all the stuff that I felt gave me my real education. (a suburban parent)

Many schools are initiating rigid, punitive, and exclusionary discipline policies that support, even encourage, suspending students or depriving them of instruction. Other punitive policies retain children in grade for a second year with no attempt to remediate their academic deficiencies and no chance to return to their original grade as soon as their academic deficiencies are corrected. School records from California indicate that 50% of those children retained once and 90% of those retained twice eventually drop out of school. Cleveland, Ohio, newspapers report that more students dropped out of Cleveland City Schools in 1985 (3,230) than graduated (3,077). There seems to be a high correlation between the dropout rate and the number of unremediated failures and repetitive retentions.

> About 52% of our high school students had at least one F on their final report. Interestingly, the dropout rate from 9th to 12th grade seems to be the same — 52%. Now that the local newspapers have picked up that statistic, maybe something will be done. (a central office administrator, Dallas Independent School District)

It is no secret that test score averages will increase if a large enough number of low-achieving students are suspended from school, or if they voluntarily leave school. As a result, higher averages can occur *without any student achieving more.*

> At a time when our dropout rate is inching upward, when more hard-to-educate youngsters attend our schools than ever before, the commission's emphasis on *rigor* presents to both educators and the public a welcome diversion. Those students who drop out of school can now be explained away: they are, for whatever reasons, unwilling or unable to meet the new and rigorous standards demanded by society. The schools are therefore absolved. (Albrecht 1985, p. 685)

Many proposals for achieving excellence are indeed exclusionary and punitive. Even the President of the United States has praised a principal for suspending 300 students during the first few weeks of school and for carrying a bullhorn to maintain order (Hyman and D'Alessandro 1984). While unusual circumstances may require such stringent measures, no school we have ever seen should require so many suspensions to maintain order. Even if a school did require such extreme measures, it should be for short-term

94

effect until more permanent means for eliciting cooperation could be nurtured and developed. It should be noted that the school praised by the nation's chief executive had a dropout rate of 50% in 1982-83. Test score averages will rise if half the students leave, but the gains could scarcely be called excellence.

One Final Caution

We have argued that some of the reform reports' recommendations can be faulted for their lack of a research base and for being too simplistic in their solutions to complex problems. In retrospect, it seems clear that the reports have benefited from trends that already were in motion long before any of their recommendations were made. Nevertheless, they are claiming the same kind of credit that Pogo's sidekick, Albert the Alligator, claimed for breaking a drought when he declared, "The rainstorm happened during my administration."

Those who criticize the reform reports by mere carping or by pretending that the conditions of our schools prior to release of the reports were satisfactory do little to advance the cause of quality education. If educators had made appropriate responses to the War on Poverty and the civil rights movement with its efforts to eradicate classism, racism, and sexism, there would have been little support for reforms proposed by the elitists.

What we need to remember is that the reform reports are only the most recent manifestation of an ongoing historical debate about the role and function of the public schools in America. They do voice sincere concerns about some long-standing deterents to true excellence (however excellence is defined), and they have opened yet another "window of opportunity" for educators to eradicate systemic barriers to educational excellence and equity.

References

Albrecht, James E. "A Nation at Risk: Another View." *Phi Delta Kappan* 65 (June 1984): 684-85.

Anrig, Gregory R. "Educational Standards, Testing, and Equity." *Phi Delta Kappan* 66 (May 1985): 623-25.

Association for Supervision and Curriculum Development. "Computer Integration into Instruction Is Stuck: Experts Blame Unclear Optimal Uses and Three Implementation Problems." *Update* 27 (Summer 1985).

Ball, Doris, and Paulson, Darryl. "Back to Basics: Minimum Competency Testing and Its Impact on Minorities." *Urban Education* 19 (April 1984): 5-16.

Brooks, David. "Public Mess, Private Function." *National Review,* 14 June 1985, pp. 42-43.

Bunzel, John H., ed. *Challenge to American Schools: The Case for Standards and Values*. New York: Oxford University Press, 1985.

Cardenas, Jose A. "The Role of Native-Language Instruction in Bilingual Education." *Phi Delta Kappan* 67 (January 1986): 359-63.

Committee on Education and Labor, U.S. House of Representatives. *Report of the Merit Pay Task Force*. Washington, D.C.: U.S. Government Printing Office, February 1984.

Culbertson, Jack A., and Cunningham, Luvern L. *Microcomputers and Education*. Chicago: University of Chicago Press, National Society for the Study of Education, 1986.

"Equity Is Still a Goal in School Spending: ECS." *Phi Delta Kappan* 66 (October 1984): 157.

Gallegos, Arnold M. "The Negative Consequences of Teacher Competency Testing." *Phi Delta Kappan* 65 (May 1984): 631.

Gardner, John W. *Excellence: Can We Be Equal and Excellent Too?* 2nd ed. New York: W.W. Norton, 1984.

Glenn, Beverly Caffee. "Excellence and Equity: Implications for Effective Schools." *Journal of Negro Education* 54, no. 3 (1985): 289-300.

Goodman, Kenneth S. "Equity and Quality: A Critique of the Report of the National Commission on Excellence in Education and a Progressive Alternative." Paper presented at annual conference of the International Reading Association, Atlanta, Georgia, May 1984.

Gross, Jacqueline. *Make Your Child a Lifelong Reader*. Los Angeles: Jeremy P. Tarcher, 1986.

Grossnickle, Donald R. *High School Dropouts: Causes, Consequences, and Cure*. Fastback 242. Bloomington, Ind.: Phi Delta Kappa Educational Foundation, 1986.

"How Can Computers Best Be Used to Individualize Instruction?" *ERIC Clearinghouse on Educational Management* (Spring 1986).

Howe, Harold. "Education Moves to Center Stage: An Overview of Recent Studies." *Phi Delta Kappan* 65 (November 1983): 167-72.

Hyman, Irwin A., and D'Alessandro, John. "Good, Old-Fashioned Discipline: The Politics of Punitiveness." *Phi Delta Kappan* 66 (September 1984): 39-45.

Johnston, William J., ed. *Education on Trial: Strategies for the Future*. San Francisco: Institute for Contemporary Studies Press, 1985.

Karweit, Nancy, and Slavin, Robert. "Time-on-Task: Issues of Timing, Sampling and Definition." *Journal of Educational Psychology* 74 (December 1982): 844-51.

Kirst, Michael W. "Sustaining the Momentum of State Education Reform: The Link Between Assessment and Financial Support." *Phi Delta Kappan* 67 (January 1986): 341-45.

Komoski, P. Kenneth. "Instructional Materials Will Not Improve Until We Change the System." *Educational Leadership* 42 (April 1985): 31-38.

Lapointe, Archie E. "The Good News About American Education." *Phi Delta Kappan* 65 (June 1984): 663-67.

Lasch, Christopher. " 'Excellence' in Education: Old Refrain or New Departure?" *Issues in Education* 3 (Summer 1985): 1-12.

96

Lauderdale, William Burt. *Educational Reform: The Forgotten Half.* Fastback 252. Bloomington, Ind.: Phi Delta Kappa Educational Foundation, 1987.

Lipkin, John P. "Equity in Computer Education." *Educational Leadership* 41 (September 1983): 26.

Molnar, Alex. "The Equality of Opportunity Trap." *Educational Leadership* 43 (September 1985): 60-61.

Moock, Peter R. "Education and the Transfer of Inequality from Generation to Generation." In *Families and Communities as Education,* edited by Hope Jensen Leichter. New York: Teachers College Press, 1979.

National Coalition of Advocates for Students. *Barriers to Excellence: Our Children at Risk.* Boston, 1985.

National Committee for Citizens in Education Commission on Educational Governance. *Public Testimony on Public Schools.* Berkeley, Calif.: McCutchan, 1975.

National Staff Development Council. "Staff Developers Respond to the National Reports on Education." *The Journal of Staff Development* 5 (December 1984).

New York Times, "Educational Supplement," 13 November 1983.

Oakes, Jeannie. "Keeping Track, Part 1: The Policy and Practice of Curriculum Inequality." *Phi Delta Kappan* 68 (September 1986): 12-17.

Odden, Allan. "Financing Educational Excellence." *Phi Delta Kappan* 65 (January 1984): 311-18.

Ovando, Carlos J. "Bilingual/Bicultural Education: Its Legacy and Its Future." *Phi Delta Kappan* 64 (April 1983): 564-68.

Parkay, Forrest W. "The Authoritarian Assault upon the Public School Curriculum: An Additional Indicator of Risk." *High School Journal* 68 (February-March 1985): 120-27.

Passow, Harry E. "Tackling the Reform Reports of the 1980s." *Phi Delta Kappan* 65 (June 1984): 674-83.

Peterson, Paul E. "Did the Education Commissions Say Anything?" *Brookings Review* (Winter 1983): 3-11.

Pipho, Chris. "Legislators Pit Excellence Against Economy." *State Education Leader* 3 (Winter 1984): 1-3.

Rosenholtz, Susan J. "Political Myths About Education Reform: Lessons from Research on Teaching." *Phi Delta Kappan* 66 (January 1985): 349-55.

Rotberg, Iris C. "A New Perspective on Math and Science Education." *Phi Delta Kappan* 65 (June 1984): 668-73.

Samway, Katharine. "And You Run and You Run to Catch Up with the Sun, But It's Sinking." *Language Arts* 63 (April 1986): 352-57.

Scott-Jones, Diane, and Clark, Maxine L. "The School Experiences of Black Girls: The Interaction of Gender, Race, and Socioeconomic Status." *Phi Delta Kappan* 67 (March 1986): 520-26.

Serow, Robert C., and Davies, James J. "Resources and Outcomes of Minimum Competency Testing as Measures of Equality of Educational Opportunity." *American Educational Research Journal* 19 (Winter 1982): 529-39.

Toch, Thomas. "The Dark Side of the Excellence Movement." *Phi Delta Kappan* 66 (November 1984): 173-76.

Vargas, Julie S. "Instructional Design Flaws in Computer-Assisted Instruction." *Phi Delta Kappan* 67 (June 1986): 738-44.

Wehlage, Gary, and Rutter, Robert. "Dropping Out: How Much Do Schools Contribute to the Problem?" Paper presented at the meeting of the American Educational Research Association, Chicago, April 1985.

White, Merry I. "Japanese Education: How They Do It." *Principal* 64 (March 1985): 16-20.

Whittaker, Douglas, and Lutz, Jay. "Excellence by the Book." *Principal* 65 (January 1986): 34-37.

Willie, Charles V. "Educating Students Who Are Good Enough: Is Excellence an Excuse to Exclude?" *Change* 14 (March 1982): 16-21.

Willis, Harriet Doss. *Students at Risk: A Review of Conditions, Circumstances, Indicators, and Educational Implications.* Elmhurst, Ill.: North Central Regional Educational Laboratory, 1986.

CHAPTER SIX

Latent Causes for Public Concern About Schools: Bases for Substantive Reforms

There can be no real liberty without a wide diffusion of real intelligence . . . the members of a republic should all be alike instructed in the nature and character of their equal rights and duties, as human beings, and as citizens. . . . education, instead of being limited as in our public poor schools, to a simple acquaintance with words and ciphers, should tend, as far as possible, to the production of a just disposition, virtuous habits, and a rational self governing character.

> — "Report of the Working-men's Committee of Philadelphia"
> *Working-man's Advocate*, New York, 6 March 1830

Why did the wave of reform reports that began with *A Nation at Risk* capture the public's attention? Why did governors and state superintendents rush to show that they were responding to the recommendations made by national commissions and foundations? There is no question that these reports touched the public's conscience in ways that sparked strong interest and vigorous response.

The publicity accorded the reform reports can be explained partly by a combination of political and economic factors. Educational excellence was good fodder for the 1984 presidential campaign. And several governors in states pushing for new economic growth seized the opportunity to gain public support for improved schools, because they knew that economic growth requires the foundation of a good education system.

Indeed, economic forces had wrought genuine changes in the dominant international role the United States had enjoyed since the end of World War II in 1945. Some policy makers knew the cold facts: the new world economy had made the U.S. production system obsolete, including the undereducated labor force that staffed it. Education costs had risen sharply with no gains in achievement. At the same time, poorly educated laborers in developing nations were taking jobs once held by poorly educated laborers in industrialized nations – and at a much lower wage. Economic adjustments were affecting every segment of American life, and formerly comfortable arrangements were crumbling before internal and external shifts in the world economy. Clearly, the implications of these economic forces will require major changes in our schools and universities.

However, these factors do not account for the unprecedented public response to the educational reform movement. The reports must have touched deeper concerns in the public's mind.

What the public wants from its schools may be difficult for the average citizen to articulate. The reform reports themselves do not identify the true concerns, nor are they discernible to outsiders who are unfamiliar with the workings of schools. Because Goodlad, Boyer, and Sizer have an "insider's" view of the schools, their books come closest to identifying the problems whose solution would bring about authentic educational reform.

We suggest that the real concerns of the public arise from historical deficiencies in American education that are not amenable to easy change. This chapter presents some possible causes for the public's concerns. Our observation is that every school or school system with a reputation for excellence has done something by design or intuition that not only addresses these problems but overcomes their negative impact on student achievement, discipline, staff morale, and public confidence.

1. Too Many Schools Seem to Have No Clear Sense of Purpose

A school, like any social enterprise, must have some sense of purpose to focus its decisions, to give integrity to its actions, to gauge its progress, and to legitimate its existence. In good schools, one not only senses purposiveness, but the people there can articulate a purpose. And they act with the confidence that comes from knowing what they are doing and why. Nothing is done just because it always has been done that way. Excellence in education cannot occur without purpose guiding action.

American education has long suffered from an essential conflict in its purpose. Political struggles in the 1980s to control the schools are merely the latest version of a debate that has gone on since the earliest days of this nation. Our education system was born of an uneasy compromise between two opposed social philosophies concerning the nature of people and society. At stake was the type of education to be given the common citizen. On the one hand was the classical liberal education of aristocratic gentlemen. Such an education was seen as necessary for those presumed destined for leadership. On the other hand, education for the poor and working class was designed to give them specific skills for existing jobs. As some of these lower-class groups gained economic power, they were offered a broader education in order to placate their demands for social equality and mobility.

Many members of the propertied class believed that only the well-to-do should be broadly educated. They reasoned that those who had the ability to acquire property contributed the most to society and to the welfare of other citizens; therefore, those select few "deserved" to control government. They wanted no public schools and saw no reason to pay taxes to educate someone else's child.

These elitists were willing to support pauper schools in order to instill some degree of civil order, but essentially they regarded the poor as threats to their property. Indeed, in 1805 DeWitt Clinton and a committee of property owners used the threat of social disintegration as an argument for funds to teach children of the poor to be obedient citizens and workers:

> This neglect [of religious and moral instruction] may be imputed either to the extreme indigence of the parents of such children, their intemperance and vice, or to a blind indifference to the best interests of their offspring. The consequences must be obvious to the most careless observer. Children thus brought up in ignorance, and amidst the contagion of bad example, are in imminent danger of ruin; and too many of them, it is to be feared, instead of being useful members of the community, will become the burden and pests of society. Early instruction and fixed habits of industry, decency, and order, are the surest safeguards of virtuous conduct. . . . It is certainly in the power of the opulent and charitable . . . if not wholly to prevent, at least to diminish, the pernicious effects resulting from the neglected education of the children of the poor. (DeWitt Clinton et al., *Address of the Trustees of the Society for Establishing a Free School in the City of New York, for the Education of Such Poor Children as Do Not Belong to, or Are Not Provided by Any Religious Society,* 18 May 1805)

After resisting for half a century, opponents of universal education did agree to support free public schools because they saw them as a means of controlling the swelling immigrant population as well as the children of the common working classes. At different times they emphasized subject matter learning, textbook-centered instruction, obedience to authority, iso-

101

lated skills needed in the workplace, and a strong dose of patriotism as hallmarks of a good education for the common people. They advocated either local or state control of the curriculum to be taught by minimally trained teachers. They believed that the schools could develop good American citizens better than immigrant and poor parents could, so they encouraged little contact with parents.

Proponents of free public education for all children argued that the foundation of any government rests on the contributions of the working class as well as the property owners. They wanted free public schools so that all citizens would be educated enough to contribute their best to social advancement. The rationale for free education was powerfully stated by one of the Workingmen's Societies:

> The original element of despotism is monopoly of talent, which consigns the multitude to comparative ignorance, and secures the balance of knowledge on the side of the rich and the rulers. If then, the healthy existence of a free government be . . . rooted in the will of the American people, it follows as a necessary consequence . . . that this monopoly should be broken up, and that the means of equal knowledge (the only security for equal liberty) should be rendered, by legal provision, the common property of all classes. ("Report of the Working-men's Committee of Philadelphia," *Working-man's Advocate*, New York City, 6 March 1830)

As the idea of a free universal public education became accepted and common schools were established, the philosophical descendants of these early advocates tended to emphasize a broad curriculum, experiential education, educating the "whole child," close relationships between home and community, better trained teachers, pluralistic concepts of society taught in heterogeneous settings, legal interventions to expand local services to neglected populations, self-discipline, and social responsibility as hallmarks of a good education for all persons.

The current debates over the Excellence Movement are merely an extension of the long-time controversy over who gets what kind of education. The reform reports attempt to define what curricular content is most important and what outcomes are to be pursued. They try to identify what is enduring and basic for the next generation to know.

Some of the reformers have tried to narrow the schools' purposes, but a reading of all the reports soon reveals that little narrowing has been accomplished. Clearly, education in a democracy has multiple purposes. In 1944 a British observer made an astute commentary on the multiple purposes of American schools:

The social and political role of American education cannot be understood if it is thought of as being primarily a means of formal instruction. If it is so thought of, it will be overrated and underrated . . . overrated because [the number of students served] will dazzle the visitor used to seeing opportunities for higher education doled out . . . on a combined class-and-intellectual basis . . . underrated if, at any stage below the highest . . . the academic standards are compared with those of [good foreign schools]. If these millions of boys and girls are to be judged by their academic accomplishments, they will be judged harshly. But they are not to be so judged, for their schools are doing far more than instructing them: they are letting them instruct each other in how to live in America. (Brogan 1944)

The attitudes, values, and skills of fully functioning citizens are not all taught through formal classroom instruction; they are often learned through informal contacts with caring mentors in hallways, playgrounds, gymnasiums, and other less-structured places. It is a mistake to think that all education occurs in classrooms taught by adults with special competence in some subject (Sarason 1983). Educating for effective citizenship does not necessarily require adding more courses or employing more instructional specialists.

Defining the mission for education in simplistic terms is a favorite ploy of some educators and politicians, especially if that mission appeals to some portion of the voting public. Yet, public opinion varies widely on what constitutes an adequate education, who should receive it, and who should pay for it. Still, every school must define what it is doing and communicate it to the public. The public will not have confidence in or provide support to the schools if they appear to have no purposes.

2. Too Many Schools Exhibit Dysfunctional Bureaucratic Characteristics

All organizations tend to suffer from predictable bureaucratic dysfunctions, which cause them to perform poorly (Merton 1957). Public concern about our schools may be partially understood if we examine some of the bad habits one sees in some schools.

Insulation from Criticism and Change. Schools, like many organizations, often close themselves off from outside influences, thus becoming unable to respond to changing conditions outside their boundaries. This inability to see the need for change or to respond to requests or even demands for improvement is what causes many to become hostile toward the school bureaucracy. Outsiders have to exert extreme pressures in order to bring about even the smallest changes.

Because organizations tend to isolate themselves from outside criticism and to discipline insiders for making problems public, they are oblivious to problems that cry out for change. As a result, they frustrate both sincere critics and irrational cranks, whom they come to view as meddlesome and "enemies" of the system. Even insiders are often disciplined if they make suggestions for correcting problems in the school.

> All I did was try to point out that the new plan was not going to help children, though it looked good on paper. They moved me to another school as punishment. The parents protested, so I was called in and told to cancel the parent meeting or I'd never get a promotion for the next 40 years.
>
> — Elementary principal

> I tried to warn them that we had a serious dropout problem developing, but the other assistant superintendents told me the old man didn't want to hear it and I should forget it. When I brought it up, they all said the data was wrong. This year the newspapers dug it up and all hell broke loose.
>
> — Assistant superintendent

Unexamined Folklore. Organizations frequently canonize certain practices as excuses for not making changes. Practices become institutionalized even though they may be contributing to failure or retarding success. These practices become standard operating procedure and become part of the professional litany whether or not they have any basis in fact. Schools have not escaped this dysfunction of unexamined folklore, which, for example, permits educators to believe that children perform poorly because of:

poor home background	bad principal
low socioeconomic status	large class size
poor neighborhood	lack of materials
lack of motivation	teacher contract
bad curriculum	television
peer group	drugs

Through repetition, such excuses for low performance become accepted; and few ever bother to question or test them. As a result, professional commitment erodes to the point that many children suffer, because school personnel do not try to find ways to improve students' performance. The folklore both excuses poor performance and prevents searching for better practice; the excuses have become self-fulfilling.

Substituting Means for Ends. Some people in organizations come to believe that the *way* things are done is more important than the outcomes to be achieved. This glorification of means at the expense of educational outcomes results in absurdities in some schools.

> My daughter is a good reader. She reads everything in sight, but she got a D on the report card because she hadn't done all of the worksheets they hand out to keep the kids quiet.
>
> — Parent

> My kid got all 95's and 100's on the spelling tests but a D for the year in spelling because she hadn't handed in the workbook pages on time.
>
> — Parent

> We have children who are reading more than two years below grade level on the average; teacher turnover has been more than 40% per year. The parents wanted to burn the building down. The first month I was on the job, central office sent all the attendance books back to be done over because attendance hadn't been marked in blue ink and absences in red.
>
> — Principal

Too many educators have succumbed to the bureaucratic ploy of substituting means for ends. Principals spend endless amounts of time debating whether the school should have seven or eight periods but seldom consider whether such restrictive scheduling may contribute to the apathy and lowered achievement that marks many junior and senior high schools. The 50-minute period and departmentalization in the comprehensive secondary school have been sacred for many years (Trump and Baynham 1961), despite the strictures they impose on collaborative and integrative styles of teaching and learning.

Public eagerness to embrace the reform reports could well be a reaction against a curriculum that depends too much on textbooks, workbooks, and other packaged materials as the primary vehicles for delivering content. The public is less interested in the *means* by which children will be organized or instructed than in the *ends* (outcomes) of what they have learned. The public is seeking ways to judge educational productivity based on student outcomes rather than means devised for teacher convenience or administrative efficiency. This emphasis on outcomes rather than means is revolutionary in reform movements.

Standardization. Although teaching and learning are highly individual functions, schools persist in trying to standardize the curriculum. Recent reform proposals calling for prescribed content and rigid schedules are made without examining what less restrictive practices might produce. The 50-minute period, the extended school day, the 200-day school year, the age-grade lockstep — all reflect and reinforce the folklore that one is educated if those time requirements have been fulfilled. All standardized practices should be examined to determine whether they lower achievement, increase apathy and discipline problems, lower staff morale, and reduce public confidence.

Depersonalization. Organizations, especially larger ones, have a tendency to depersonalize their employees as well as their customers or clients. Everybody and everything has a number. Regrettably, many schools have fallen prey this same syndrome. People who attended a small town school in the 1940s or 1950s would be dismayed to see how impersonal many schools have become. Too often staff members are treated like mechanical parts that can be replaced by daily substitutes who are strangers in the school. Staff members interact with one another only infrequently during the workday, often not at all outside the school. Not uncommonly, especially in large schools, staff members may not know one another's names; consequently, they know little about one another either as professionals or as persons. Citing central office regulations or legal restrictions, school administrators may handle even delicate personnel functions in cold and impersonal ways:

> In 1981, the district reduced the force by 215 teachers. Even though rumors started three months before, nothing official was said and nothing done to prepare anyone. Of course, many teachers were anxious about it. The first word I got that I was one of the ones out of a job was on the Friday before. When I picked up my check, it had a Xeroxed note with just two lines on it, saying that I was no longer employed by the district. I should clean out my desk and not return to the building.
>
> — Teacher, Midwestern city

Students, too, suffer depersonalization, especially in secondary schools. Some teachers will not know the names of all the students in their classes and can make few discerning comments about them without referring to a record book. Staff members may know little about the students' homes or even the community or neighborhood in which they live.

> We went to the open house. That is when the teachers are supposed to be on their best behavior and when they are supposed to make us feel good about the school. We met eight teachers, not a single one introduced themselves by name. Not one could remember whether our daughter was in the class or not. One of them even told us it would take him 12 weeks to tell what the kid didn't know about math assignments. We were not impressed.
>
> — Parent, Midwestern city

106

Our kid was involved with a bad little group that was against school-
work and against parents. We went to school to get some advice and
help. She had eight teachers and not a single one could tell us who
our kid played with on the playground.

— Parent, Eastern seaboard city

I retained seven children last year. Or was it nine? Nine, I believe.
I really can't remember who they were.

—First-grade teacher, Midwestern city

In such schools, individuals are stereotyped according to categories. Students may be known and treated as "third-graders," "jocks," "bussed-in kids,"
"winners," "losers," "preppies," or "punks."

Such depersonalization undermines motivation, loyalty, commitment, and
learning. Impersonal treatment of adults and students has been linked with
disruptive behavior (PDK Commission on Discipline 1982), and is closely
related to poor morale. Impersonal treatment of students, parents, and visitors lowers public confidence in schools (Wayson et al. forthcoming). This
organizational dysfunction indeed may be the single most potent factor causing public unrest about the education establishment.

3. Too Many Schools Are Unstable, Unpredictable Places

Learning cannot occur without some degree of stability. True, life today
is constantly changing. Families, communities, and institutions disintegrate
while we watch (or try not to watch). But if children are to learn, they must
be provided an environment with enough stability to give them confidence
in their teachers and in themselves. Too many children today, especially
those most in need of stability, have to attend schools that mirror the instability that pervades their lives outside of school.

There was a time when children entering first grade would know who
their sixth-grade teacher would be. They knew the principal in the high
school. They knew which teachers were "mean" and which had bad breath.
Now, they may not know who their teacher will be until the opening day
of school, and that teacher may change several times during the year.

Teacher absenteeism is nearly as high in some schools as student absenteeism; and with each teacher absence comes a substitute, who more than
likely is a stranger to the school and to the students. In some schools, typically in areas where children most need stability, substitutes constitute the
majority of the staff on any given day. Instability also occurs through disruptions in the classroom schedule. Fire drills, emergency announcements,
and ringing bells combine to disrupt the concentration of teachers and students alike. In many high schools students have only one thing to call their

own – a locker, which often is shared with another student. Often they do not have even a desk they can call their own. They may have no homeroom teacher; or if they have one, the homeroom period is simply an administrative arrangement for taking attendance and making announcements and does not foster a sense of belonging.

The staff may complain about the breakdown of the family and the problems it makes for them, but they often do little on their own to mitigate these problems. On a more positive note, some schools are developing innovative ways to establish a "family" atmosphere in the school. For example, the U-32 High School in Montpelier, Vermont, assigns every adult in the school to serve as a "parent surrogate" to 12 students. Their assignment is to give the student a boost when necessary and to protect the student from unfair treatment in the school. Thus, every student has an adult with whom to interact. Moreover, the assignments last for the full six years that the student is in the school, resulting in an ongoing personal relationship between adults and teenagers.

Establishing stability in the school is made more difficult because of changing personnel at the policy-making levels. The composition and philosophy of school boards may change in one election. Also, many superintendents change districts about every three to four years, disrupting the entire system for a year before they leave and for two years after a new superintendent arrives on the scene. Districts often transfer principals from school to school with little consideration for the impact it will have on either school. Many children will have two or more principals, with as many changes in philosophy and procedures, during their years in a school. Clearly, students would learn more and public confidence would be restored if the learning environment were stabilized.

4. The Profession Defines Teaching too Narrowly

Too often teachers have been trained to be "walking textbooks," whose sole purpose is to transmit information to students. Moreover, an increasing number of specialists have taken over functions from teachers, thereby fragmentizing students' learning as well reducing teachers' status in the school and community:

> Current teaching practices emphasize the passivity of the learner,
> especially at the secondary level. Teachers lecture or pass out work-
> sheets. Students listen or fill in blanks. Little interaction or engage-
> ment characterizes the teaching approach. The focus is on topics rather
> than concepts. Subjects are covered; little is uncovered or mastered.
> Moreover, schools do not design learning activities to connect students

108

with the structure and ways of thinking that characterize a field of inquiry. Students, in other words, are not learning how to learn. . . . Students who are prepared merely for passive acceptance have not learned to think no matter how many years of subject matter they have taken, how many credits they have, or how high they score on standardized tests. (NCAS 1985, pp. 50-51).

The current debate over educational reform is fueled by poor outcomes resulting from a narrow view of instruction characterized by teachers talking and students listening passively. Morever, educators themselves have actively supported narrower roles, often with good justification. Teachers understandably are impatient with many of the custodial functions of schooling mandated by school policies and expected by the community. "Covering" or "supervising" students on the playground, in study halls, and in lunchrooms becomes a policing activity in many schools. The atmosphere is hardly a stimulating learning environment for either teachers or students.

The traditional definition of teaching is an adult working with a group of children. Teachers who operate within this narrow definition see activities not involving children as something "extra," not teaching. When confronted with a child with a learning problem, they are quick to refer the child to a specialist to diagnose and treat the problem, which frequently yields unsatisfactory results because the treatment is not integrated into the regular instructional program when the child returns to the classroom. With a broader definition of teaching that included skills of diagnosis and time away from children to formulate plans for alleviating the learning problem, the teacher's status as a professional would be enhanced.

Actually, effective teachers always have engaged in many activities beyond direct instruction (see Chapters Eight and Nine). Working with administrators and other staff to solve problems that affect children's learning takes time and thought. Working with individual children and their families takes time. So does instructional planning. Even some of the so-called custodial functions of teachers on the playground or in the lunchroom provide informal contacts that can have a positive influence on students. Yet teacher training institutions and school systems continue to perpetuate a narrow definition of teaching.

To implement a broader definition of teaching, there will have to be changes in all the policies and practices currently used in the selection, training, certification, and assignment of teachers. Prospective teachers must be aware of these broader functions. Their training programs must prepare them for these functions. Certification requirements must recognize these functions. And teacher contracts and personnel practices must incorporate these functions. Only then will we have schools that are truly excellent.

5. Too Many Schools Lack Effective Leadership

Given the increased certification requirements, the longer preparation programs for teachers and administrators, and the increasing number of
teachers, administrators, and other staff holding doctoral degrees, one might
assume that our schools are staffed by a corps of professionals who know
how to make schools work. If so, then why did the Excellence Movement
have to occur at all? What went wrong?

We would contend that the central problem is a lack of leadership. There
are, of course, many school systems led by outstanding educators with a
clear sense of purpose and a dedication to help all children achieve that
purpose. Some of the schools we studied for this report are led by such
educators. But there are too few of them. And they frequently are frustrated from doing what they know is right by those who propose superficial solutions to educational problems.

During the last 30 years, we have seen an infusion of social science theory into programs for preparing school administrators. This move to provide a scientific base has been productive for the field and has given increased
academic status to departments of educational administration in colleges
and universities. Financial and political management of schools has improved. Administrators receive higher salaries, and those with doctorates
have achieved a tenuous status among businessmen and politicians.
Nevertheless, such increases in academic and professional status have not
automatically created educational statesmen who can mobilize their facul-
ties or communities to implement superior educational programs. Their training may have helped them to describe what *is* but not to envision what *ought*
to be in our schools. Too many have become fixated on the mechanical,
easily measurable elements of management to the neglect of learning processes and outcomes.

> We need to raise up a new kind of educational leader in this country
> if the great questions of educational purpose are to receive intelligent
> discussion. . . . He or she will need . . . to develop a clear and com-
> pelling vision of education and of its relation to American life. . . .
> Only as educators begin to think deeply about the ends of learning will
> the politics of popular education . . . become . . . a constant reaching
> for the good society. (Cremin 1965, p. 188)

Good leaders are good managers, although the reverse is not necessarily
true. Management harms education whenever it limits choices, substitutes
procedures for individual creativity, lulls people into complacency, or
deprives persons of responsibility or respect. Effective leaders use management tools such as problem-solving processes that involve widespread par-

ticipation to get things done. Effective management requires the daily expression of leadership. Effective leaders do not assume that their behavior is governed by others; they take responsibility for their own actions, and they help others to move themselves and their institutions forward.

6. Too Many Adolescents Are Separated from Adult Society

A growing number of teenagers today have no significant interaction with adults either at home, in school, or in the community. Our society has changed. In 1935 about 33% of American households were in rural areas or small towns. Even in larger towns, children were in close touch with adults; they could observe adult occupations firsthand. They saw and questioned; they acted and got immediate feedback. They had models close at hand to illustrate the full range of human enterprise. By 1957, only 10% of American households were in such places; they had moved to cities or to isolated bedroom suburbs (see Glenn and Warner 1977). Fathers worked greater distances from home. By 1950, 40% more people lived in urban areas than in 1930. The rapid urbanization of society changed every aspect of life.

Families changed. Families probably never were what current nostalgia would have us believe, but they were different. In the 1930s extended families were the norm. Relatives lived in the same house or nearby, providing children with adult models and involving them in discussions covering the full spectrum of family disasters and joys. Some respected adult usually was nearby to instruct the child in the ways of life, to interpret experience, to buffer them from potential harm, and to encourage and guide their experimentation.

In those days children had chores that were essential for carrying out the life of the family. Adults took the time to teach them how to do those chores and to see that they were carried out. If they were not performed, children experienced the consequences when the family suffered because of their failure to contribute.

> I was driving a tractor when I was only 12. Dad always told me not to take it into the back field when it rained or it would bog down. One day I thought I was big, so I drove it back there; and she bogged down up to the hubs. I hightailed back to the barn and asked Dad what we were going to do now. He looked straight at me and said, "Well, I'm going to wash up, go in to eat, and then go to bed. You are going to take that shovel there and dig that tractor out." I never forgot the lesson.
>
> — School superintendent

111

Families worked together, played together, celebrated together, grieved together. There was connection between adults and children.

By the late 1970s, members of the average family spent about 15 minutes a day interacting. One estimate is that much of that time is adversarial interaction (Glenn and Warner 1977). Some middle-class fathers spend no more than a few minutes a week interacting with each child. There are few extended families; relatives live many miles apart. Nearly 40% of children live in single-parent families, and 50% of the rest have both parents working. Only about 7% to 8% of families now fit the traditional model of a working father and a homemaker mother. Children seldom see their fathers at work; most cannot even describe what their fathers do for a living. The same is true when mothers work outside the home. Television, videogames, or other diversions interfere with family interaction. Most teenagers are as overscheduled outside the home as their parents are. Parents usually fulfill material needs; their children often are not expected to contribute to the family chores, and so they never learn how.

Schools have changed. Staff members in many schools seldom enter into the personal interactions with students that help them learn adult roles. Specialists have taken over the counseling function from the teacher. Yet many of them have too heavy a caseload to become mentors or confidants for students. Many children have no teacher or other adult in the school who feels responsible for them. The result is that many children, especially those in the secondary schools, have no adult to whom they can, or will, turn for personal advice or support. Adults leave them alone with peers. Is it any wonder that youth get their models and their support from peers.

One result of all these changes is that youth, with their involvement with drugs, alcohol, and sex, seem to grow up too soon; but the appearance is deceptive. In reality, society has conspired with schools to extend adolescence well into the twenties. What the effect of this prolonged adolescence will be on society is uncertain, but parents and communities are beginning to express concerns. And their concerns naturally turn toward the schools, which they see as both a cause of and a possible solution for the problems. The solution, of course, encompasses more than the schools can do. Society in general has to find better ways to help youth make the transition to responsible adult roles.

7. Many Schools Assume that Lower-Class Children Cannot Learn

Many accepted school practices are based on a pervasive attitude that children from lower socioeconomic homes cannot learn; hence, these children are considered hard, perhaps impossible, to teach.

Some children just can't do things with their brains. It's in the blood, and the school just can't change it; and I don't think we should try. But we should know what they can do and try to help them do it better.

— Retired principal

There is little argument that children from middle-class homes come to school better prepared to learn the standard curriculum because, for the most part, it is a middle-class curriculum. Children not fortunate to come from middle-class homes are more likely to receive custodial care rather than an education. As long as teachers operate within this middle-class mode, it reinforces their social class biases.

In the 1960s, studies by James Coleman (1966) and Christopher Jencks (1972) concluded that schools did not have much impact on overcoming a child's socioeconomic background.

Educators who interpreted Coleman to say that schools *could not* make a difference were merely seeking excuses for doing nothing. They were like doctors who looked at the death and crippling rate for polio in 1948 and decided to invest in funeral parlors.

— Inner-city high school principal

Probably few educators used Coleman as an excuse for doing nothing. Rather, the failure in the last decade to improve educational outcomes for children who came from homes different from the "Dick and Jane" model continued because there were no serious policy actions to make it happen. Political and economic pressures for improvement were too small and too short-lived to cause change in the average school and classroom.

Yet, experience in many schools demonstrates that progress is possible (see Chapters Eight and Nine). In these schools, staff members question procedures that are based on beliefs about who can learn and who cannot. In too many schools, tracking, special education placements, grading policies, and promotion and retention policies all are used to justify the belief that some children cannot learn. Such beliefs deter teachers from using instructional strategies known to be effective with disadvantaged students, and these beliefs sustain expectations for low achievement in schools serving lower socioeconomic communities. Such beliefs, when reinforced by official sanctions, lead to self-fulfilling prophecies that affect both students and teachers. Overcoming those prophecies will be essential before schools can serve the majority of their clients in the next decade.

8. Many Schools Fail to Use Effective Teaching Methods

Frequently debates among reformers center on how best to instruct students. Each side tries to muster arguments that feed on the failures of the other, but neither acknowledges the complexity of how learning takes place. Humanistic educators want no drill; yet, learning some things — addition facts, multiplication tables, rules of punctuation — are learned best if they are repeated and practiced. On the other hand, conservatives who are so fond of drill fail to see how sterile such learning is.

Many things are learned easiest through coaching — having a knowledgeable adult (or other student) ready to correct a student immediately during the act of learning, whether it be shooting free throws in the gym or doing an experiment in the science lab. Far too little direct coaching is used as an instructional technique in our classrooms.

Some of the most powerful learning occurs during a family dinner-table conversation, on a fishing outing with grandfather, on a shopping expedition to buy school clothes, or in a father-daughter chat before the prom. Yet, these models are seldom emulated in the school setting. They are difficult, but not impossible, to emulate in the lockstep of the modern school. Some coaches, music teachers, and vocational teachers (particularly in home economics and agriculture) establish such relationships with individual youngsters and make lasting impressions on these young lives

Notes on Probable Success

Many schools have surmounted the problems we have discussed here. We shall describe some of them in Chapters Eight and Nine. Their success demonstrates that change is possible. But the restraints under which they work also show that the struggle most likely will be won on a school-by-school basis rather than on any broad front.

Calls for radical restructuring of our schools, no matter how desirable or how well orchestrated, will not succeed without a radical restructuring of the relationships among all those parties with a vested interest in the status quo — a process difficult to begin and even more difficult to sustain. This is even more true in higher education, where the intransigence of colleges of education makes them nearly completely impervious to any outside stimulus for reform. Reforming higher education, or finding ways to bypass it to select and prepare educators, would be essential for any large-scale reform to succeed. Indeed, the Excellence Movement has spawned a second wave of reports directed toward teacher education (Feistritzer 1984; Holmes Group 1986; Carnegie 1986); but implementing their recommendations will be much more difficult than implementing those proposed for elementary and secondary education.

Each reform movement is the genesis of new problems leading to unrest, which becomes the basis for the next reform. Many of the current problems in education, which the Excellence Movement is attempting to address, stem from misguided reforms following the launching of Sputnik in 1957. Post-Sputnik reforms intensified the rigidities of the education system; they depersonalized the educational process; they weakened the profession by creating splits between educators; they glorified specialization by elevating teachers to positions of dominance over other teachers; they narrowed roles for teachers; and they diminished power and respect for those who work most closely with children. Rather than ameliorating problems, the post-Sputnik reforms exacerbated the endemic problems discussed in this chapter.

In the hands of those who oppose free universal education, the slogans of the Excellence Movement could become instruments for undermining the public school system as we know it. True, the Excellence Movement has put education back on the front pages and on state and national agendas; but if free universal education is to remain the foundation of our free society, educators must address the continuing problems that feed public dissatisfaction with our schools.

References

Anyon, Jean. "Social Class and the Hidden Curriculum of Work." *Journal of Education* 162 (Winter 1980): 67-92.

Brogan, Denis W. *The American Character*. New York: Alfred A. Knopf, 1944.

Carnegie Forum on Education and the Economy. *A Nation Prepared: Teachers for the 21st Century*. Washington, D.C., 1986.

Coleman, James S.; Campbell E.; Hobson, C.; McPartland, J.; Mood, A.; Weinfield, F.; and York, R. *Equality of Educational Opportunity*. Washington, D.C.: U.S. Government Printing Office, 1966.

Cremin, Lawrence A. "Family-Community Linkages in American Education: Some Comments on the Recent Historiography." In *Families and Communities as Education,* edited by Hope Jensen Leichter. New York: Teachers College Press, 1979.

Cremin, Lawrence A. *The Genius of American Education*. New York: Vintage Books, 1965.

Cremin, Lawrence A. *The Transformation of the School*. New York: Alfred A. Knopf, 1961.

Feistritzer, Emily C. *The Making of a Teacher: A Report on Teacher Education and Certification*. Washington, D.C.: National Center for Education Information, 1984.

Foxley, Cecilia H. "Sex Equity in Education: Some Gains, Problems, and Future Needs." *Journal of Teacher Education* 33 (September-October 1982): 6-9.

Gardner, John. "The Anti-Leadership Vaccine." *Annual Report to the Carnegie Corporation*, 1965.

Gay, Geneva. "Multiethnic Education: Historical Developments and Future Prospects." *Phi Delta Kappan* 64 (April 1983): 560-63.

Glenn, H. Stephen, and Warner, Joel W. *The Developmental Approach to Preventing Problem Dependencies.* Bloomington, Ind.: Social Systems Inc., 1977.

Good, L. V., ed. *A Nation of Learners.* Washington, D.C.: U.S. Government Printing Office, 1976.

Hawley, Willis D. "Improving Schools by Ending Poverty." *Educational Digest* 49 (April 1984): 20-22.

Holmes Group. *Tomorrow's Teachers: A Report of the Holmes Group.* East Lansing, Mich., April 1986.

Jencks, Christopher S.; Smith, M.; Ackland, H.; Bane, M.J.; Cohen, D.; Ginits, H.; Heyns, B.; and Michelson, S. *Inequality: A Reassessment of the Effect of Family and Schooling in America.* New York: Basic Books, 1972.

Jones, Beau Fly. "Quality and Equality Through Cognitive Instruction." *Educational Leadership* 43 (April 1986): 4-12.

Judge, Harry. *American Graduate Schools of Education: A View from Abroad.* New York: Ford Foundation, 1982.

Jung, Carl G. *The Undiscovered Self.* New York: Mentor Books, New American Library, 1959.

Keesby, Forrest E. "Who Wrecked the Schools? Thirty Years of Criticism in Perspective." *Educational Theory* 34 (Summer 1984): pp. 209-17.

Kirst, Michael W. "Loss of Support for Public Schools: Some Causes and Solutions," *Daedalus* (Summer 1981): 45-68.

Merton, Robert K. *Social Theory and Social Structure.* Glencoe, Ill.: Free Press, 1957.

Methvin, Eugene H. "Guess Who Spells Disaster for Education." *Readers Digest* 124 (May 1984): 89-94.

National Coalition of Advocates for Students (NCAS). *Barriers to Excellence: Our Children at Risk.* Boston, 1985.

Neff, Walter S. *Work and Human Behavior.* New York: Aldine, 1985.

Ornstein, Allan C. "Urban Demographics for the 1980s: Educational Implications." *Education and Urban Society* 16 (August 1984): 477-96.

Phi Delta Kappa Commission on Discipline. *Handbook for Developing Schools with Good Discipline.* Bloomington, Ind.: Phi Delta Kappa, 1982.

Pipho, C. "Education Reform Continues to Command Attention." *Phi Delta Kappan* 67 (October 1985): 101, 175-76.

Powell, Arthur G. "Being Unspecial in the Shopping Mall High School." *Phi Delta Kappan* 67 (December 1985): 255-61.

Robertson, Wilmot. *The Dispossessed Majority.* Cape Canaveral, Fla.: Howard Allen Enterprises, 1981.

Rury, John L. "Race and Common School Reform: The Strange Career of the NYS-PECC, 1847-1860." *Urban Education* 20 (January 1986): 473-92.

Rutter, Michael. "School Influences on Children's Behavior and Development." *Pediatrics* 65 (February 1980): 208-20, 361.

Sarason, Seymour B. *Schooling in America: Scapegoat and Salvation.* New York: Free Press, 1983.

Schlesinger, Arthur M., Jr. *The Age of Jackson.* Boston: Little, Brown and Company, 1950.

Sorenson, Gail Paulus. "Indoctrination and the Purposes of American Education: A 1930s Debate." *Issues in Education* 3 (Fall 1985): 79-98.

Stringfellow, William. "The Demonic in American Society." *Christianity and Crisis* (September 1969): 247.

Trump, J. Lloyd, and Baynham, Dorsey. *Focus on Change: Guide to Better Schools.* Chicago, Rand McNally, 1961.

Wayson, William W.; Achilles, Charles; Pinnell, Gay Su; Cunningham, Luvern; Carol, Lila; and Lintz, Nan. *Handbook for Developing Public Confidence in Education.* Bloomington, Ind.: Phi Delta Kappa Educational Foundation, forthcoming.

Weller, H. N. *Education, Public Confidence and the Legitimacy of the Modern State: Is There a Crisis Somewhere?* Institute for Research on Educational Finance and Governance Program Report No. 82-B4. Stanford, Conn., June 1982.

Woodring, Paul. *The Persistent Problems of Education.* Bloomington, Ind.: Phi Delta Kappa Educational Foundation, 1983.

CHAPTER SEVEN

How Has the Excellence Movement Affected Schools?

Their discussion turned to the story of the Garden of Eden. Why was it, the official asked, that a God who was all-knowing had to call out when Adam was hiding and ask him, "Where art thou?"

"You do not understand the meaning of the question," the rabbi answered. "This is a question God asks of every man in every generation. After all your wanderings, after all your efforts, after all your years, O man, where art thou?"

— Charles Silberman
Crisis in the Classroom, 1970

Secretary of Education Terrel Bell's adroit planning made good use of the 1984 presidential election to create a bandwagon for educational reform. As if on cue, national commissions released their reports in rapid succession; national media publicized each one, surrounding the public with what appeared to be a seamless garment of recommendations about education. Governors and state legislators began frenzied action to improve education in their states. Education spokespersons and professional associations seemed to support the movement more than they opposed it, but none of them ignored it. Both state and local superintendents of schools created commissions and issued various reports to show that they were not only aware of the problems raised in the reports but had already initiated action months or years before to overcome them. School district officials were under

118

tremendous pressure to get on board the bandwagon or face a public whose curiosity, if not its animosity, had been aroused by a blitz of news about the need for excellence.

In the fall of 1984 we asked state education departments and others to nominate school districts that were considered excellent. Our purpose was to gain information about their programs, to question educators in these districts about the reports, and to see to what degree these "excellent" school districts reflected the reforms recommended by the commissions and scholars who were calling for excellence. We also wanted to gather descriptions of exemplary activities that might be used by other districts striving to become excellent.

All but two states nominated at least one district. We sent all nominated districts a questionnaire about how they had responded to the most frequently mentioned recommendations from the reform reports. A total of 59 districts, representing all but three states, returned questionnaires by January 1985. Nearly one-fourth were suburban districts; one-fifth were small cities with under 50,000 population; the others were evenly distributed among large urban districts with predominantly lower socioeconomic students, large urban districts with predominantly middle-class students, and rural districts. One-third had 5,000 or fewer students; one-fourth had from 5,000 to 10,000; about a third ranged from 10,000 to 50,000; one had between 50,000 and 75,000; and one had more than 75,000. Responding districts represented those identified as examples of excellence. Their programs were intended as gauges both of how deeply the movement was penetrating local districts and as exemplars for what other districts could do.

Evidence of the Excellence Movement's Immediate Impact on Schools

The questionnaire listed 49 specific recommendations gleaned from 21 of the earliest reform reports. We asked school officials whether their district had ignored, had considered and rejected, or had planned and/or implemented actions relative to each of the recommendations. They also were asked to specify when the action was initiated, if it was in the planning stage, or if it was already fully implemented. In analyzing the questionnaire returns, we had two basic questions in mind:

1. What recommended actions were most frequently planned or implemented by these exemplary school districts?
2. Of those actions, which were initiated prior to May 1983 and which were initiated after?

The tables that follow summarize what the districts reported doing by 1985 relative to recommendations in five areas: 1) curriculum reform, 2) testing student achievement, 3) teachers' status and performance, 4) organization and management, and 5) discipline. The tables show the percentage of districts (n = 59) that 1) had ignored or rejected each recommendation, 2) had initiated some action related to each recommendation prior to May 1983, and 3) had taken action after May 1983.

The responses from these 59 districts do not tell us how the reform reports affected most districts in the United States. However, since they were designated as "excellent" school districts, one can assume that they would be leading and influencing rather than simply following the movement's mandates. Furthermore, school officials, like other skillful public officials, are adept at describing what they already are doing in terms most acceptable to public opinion; they may use the rhetoric of the Excellence Movement to describe programs that have been in place for some time. Consequently, when these "excellent" school districts report an activity recommended by the Excellence Movement, the activity is not necessarily a direct result of the movement, especially if it was initiated before May 1983. At best, the movement may have breathed new life into activities that might have been abandoned or neglected had the movement not occurred. Of course, if the activity was planned or initiated after the publication of *A Nation at Risk*, one can speculate that the movement may have stimulated the activity.

District Actions Related to Curriculum

Most of the commission reports and their proponents emphasized the need for curriculum reforms in order to achieve excellence. They called for increasing requirements in some academic areas and reducing nonacademic or "frill" programs. Districts were challenged to monitor student progress, increase homework, and develop computer literacy. School officials were admonished to adopt new materials and textbooks or special methods of teaching in particular courses or at special schools. Some reports recommended expanding bilingual programs; others recommended a cutback. Table 7.1 shows how districts responded to specific recommendations related to curriculum.

Of the curriculum recommendations listed, the ones most frequently reported by these districts with a reputation for being excellent were adding courses in computer literacy (100%); adopting textbooks with no stereotypes (92%); adopting special textbooks for disadvantaged or gifted students (90%); increasing requirements in math (90%), science (76%), and English (71%); offering foreign languages to elementary students (62%); and

Table 7.1. School District Responses to Recommendations Related to Curriculum — 1984

Recommendation	Not Considered/ Rejected	Adopted Before May 1983	Adopted After May 1983
1. Establish computer literacy courses	0%	77%	23%
2. Use new non-stereotyped textbooks	8	92	0
3. Use special textbooks for special groups	10	90	0
4. Increase math requirements	12	50	40
5. Increase science requirements	24	36	40
6. Increase English requirements	29	50	21
7. Increase homework	38	33	29
8. Foreign language in elementary grades	38	45	17
9. Reduce academic offerings	43	36	21
10. Increase foreign language requirements	57	17	26
11. Initiate special methods	60	31	9
12. Eliminate non-academic offerings	64	19	17
13. Expand bilingual programs	79	14	7
14. Cut back bilingual programs	95	0	5

Note: Percentage totals may be slightly above or below 100% because of rounding.

increasing homework (62%). Other recommendations that were in operation in more than a third of these districts were reducing academic offerings (57%); increasing requirements for foreign languages (43%); initiating special methods of instruction (40%); and eliminating non-academic offerings (36%). Additional curricular actions not included in the questionnaire but written in by school districts were focusing decision-making at the school building level and increasing credits required for graduation.

By far the largest proportion of the activities reported had been initiated before May 1983. All districts reported computer courses, but 77% had begun these before 1983. Half of the districts already had increased requirements for math and English composition by the time the reports were published. The only recommended curriculum change that more districts adopted after publication of *A Nation at Risk* than before was increasing graduation requirements for science (40%). The other actions initiated most frequently after May 1983 were increasing math requirements (40%) and homework (29%), adding courses in computer literacy (23%), and increasing requirements for foreign language (26%) and English (21%). Some of these no doubt can be attributed to the stimulus provided by the Excellence Movement.

121

The recommendations for curriculum reform least acceptable to these districts were cutting back bilingual programs (rejected by 95%), expanding bilingual programs (not considered by 79%), and eliminating non-academic offerings (rejected by 64%).

District Actions Related to Testing Students

The reform literature contains many recommendations for improving and testing student competence in basic skills. What these districts reported related to this area is reported in Table 7.2.

Table 7.2. School District Responses to Recommendations
Related to Testing Student Achievement — 1984

Recommendation	Not Considered/ Rejected	Adopted Before May 1983	Adopted After May 1983
1. Monitor student progress schoolwide	5%	74%	21%
2. Require standardized tests at transition points	10	23	67
3. Promote/graduate based only on academic progress	36	50	14
4. Require minimum competency for diploma	71	5	24
5. Concentrate on basics until minimum competency achieved	78	5	17

Activities related to improving and testing student competence in basic skills reported most frequently were monitoring student progress on a school-wide basis (95%), requiring standardized testing at transition points (90%), and promoting/graduating based only on academic progress (64%). However, note that 74% of the districts had monitored student progress and 50% had promoted or graduated only on academic merit before May 1983. Evidently, the Excellence Movement's greatest impact was increasing standardized testing at transition points in the student's career.

Almost three-fourths of the districts rejected or were not considering requiring minimum competency as a basis for a diploma, nor were they planning to concentrate on basic skills until minimal test scores were achieved. One could assume that the reports stimulated one in four districts to establish minimum competencies for graduation and one in five to concentrate on the basics until students could pass minimum competency tests.

Some of the "other" activities reported by these districts emphasized locally designed assessment procedures and lists of competencies for use in diagnosing students' learning problems.

District Actions Related to Teachers' Status and Performance

The reform reports identified teachers as the key to improving education. Table 7.3 shows how school districts responded to the major recommendations for improving teachers' status and performance.

Table 7.3. School District Responses to Recommendations
Related to Teacher Status — 1984

Recommendation	Not Considered/ Rejected	Adopted Before May 1983	Adopted After May 1983
1. Reduce teachers' non-instructional tasks	33%	46%	21%
2. Compensate master teachers at higher rates	67	26	7
3. Create new teacher education programs	70	21	9
4. Create differentiated status to encourage achievement	74	21	5
5. Increase teacher pay based on 11-month contract	81	17	2
6. Employ non-credentialed teachers to meet special needs	86	4	10
7. Pay higher salaries for math/science teachers	90	5	5
8. Link salary raises to student achievement	93	7	0

Most of the recommendations related to teachers' status and performance had not been considered or had been rejected by the districts. The one exception was the recommendation about reducing non-instructional tasks, which had been implemented by more than 67% of the districts. The next most frequently reported actions relative to these recommendations were compensating master teachers at higher rates (33%), creating new teacher education programs (30%), and differentiating status among teachers (26%).

Most of the actions taken by the districts began before May 1983. The most frequent actions that could be attributed to the reports were reduction of non-instructional tasks for teachers (21%) and employment of non-credentialed teachers to meet special needs (10%).

It seems that the reports' recommendations for improving teachers' status and performance had little influence on these "excellent" districts during the first year and a half after publication of *A Nation at Risk*.

District Actions Related to School Organization and Management

The reform reports contained many recommendations for changing organization and management practices in schools and school districts. What the districts did relative to these recommendations is reported in Table 7.4.

Table 7.4. School District Responses to Recommendations
Related to Organization and Management — 1984

Recommendation	Not Considered/ Rejected	Adopted Before May 1983	Adopted After May 1983
1. Strengthen principals' management skills	5%	76%	19%
2. Computerize administrative function	7	63	30
3. Establish school-business partnerships	14	56	30
4. Reduce class size	21	61	18
5. Create alternative schools	37	51	12
6. Create assistance centers to promote good programs	42	37	21
7. Initiate grouping and tracking	48	38	14
8. Lengthen school day	69	12	19
9. Eliminate grouping and tracking	76	12	12
10. Lengthen school year	84	2	14

The recommended organizational and management practices most frequently reported by these exemplary districts were strengthening principals' management skills (95%), computerizing administrative functions (93%), and developing partnerships with businesses (86%). Nearly 80% reported reducing class size. Other actions reported by more than a third of the districts included creating alternative schools (63%), providing assistance centers to promote good programs (58%), and instituting tracking or grouping of students (52%).

Very few districts reported lengthening the school year (84% had rejected the idea), perhaps because of the higher costs involved or because of widespread opposition to the proposal. Three out of four had made no move to eliminate grouping and tracking; and more than two-thirds did not consider lengthening the school day.

The majority of changes in organization and management had been under way before May 1983 and were not a response to the reform report recommendations. Actions taken after May 1983, which could be seen as responses to the reform movement, included undertaking partnerships with businesses (30%), computerizing administrative functions (30%), opening centers to assist in promoting good programs (21%), lengthening the school day (19%), and strengthening principals' management skills (19%).

District Actions Related to Discipline

School discipline had received considerable public attention for some time before the Excellence Movement began. In spite of this great attention, it remains one of the most widely misunderstood areas of educational policy making (Wayson 1985). For many years the Phi Delta Kappa/Gallup Poll of Public Attitudes Toward Education found discipline to be at the top of the list of school problems. In 1986 it dropped to second place after drug abuse (which also is a problem of discipline). The reform reports' recommendations for dealing with discipline and the exemplary districts' responses to these recommendations are reported in Table 7.5.

Table 7.5. School District Responses to Recommendations
Related to Discipline — 1984

Recommendation	Not Considered/ Rejected	Adopted Before May 1983	Adopted After May 1983
1. Initiate parent involvement, counseling for disruptive students	5%	88%	7%
2. Develop and enforce stricter discipline codes	14	76	10
3. Remove highly disruptive students from school	17	73	10
4. Create alternative programs for disruptive students	21	64	15
5. Reduce teachers' personal liability	64	36	0
6. Hire more guidance counselors	78	7	15
7. Limit legal rights regarding suspension	92	5	3

The districts' most common actions were involving parents in counseling for disruptive students (95%), developing stricter discipline codes (86%), removing highly disruptive students from school (83%), and providing alternative programs for disruptive students (79%). Nearly all those actions took effect prior to May 1983. Very few of the districts reported any actions related to discipline that could be attributed as a response to the reform reports. After May 1983, a few districts hired more counselors (15%), created alternative programs — mostly in-school suspension programs — for disruptive students (15%), and removed disruptive students from school (10%). In spite of widespread assertions that students' "legal rights" limit school officials' ability to enforce good discipline, only a few of the districts attempted to limit the rights of children facing suspension. As one respondent remarked, "We have no jurisdiction to limit these rights."

Conclusions About Early Impact of the Reform Reports on "Excellent" School Districts

1. Most actions recommended by the reform reports had begun in some of these "excellent" school districts before the publication of *A Nation at Risk* in May 1983.

2. The recommendations from the reform reports found most frequently in the "excellent" districts (at least 90% of the districts reporting) were instituting computer literacy courses, using non-stereotypic textbooks, monitoring student progress, strengthening principals' management skills, involving parents in counseling for disruptive students, computerizing administrative functions, acquiring special textbooks for students at risk or for gifted students, and using standardized testing at transition points in schooling.

3. The next recommendations of the reform reports found most frequently in the "excellent" districts (at least two-thirds of the districts reporting) were increased math requirements, partnerships with business, strong discipline codes, removal of disruptive students from school, alternative programs for disruptive students, reductions in class size, increased requirements for science and English, and fewer non-instructional tasks for teachers.

4. Recommended activities found in from one-half to two-thirds of the districts included promotions and graduation based on academic performance, foreign language in elementary schools, increased homework, alternative schools, assistance centers to promote new programs, reductions in academic offerings, and tracking of students.

5. Recommendations most frequently implemented after publication of *A Nation at Risk* were standardized testing at transition points in school-

ing, increased requirements in math and science, school-business partnerships, and computerizing administrative functions.

6. Most of the impact of the reform reports was in the area of curriculum and instruction.

7. The recommendations least frequently found in the "excellent" districts (rejected or ignored by at least 80% of the districts) were cuts in bilingual programs, linking teachers' salary increases to improved student achievement, higher salaries for math or science teachers, limiting rights for suspended students, employing non-credentialed teachers for areas of scarcity, 11-month contracts for teachers, and lengthening the school year.

How Schools Were Affected Two Years Later

Each of the districts in our sample was asked in 1984 to identify at least two schools whose programs could be considered exemplars of excellence. Representatives in these schools thus became part of the sample from whom we gathered the characteristics of exemplary excellent schools described in Chapter Eight. In December 1985, 51 of the districts and 88 of the school representatives responded to a new questionnaire asking: 1) What had they done since June 1984 that might be attributed to the reform reports? 2) What positive effects had the reports made in their schools? and 3) What negative effects had they made in their schools?

Returns were analyzed separately for elementary, junior high, and high schools and by districts, so we could identify any differences that occurred at each level. At least for these schools and districts identified as being "excellent," the Excellence Movement has affected elementary, junior high, and high schools in similar ways, except for a few recommendations, such as increased graduation requirements, that apply only to high schools. The changes reported to us varied from the superficial to the profound, but the same variations occurred at all grade levels. High schools and elementary schools reported more changes than junior high and middle schools. However, when junior high schools were affected, the changes seemed to be the same ones seen at the other levels.

The following discussion will focus on the effects on individual schools unless we specifically mention districts. However, we must keep in mind that these schools were already reputed to be outstanding when the movement started; so their responses may not tell much about what, if anything, is happening in other schools. Nevertheless, the generalizations we can draw from their experiences are useful for analyzing policy effects and for guiding those who wish to improve their schools even after the Excellence Movement has faded from the scene and become another forgotten fad.

What Was Done Between 1984 and 1985?

Since the spring of 1984, three-fourths of these "excellent" schools had taken some actions, which they reported was a response to the reform reports. Many districts appointed a task force or commission that made recommendations resulting in changes in local schools.

> The Board of Education appointed a Task Force on Excellence comprised of 23 lay citizens. The impetus for this was *A Nation at Risk.* As a direct result of the Task Force recommendations, in December 1984, several actions have been taken. The major ones are:
>
> 1. Initiated a summer school enrichment program that has received a commendation from the Kentucky Department of Education.
> 2. Established a Computer Committee that has developed a plan for the increased use of the computer in the instructional program.
> 3. Increased the art instruction program in our elementary schools.
> 4. Established a committee that is currently studying the salaries paid to our teachers.
> 5. Created a committee that recommended procedures for increasing the number of volunteers in our schools.
>
> — Fort Thomas (Kentucky) School District

Generally, no more than a third, and usually fewer, of the schools reported making the same changes. This seems to indicate that local conditions and needs strongly influence what is being done in response to the reform report recommendations.

> Locally, we have increased standardized testing to cover three more grade levels. We held three Administrative Academies designed to make all principals instructional leaders, implemented a new curriculum development model, adopted a new attendance policy, and instituted an academic awards program. We increased graduation requirements to 19 credits, increased staff in math and science, and added new science facilities. We also started a "Know Your Schools" month with weekly breakfast meetings at the Chamber of Commerce. We have provided *TESA* (Teacher Expectations and Student Achievement) training for 48 teachers and administrators, provided inservice to staff on implementing the Madeline Hunter model, and sent five administrators for training in the Effective Schools movement. We introduced teaming at the middle school and completely revised the schedule.
>
> — Ravenna (Ohio) City School District

Most schools reported that the changes they had made were initiated locally before the reform reports were issued. Of course, this is what one would expect of "excellent" schools; they are trendsetters in their regions and do not wait for policy, or politics, from on high to identify problems they want to solve.

> Our test scores are the tops in the state in all state tests. We were well on our way toward excellence before the mandates started coming down.
>
> — Gwinnett County (Georgia) Public Schools

> We do not believe the data that drive the reports are transferable to this district. We also believe that many of the recommendations are quantity responses (add classes, time, etc.) to quality problems (can't compute complex fractions, etc.).
>
> — Academy #20, Colorado Springs, Colorado

In states where mandates had been legislated, the changes were a blend of state and local initiatives. Where there were state initiatives — in most of the Sunbelt states and a few others — local schools have been affected. State mandates seem to focus on areas in response to popular public concerns: student achievement, graduation requirements, test results, evaluating teachers, lengthening school day and year (only a few states), and increasing accountability. Changes made locally, particularly in schools that already are achieving well beyond the minimal levels required by the state, tend to be less dramatic. Some have been under way for a long time, so no change is apparent. Some are marginal. Some are necessary but are not included in the "glamour" issues popularized by the reform reports.

> An economics credit will be required beginning with the graduating class of 1988. Science has been emphasized at the elementary level. Middle school time allocations for each program have been restructured by state mandate. Under local policy, algebra and pre-algebra will be offered in grades 7, 8, and 9 depending on the readiness of the student. Greater emphasis has been placed on staff development. Math Problem Solving Workshops are more prevalent. Summer school programs continue to expand due to both local and state action. Prime Time, a state and local program reducing the pupil-teacher ratio in the primary grades, is being phased into grades one through three.
>
> — Fort Wayne (Indiana) Community Schools

> The movement helped to refine some of our goals and objectives. It further gave credence to many of the educational improvements we had focused upon and developed. The majority of the state requirements had already been in place in our district before the state required them.
>
> — Consolidated Elementary School, Kennebunkport, Maine

129

In a number of states, the movement has strengthened the state's power over local education policy, producing some tension and strain between state and local officials.

> State legislatures mandate changes without involving the schools in the proposed changes. It causes increased paperwork and duplication of effort for districts already implementing many of the reforms being recommended. A lot of politicians are jumping on the bandwagon and using educational reform for personal motives.
> — Lulu M. Ross Elementary School, Milford, Delaware

> Within the State of Colorado, tremendous efforts have been made (mostly through legislation) to mandate numerous things — hours in class, preparation curriculums for administrators and teachers, increased credits in "solid" subjects, etc. At the same time, Colorado is considering reducing its fiscal support to K-12 education.
> — Academy #20, Colorado Springs, Colorado

The most common action taken in these districts has been to write new curriculum guides and courses of study. Some of these were efforts to bring the local curriculum in line with state mandates. Others were to create a clearly articulated curriculum (or the appearance of one) where there had been none, to add more specific objectives, to bring the curriculum more closely in line with testing programs, or to develop curricula for expanded programs such as gifted and talented, advanced placement, or added requirements for graduation. These new curricula tended to be more detailed and rigorous in terms of stating what and how much to cover and how to test for student achievement.

> A broadly based study committee was assigned the task of reviewing all aspects of the high school program. Its recommendations have resulted in: appointment of department chairpersons, use of improved budgeting procedures, greater emphasis on locally developed objective tests, updating the Industrial Arts Department offerings, and increased emphasis on offering teacher/administrator-planned staff development.
> — Mason (Michigan) Public Schools

One of the most popular actions taken by these schools was to add advanced placement courses and programs for gifted and talented pupils.

> An Advanced Placement Program has been initiated to provide specific instruction in chemistry, biology, American history, calculus, composition, and literature. Both state and local demands prompted us to provide these programs for college-bound students and those identi-

130

fied as gifted and talented. We expanded the enrichment program for greater emphasis on gifted and talented work at all levels with all children.

— Natrona County #1 School District, Casper, Wyoming

About one in five of these schools has added new graduation requirements.

We added specific courses to the previously expanded high school graduation requirements. The state added one-half unit in social studies; we added one-half unit in fine arts.

— Topeka (Kansas) Public Schools

Most of the efforts in our district started prior to *A Nation at Risk* and were continued in a *Report to the Legislative Delegation* (1984). Since then (among other things) we implemented a new social studies program (7-12) heavy in American history, world history, economics, and government. These courses are required of all students prior to their opting for electives.

— Natrona County #1 School District, Casper, Wyoming

About one third of the districts had added staff development activities, mostly to improve instructional methodology in areas where it was felt the staff needed help.

We have implemented a local staff development program for both certified and classified personnel. The goal of the certified training is that all present staff will acquire a reading endorsement in this state in the next three years. We began with an on-campus, week-long inservice two weeks before school opened. Teachers received a stipend, and course credit was paid by the district. So far two courses have been provided. Classified staff have been granted ten days of released time this year to receive additional training in a college course and a workshop.

— Ganado Primary School, Ganado, Arizona

Principals and teachers were provided assistance in interpreting non-referenced and objective-based test data and in writing instructional change plans, which define student skill deficiencies, reasons for skill deficiencies, and changes needed in the program. The instructional changes had a positive impact on student learning rates. This was a local initiative. Responding to research that has shown that matching instruction with individual learning styles enhances learning, Howard County has developed assessment instruments for teachers to diagnose students' skills and to assist teachers in diagnosing learning styles. Training teachers to use the results in the classroom has increased students' learning. This, too, is a local initiative.

— Howard County (Maryland) Public Schools

Some of the reported staff development sessions were workshops for evaluating and adopting new textbooks. This necessary but traditional activity carried out in most school districts did not represent any change in inservice activities that could be attributed to the reform reports. A few of the reporting schools had developed clear statements of objectives and implemented more testing procedures.

> The local project to develop districtwide objectives for each subject is now completed. We are initiating a pilot project to develop criterion-referenced tests to measure student mastery of district objectives.
> — Topeka (Kansas) Public Schools

> Our locally initiated curriculum design is measured by specific performance objectives; curriculum in all areas is designed to meet stated objectives, which are tested pre- and post- as well as at least three times per quarter on district-designed, criterion-referenced tests.
> — Apache Junction Junior High School, Apache Junction, Arizona

Some of the districts, usually in response to state mandates, were supervising and evaluating teachers more closely. Some localities had begun to evaluate administrators as well.

> Teaching acts are more observable through use of a teaching model, resulting in more precise evaluation. Teachers are receiving higher pay for instruction. This has had an overall positive impact in that teaching is beginning to be viewed as a profession.
> — Apache Junction Junior High School, Apache Junction, Arizona

Some schools, usually high schools, have established summer schools for students who need help or for academically able students who want to take electives.

> A summer school program is now in place so that there is opportunity for students failing required courses to repeat them during the summer months in order to meet increased state and local requirements for graduation. Accelerated classes also are available for students following the academic Honors Curriculum, who find that the requirements preclude taking electives during the standard school year.
> — Cape Girardeau Central High School, Cape Girardeau, Missouri

Several schools had adopted some form of the Effective Schools model, usually involving training principals and other administrators to implement programs associated with school effectiveness. Many schools in this sample had already installed some facet of the Effective Schools model before the Excellence Movement began (see discussion in Chapter Eight), so not many mentioned it on the 1985 questionnaire.

Prior to June 1984, the Jackson School District had planned and executed the effective school model in all the schools. The five correlates underlying the effective school model were being implemented concurrently. The primary initiative was local. The Mississippi Education Reform Act reinforced what the district was doing.
— Jackson (Mississippi) Municipal Separate School District

One in five of the reporting schools had been honored by some type of recognition program, usually a national or state excellence award. These awards contributed to increased morale of staff and students. They fostered greater public confidence and increased support from the community, including the school board. Even being nominated for an award was an important recognition. Both nominations and awards were mentioned as much as three times in some of the questionnaires, which is an indication of the pride that was generated. Receiving such awards also means that someone in the school — a principal or other staff member — had the initiative and energy to do all of the paperwork necessary for submitting the application for these awards.

We have had a lot of positive effects from the public relations that came from the recognition the school has received. The Kansas Department of Education has also praised our college-prep science curriculum and our mathematics curriculum.
— Topeka West High School, Topeka, Kansas

Crest Hill Elementary School was selected as the only elementary school in the State of Wyoming to be visited by the United States Department of Education for consideration as an Exemplary School (April 1986).
— Natrona County #1 School District, Casper, Wyoming

A common response from the schools was to stress more time on task and to reduce the number of interruptions to classroom instruction.

Working from local initiative, Aurora High School committed itself to "time on task" for the 1985-86 school year. To that end, paraprofessionals were hired to conduct all study halls and to supervise our daily activity period. The effect was to free faculty in order that they might tutor students who needed additional work in each subject. Also, some teachers were made available to write curriculum and conduct various committee meetings. The results of the tutoring will be evaluated through the help of Kent State University this June, 1986.
— Aurora High School, Aurora, Ohio

Many of these schools reported that they had raised expectations for student achievement and for more intensive instruction. Although few schools were linking teacher salaries to student achievement, such linkage did occur in some states with career ladder programs.

> Teachers electing to go on the state-initiated career ladder are paid based on their performance rather than on length of service or number of academic hours obtained.
> — Apache Junction Junior High School, Apache Junction, Arizona

Computers were mentioned less frequently in the 1985 questionnaire than in the previous year. Perhaps most of these schools already had installed some form of computer education. Only a few cited computers as a new program.

> Computer programs and cultural arts improvements were initiated at Neubert and funded by parents. Language arts outcomes and writing improvements were initiated by our local Language Arts Committee.
> — K.E. Neubert Elementary School, Algonquin, Illinois

Other responses mentioned by only one or two schools included: creating stronger parent groups, establishing school-business partnerships, weighting grades for different tracks, teaching higher-order thinking skills, adding drug and alcohol programs, raising certification requirements (state mandate), assigning teachers only in areas for which they were certified (local), and adding a few minutes to the school day or reallocating the day into more periods.

What Do School Personnel See as Positive Effects of the Excellence Movement?

In the 1985 survey, we asked districts and schools to list positive effects the Excellence Movement had on their schools. About one-third said there were no positive effects. No more than one-fifth mentioned any of the specific positive effects we have listed below, indicating that the effects vary according to local conditions and the school's traditions. Interviews with other educators in several states indicate that moderately good or mediocre schools with aspiring leaders have realized more positive effects than schools that already had excellent programs. Schools in communities or states that have not supported education very well in the past seemingly have received more positive effects from the public interest generated by the movement than have schools in areas with a tradition of strong support for good education.

The movement has caused local school personnel to focus on student achievement, basic skills, instruction, and curriculum.

I think it has helped me to focus on some important issues. I hope the attention the Excellence Movement has brought to schools continues. We need to know what is working and how to improve.
— Cascade Elementary School, Kennewick, Washington

All this publicity has made educators aware of areas of weakness as viewed by someone outside local districts. It has caused local districts to reexamine their own programs, practices, and direction.
— Pierce Middle School, Grosse Point Park, Michigan

The movement has made staff, students, and parents more aware of what the curriculum objectives are and has provided a clearer sense of how to attain them.

For the average student, knowing expectations and course objectives makes achieving the goal easier. Teachers know expectations and know precisely what is to be taught. They can evaluate their performance as well as the performance of their students.
— Windsor Forest High School, Savannah, Georgia

The excellence movement has focused attention once again on the importance of education and the need to raise the level of student achievement. Student achievement scores have become more important to the public; but since the students in our district achieve above state and national norms, the extra attention has been a positive experience. Having members of the community participating on parent advisory committees has also raised the level of community appreciation and support for the district's educational program.
— Mason (Michigan) Public Schools

The movement has focused students' attention on grades and test scores as the measure of academic success.

The more able students are now following a more demanding course of study. The increased graduation requirements have caused other students to become more serious, realizing there is less time for failure if they are going to complete requirements.
— Cape Girardeau Central High School, Cape Girardeau, Missouri

The movement has stimulated more stringent academic requirements, at least in quantitative terms of time and credits, and it is causing students to learn more, particularly factual information included on tests.

Student achievement has been improved. Teacher expectations are greater. The academic areas of the curriculum have been stressed more since the involvement in the effective schools model. Parent interest has improved.
— Steward Elementary School, Akron, Ohio

The emphasis on excellence has caused greater awareness of classroom interruptions and has generated efforts to reduce them.

> I think the only real change I have seen is that we now are more aware of the interruptions in the day, and we do more to prevent them. Of course, that can be bad, too, if it keeps us from doing some really educational things just to keep kids at their desks.
> — Welch Elementary School, Hamilton County, Ohio

The movement has aroused public interest in education, resulting in more funds from local sources and greater constituent support for what the schools are doing.

> The Excellence Movement has made these the "right times" to foster improvement in our schools. The public in general is more responsive to our requests to fulfill many of the needs that we have been identifying for some time.
> — Aurora High School, Aurora, Ohio

> The movement has made parents more aware, and that has helped pass needed tax increases. The climate has put more attention on obtaining better qualified teachers.
> — Milford Middle School, Milford, Delaware

The movement has provided school boards and communities with a rationale for supporting school leaders who had wanted to create better programs but could not generate sufficient community or board or staff support to carry them out. In some situations, state mandates have legitimated local efforts that were encountering resistance.

> The community has come to a greater appreciation of and a higher level of awareness of the public school students' achievement. The movement has also reinforced the teachers' beliefs that the district was on the right path to effectiveness and ultimately excellence.
> — Jackson (Mississippi) Municipal Separate School District

> Publicized criticism of public schools reinforced the fact that more "good than bad" was occurring in Howard County. That provided incentive for greater funding and involvement because of the focus on education as a national concern. That instilled enthusiasm for change.
> — Howard County (Maryland) Public School System

The movement has increased the amount of evaluation and supervision of teachers, students, administrators, and schools.

> Neubert is in the midst of a building self-study. The instrument developed for measurement focused on discovery of strengths and weak-

nesses in relation to *A Nation at Risk*. All schools in District #300 have initiated self-studies in the past two years. These studies were mandated by our local board of education.

   – K. E. Neubert Elementary School, Algonquin, Illinois

The movement has provided school staffs with the incentive for doing better and has generated enthusiasm for change.

We now see greater awareness of the educational program on the part of all citizens, resulting in increased support and interest. Teachers, principals, and school boards show greater support for new thrusts in academics. They all want greater sophistication in instruction. We've also seen stronger support for keeping the school day free of non-academic interruptions.

   – Natrona County #1 School District, Casper, Wyoming

The award has helped set a goal for us. It makes us try harder. We always try to get a little better as a result of the excellence flags hanging in our school.

   – Kenai Junior High School, Kenai, Alaska

The movement has generated pride, increased commitment, and bolstered morale for both staff and students, particularly if they have received recognition through awards.

Faculty morale is now at its highest level. The student body has become very proud of what the school stands for. The parents have openly supported both academic and social programs. The concept that we are all "family" has intensified, and there is a strong sense of belonging.

   – Wooster Intermediate School, Stratford, Connecticut

The movement has allowed good schools, good teachers, and good students to receive recognition.

Southport Elementary has been selected as one of five schools in the State of Indiana in the National Elementary School Recognition Program. Evaluation is currently under way by the United States Department of Education.

   – Southport Elementary School, Southport, Indiana

In addition to maintaining and refining existing junior/senior high programs, our elementary staff has completed an application for the United States Secretary of Education Elementary School Recognition Program. Currently we have been selected for an on-site visit.

   – Mullan School District, Mullan, Idaho

The movement has increased efforts to provide staff development with an emphasis on new instructional techniques. Some staff development is state mandated but much comes from local initiative. The most commonly mentioned packaged programs are Effective Schools (or School Improvement), *TESA* (Teacher Expectations and Student Achievement), and Madeline Hunter's instructional improvement program.

> We instituted a new district goal to inservice teachers and administrators in Madeline Hunter's Essential Elements of Effective Instruction. We also conducted a needs assessment to determine community attitudes about our program. Although 10 pages in length, we received a phenomenal 25% return. The results will give us future guidance for improving our programs.
> — Natrona County #1 School District, Casper, Wyoming

The movement has resulted in new sources of funding in some states. In some states teacher salaries increased more than what might have been expected. Staff morale and support for the movement tends to be highest in those states.

> Throughout the state of Tennessee, education has received more attention and funds as a result of the Better Schools program. In some districts there are curriculum guides for the first time. The teacher evaluation systems have improved, and funds for counselors in grades one and two have been provided.
> — Linden Elementary School, Oak Ridge, Tennessee

What Do School Personnel See as Negative Effects of the Excellence Movement?

We asked the schools sampled in the 1985 questionnaire to describe any negative effects that they felt had resulted from the Excellence Movement. Some saw no negative outcomes. No more than one-fourth agreed on any one of the negative effects listed below, again indicating wide variations in how the movement is affecting local schools and districts.

The movement has given excessive importance to standardized testing, resulting in pressures on students and staff to improve their scores.

> The movement has increased the pressure on staff for better student test scores. When people feel too pressured, performance sometimes declines and frustration sets in.
> — Milford Middle School, Milford, Delaware

> There is a "test mania" feeling among our teachers and administrators. We are probably giving too much attention to testing. However, we welcome accountability and are not worried about it!
> — Gwinnett County (Georgia) Public Schools

138

The movement has created pressures that have caused unproductive anxieties among staff.

> While teachers and administrators accept increased accountability, the present situation has raised the level of anxiety among them. Increasing high school graduation requirements has caused reduced enrollment in elective courses, may cause marginal students to become discouraged, may increase the dropout rate, and may increase the number of students needing more than four years to graduate from high school.
> — Topeka (Kansas) Public Schools

> This is the most negative and frustrating part: higher expectations and new methods and techniques of doing things — but nothing else has changed. People are expected to do more, do it better, and do it with less. And the surprising thing is — we will! The new programs have created a heavier workload for teachers and administrators without providing funding to meet the increased demands. The pressure from the public created a situation where some schools feel they must do something even without necessary skills or programs. They are trying to compete in any way to look better and to get better press!
> — Highlands High School, Fort Thomas, Kentucky

The movement is contributing to failure and frustration of students.

> More students are failing to meet the graduation requirements within four years, thereby requiring fifth year attendance. Others elect to drop out rather than meet the new demands.
> — Cape Girardeau Central High School, Cape Girardeau, Missouri

> Our district has always had a focus on academics. This increased emphasis and pressure to raise standards seriously threatens students who are low achievers and are not college bound.
> — Mason Middle School, Mason, Michigan

By emphasizing measurable outcomes rather than broader educational outcomes, the movement has detracted from the affective and creative dimensions of the curriculum and may be undermining attainment of higher-level thinking skills.

> More and more, classes look alike. There is less creativity, flair, and joy down the halls. We are presently addressing this issue.
> — Brook Park Memorial Elementary School, Brook Park, Ohio

The movement has tended to straitjacket the curriculum and instructional methods, thereby reducing flexibility and, perhaps, inhibiting efforts to reach some students.

Much of the impact tends to be based on national norms, that is, the movement is too eager to identify the 5 or 7 or 14 elements of Excellence. A local base, while much more cumbersome and, at times, ambiguous, allows for more "ownership" on the part of all the various constituents of the school community.

— Lakewood High School, Lakewood, Ohio

Negative publicity about the schools has caused some loss of public confidence, creating a poor image of schools in general, which is particularly harmful for schools that were already doing well and therefore do not appear to be changing much.

The criticism of schools gave the impression that what was wrong nationally was wrong locally, which was not true. The movement was joined by quick-fix "experts" whose pronouncements stalled creative thinking and long-range solutions to improvement programs.

— Howard County (Maryland) Public School System

Many of the weaknesses noted by the commissions did not apply to many school districts, and yet the public assumes they do. I'm afraid that many of the important humane activities may be diminished in the push for excellence.

— Aurora High School, Aurora, Ohio

The states' new assertion of authority over local districts violates traditional practice and often leads to nonproductive policy, lackluster compliance, and covert resistance.

I do not feel that the changes affected Linden positively, since we already had dealt with most of the problems that the state mandates focused on. The extra money from the state has been used to pay for programs already in place in Oak Ridge. The Linden teachers' morale has been lowered by the career ladder program. I feel that the Governor's program has caused competition instead of cooperation among schools.

— Linden Elementary School, Oak Ridge, Tennessee

That achievement test for teachers has produced more bad feeling than you can imagine. It's just that the state makes it look as though everybody is incompetent and teachers are the cause of all the problems. The biggest concern now is that teachers are so upset with Mark White [then Governor of Texas] that they will overreact and help elect people who are even worse.

— regional state education department official in Texas

An almost universal complaint is that the excellence initiatives have increased paperwork significantly for both teachers and administrators.

140

The time and effort necessary for processing the applications for awards and the subsequent visitations distract from the usual functions of the school.
                                — Mullan High School, Mullan, Idaho

We must strike a "loose-tight" relationship in terms of state mandates to improve. Excess paperwork will not create effective or excellent schools. Practitioners must be able to see the "big picture" rather than piles of paperwork.
                                — Callaway High School, Jackson, Mississippi

Funding has increased, but most of the changes are a result of increased staff efforts or reallocation of funds for different priorities. Creating, implementing, and maintaining new initiatives springing from the Excellence Movement have added to the work of teachers and others, often with no additional compensation. Some personnel have been overextended, particularly those who always have performed beyond usual expectations.

We have been able to meet changes with our own budgets. It's a matter of where the money goes. Example: less musical instruments and more computers.
                                — Pierce Middle School, Grosse Point Park, Michigan

We've added no extra personnel, just "extra energy." Additional costs would be considered with the computer expansion program, but the township is responsible for costs involved with that program.
                                — Southport Elementary School, Southport, Indiana

Declining political interest in the movement, combined with changes in the economy, has created concern that whatever gains have been made will be lost, and the extra effort expended by some school personnel will have been in vain.

Most of these changes cost money. However, so much has occurred over the past 18 months that it is difficult to separate out the costs. The recent dramatic reductions in the price of a barrel of oil will have a catastrophic effect on the budgets of Wyoming schools. As of this date, we will neither institute new programs nor expand existing ones. Our budgets will be very difficult next year and far worse the following year due to severe reductions in state funding.
                                — Natrona County #1 School District, Casper, Wyoming

Our legislature passed sweeping education bills providing for many positive accomplishments in education, then nullified them all by refusing to allocate any kind of appropriations to implement any of them.
                                — Northeast Elementary School, Kearney, Nebraska

What Do Educators Think the Excellence Movement Has Wrought?

Although the "excellent" schools in our sample are not representative of all schools, we wanted to know if their opinions about the positive and negative effects of the Excellence Movement were shared by other educators. To make this comparison, we gathered data from several samples. In December 1985, we asked the schools and districts that had responded to our original survey in 1984 to tell us whether they agreed or disagreed with several generalizations that had been made about the impact of the Excellence Movement on schools and districts. Then in April 1986, we asked a sample of elementary and secondary school principals from Texas to respond to the same instrument; and in June 1986, we used the same instrument with teachers and administrators in Nebraska.

Table 7.6 shows the percentage of each of the three samples that replied as either "agree" or "strongly agree" to each of the generalizations.

The results show that nearly all respondents from the "excellent" schools and districts felt that the movement influenced schools to pay more attention to academic achievement. Fewer respondents from the Texas sample agreed, and still fewer from the Nebraska sample agreed. But all confirmed that a focus on academic achievement was the most prevalent or second most prevalent result of the movement.

From two-thirds to three-fourths of the total sample felt that, as a result of the movement:

- The public is giving greater attention to education.
- States have greater power over local schools and districts.
- Educators are reducing interruptions in classrooms.

About the same percentage of the Texas sample agreed that these outcomes had occurred, but a smaller percentage of the Nebraska sample agreed. Nevertheless, the Nebraska sample reported that these outcomes were among the most frequent in their state.

From 54% to 63% of the "excellent" school respondents felt that:

- Tests dominate the curriculum more than ever.
- Children are learning more.
- The public has more confidence in education.

Fewer of the Nebraska sample felt that these three outcomes had occurred in their schools. The Texas sample, which had just experienced the imposition of competency tests for both teachers and students, disagreed; they felt that tests dominated the curriculum more, children were learning less, and public confidence had waned.

Table 7.6. Educators' Opinions About How the Excellence Movement Has Affected the Schools and Districts

Reported Effects of the Excellence Movement	Percent "Agree" and "Strongly Agree"						
	"Excellent" Schools						
	Total	Elem.	Jr.	HS	Dist.	NE	TX
1. Schools are giving more attention to academic achievement.	90	95	75	95	93	53	82
2. Public is giving more attention to education.	77	70	67	90	93	64	71
3. States have been given more power over local schools.	71	80	50	75	57	45	76
4. Schools are reducing non-instructional interruptions.	69	60	67	80	61	38	65
5. Children are learning more.	63	65	58	65	71	29	29
6. Tests are dominating the curriculum more than ever.	62	70	58	55	57	45	84
7. Public confidence in education has been improved.	54	30	75	65	71	27	29
8. Teacher salaries have risen more than they would have otherwise.	42	35	50	45	64	15	27
9. Curriculum has become more textbook oriented.	42	60	33	30	37	38	63
10. Most of the changes attributed to the Excellence Movement were already taking place.	41	35	42	45	43	57	47
11. More funds for education are available than would have been otherwise.	35	35	42	35	32	04	12
12. Status of teachers has been diminished by "top down" supervision models and mandated change.	29	35	25	25	21	41	64
13. Programs are becoming more punitive, exclusionary, or elitist.	25	20	42	20	43	25	57
14. Effect of state mandates has been negative or of little consequence to students.	25	25	25	25	22	45	47
15. Disadvantaged students are receiving less attention.	25	30	17	25	07	29	27
16. Students have been affected positively by less involvement of federal government in education.	24	21	33	21	07	16	08
17. Changes have not greatly affected practice in classrooms.	19	30	08	05	19	37	16
18. Paperwork has been reduced for administrators and teachers.	15	30	08	05	04	04	04

About 35% to 42% of the "excellent" school respondents felt that:

- The curriculum now focused more on textbook learning.
- Teacher salaries were higher than they otherwise would have been.
- Most changes had been under way before the reform reports came out.
- More money was available than otherwise would have been.

More Nebraskans than Texans (57% to 47%) felt that changes attributed to the Excellence Movement had already been under way. Far more Texans than Nebraskans (63% to 38%) felt that textbooks had become more central to the curriculum. Far fewer of both groups felt that general funding or salaries were higher than would have been expected; although both felt that salaries had been affected more than general funds.

Nearly 30% of the "excellent" school respondents felt that the status of the teacher had been diminished and 21% of the district respondents felt the same way. In Texas 64% and in Nebraska 41% of those responding felt that teachers had lost status.

If we look at those who did not agree that the remainder of the movement's outcomes listed in the questionnaire had occurred, it appears that a majority felt that outcomes:

- Had neutral or positive consequences for students.
- Had not caused programs to become more punitive or elitist.
- Had not diminished efforts to serve disadvantaged students.

Texas respondents, with more experience in the movement, felt more than the other groups that the outcomes had negative consequences for students and that programs were more punitive and elitist. Nebraska respondents agreed with those from Texas about the negative outcomes, but the Nebraska respondents agreed with the "excellent" school respondents that the programs were not punitive and elitist. Both the Texas and Nebraska respondents agreed with the "excellent" school respondents that disadvantaged students were not being ignored.

When interpreting the responses to the questionnaire, it is important to keep in mind the respondents' individual perspectives. For example, the "excellent" schools might already be doing a lot with disadvantaged students, so they might feel that their efforts had not been diminished by the movement. Other school respondents might not have been doing much for disadvantaged students; or they might have interpreted "disadvantaged" to mean black students, and there were few if any black students in their schools. Therefore, they would report little change in what was being done as a result of the movement. The same perceptual or semantic factors also may bear on the question about punitive or elitist programs and even on the question about teachers' status.

About 75% of the excellent school respondents, most of the Texas and Nebraska respondents, and about 90% of the district respondents did not agree that students have been affected positively by the federal government's withdrawal from education. Many respondents wrote comments on this item to the general effect, "You've got to be kidding!" While it may be true that many in the general population feel that federal programs were ineffective or unwelcome (see Clark and Astuto 1986), most educators, including those in "excellent" schools, did not.

Most respondents from all groups in the sample felt that the outcomes of the Excellence Movement had affected classrooms. From the data reported in this chapter, the movement had both positive and negative effects. For example, more than 90% of all respondents and about 65% of elementary school respondents felt that paperwork was as heavy or heavier than ever. Notes written on the questionnaires stated that paperwork has greatly expanded for teachers and principals. It appears the blame for the increased paperwork has shifted from federal to state and local levels. The paperwork no longer is to monitor compliance with issues of equity but now is to monitor student achievement and to document instructional practices.

Conclusion

By 1986 the Excellence Movement had generated enough public pressure and state legislative action to affect districts in some way. The impact varied in both quality and intensity depending on local conditions. As might be expected, it had both positive and negative effects. And sometimes what was negative for one school was positive for another. However, we did find some agreement among educators in several parts of the country on some positive and some negative outcomes.

The movement's greatest impact was on curriculum and instruction and, as a result of state mandates, on requirements for graduation and the development of curriculum guides and courses of study. Some states instituted competency testing standards for students and career ladders or other incentive programs for teachers.

The Excellence Movement gave great visibility to the importance of public education. It caused educators to give more attention to academic outcomes and to reduce interruptions in classrooms. Some children seemed to learn more of what is tested on standardized tests, and some of the public may have gained more confidence in education.

On the other hand, the reforms associated with the movement increased state dominance over local districts, thus increasing tensions between state officials and local school districts and adding obligations that distracted from the programs in good schools. Tests and textbooks determined the curriculum in some schools. Some excellent schools reported some loss of public confidence. Opinions were equally divided as to whether children had learned more.

Opinion was divided as to whether the movement helped to increase teacher salaries or made more funds available to schools. Many costs of the reforms were absorbed by increasing the workload of teachers and administrators or by reallocating funds from other purposes.

Most respondents felt that the movement had affected children positively or not at all, that programs were not more punitive for children, and that disadvantaged students had not suffered. About a third reported negative effects on children, more punitive and elitist programs, and losses for disadvantaged children. Most felt that federal withdrawal from education had harmed children and agreed almost universally that the movement had increased paperwork and routine administrative functions.

References

Al-amin, Daian. "Survey of State Education Reforms." Leaflet. Children's Defense Fund, Education Division, 122 C Street, N.W., Washington, DC 20001. February 1985.

Anderson, Beverly, and Odden, Allan. "State Initiatives Can Foster School Improvement." *Phi Delta Kappan* 67 (April 1986): 578-81.

Association for Supervision and Curriculum Development. "Toward More Effective Schools." *Educational Leadership* 40 (December 1982).

Bondi, Joseph, and Wiles, Jon. "School Reform in Florida: Implications for the Middle School." *Educational Leadership* 44 (September 1986): 44-49.

Boal, W. John. "Business Gets an 'A'." *Western's World* 15 (April 1984).

Bridgman, A. "States Launching Barrage of Initiatives, Survey Finds." *Education Week,* 6 February 1985, pp. 1, 31.

Brookover, Wilbur B. "Distortion and Overgeneralization Are No Substitutes for Sound Research." *Phi Delta Kappan* 69 (November 1987): 225-27.

Children's Defense Fund. "Education Reports Prompt State Reform," *CDF Reports* (December 1984/January 1985): 1.

Clark, David L., and Astuto, Terry A. *The Significance and Permanence of Changes in Federal Education Policy, 1980-1988.* Bloomington, Ind.: Policy Studies Center of the University Council for Educational Administration, Indiana University, January 1986.

Clark, Terry A., and McCarthy, Dennis P. "School Improvement in New York City: The Evolution of a Project." *Educational Researcher* 2 (April 1983): 17-24.

Cuban, Larry. "Changing Course: A 50-State Survey of Reform Measures." *Education Week,* 6 February 1985, pp. 11, 30.

Cuban, Larry. "Transforming the Frog into a Prince: Effective Schools Research, Policy, and Practice at the District Level." *Harvard Educational Review* 54 (1984): 129-51.

Danzberger, Jacqueline P., and Usdan, Michael D. "Building Partnerships: The Atlanta Experience." *Phi Delta Kappan* 65 (February 1984): 393-96.

Dougherty, Van. *State Programs of School Improvement, 1983: A 50-State Survey.* Denver: Education Commission of the States, 1983.

Dougherty, Van, and Odden, Allan. *State Programs of School Improvement: A 50-State Survey.* Denver: Education Commission of the States, 1982.

Education Commission of the States. *Directory of State Task Forces on Education Issues.* Denver, 1983.

Farrar, Eleanor; Miles, Matthew B.; and Neufeld, Barbara. *Review of Effective Schools Programs: The Extent of Adoption of Effective Schools Program.* Vol. 2. Cambridge, Mass.: Huron Institute, 1983.

Education Research Service. *Needs Assessment of AASA Members, 1983-84: Summary of Responses to a Survey of AASA Members.* Arlington, Va., February 1984.

Finn, Chester E. "Toward Strategic Independence: Nine Commandments for Enhancing School Effectiveness." *Phi Delta Kappan* 65 (April 1984): 518-24.

Flakus-Mosqueda, Patricia. *Survey of States' Teacher Policies.* Denver: Education Commission of the States, 1983.

Griesemer, J. Lynn, and Butler, Cornelius. *Education Under Study: An Analysis of Recent Major Reports on Education.* 2nd ed. Chelmsford, Mass.: Northeast Regional Exchange, November 1983.

Hanes, Robert C., and Mitchell, Kay F. "Teacher Career Development in Charlotte-Mecklenburg." *Educational Leadership* 43 (November 1985): 11-13.

Kirst, Michael W. "The Changing Balance in State and Local Power to Control Education." *Phi Delta Kappan* 66 (November 1984): 189-91.

Minneapolis Board of Education. "The Mission to Ensure Equity and Excellence in the Minneapolis Public Schools." Adopted 8 June 1982.

Murphy, Joseph F. "Effective Schools: What the Research Reveals." *APEX Case Report* 1, no. 5 (February 1985). Available from APEX Center, 1310 S. Sixth Street, Champaign, Illinois 61820.

National Commission on Excellence in Education. *Meeting the Challenge: Recent Efforts to Improve Education Across the Nation.* Washington, D.C.: U.S. Department of Education, 1983. Includes supplement.

Rogus, Joseph; Severino, D. Alexander; and Thompson, Arlene. "Education as a Response to Developmental Needs: Preventing Truancy and School Dropout." In *Preventing Adolescent Alienation,* edited by L. Eugene Arnold. Lexington, Mass.: Lexington Books, 1983.

Rutter, Michael, et al. *Fifteen Thousand Hours: Secondary Schools and Their Effects on Children.* Cambridge, Mass.: Harvard University Press, 1979.

Schlechty, Phillip C. "Evaluation Procedures in the Charlotte-Mecklenburg Career Ladder Plan." *Educational Leadership* 43 (November 1985): 14-19.

Siegel, Peggy M. *Survey of 1983 State Efforts to Improve Education.* Denver: National Conference of State Legislatures, 1983.

Silberman, Charles E. *Crisis in the Classroom: The Remaking of American Education.* New York: Random House, 1970.

Stedman, Lawrence C. "It's Time We Changed the Effective Schools Formula." *Phi Delta Kappan* 69 (November 1987): 215-224.

Stedman, Lawrence C. "A New Look at the Effective Schools Literature." *Urban Education* 20 (October 1985): 295-326.

United States Department of Education. *Meeting the Challenge: Recent Efforts to Improve Education Across the Nation.* Washington, D.C.: U.S. Department of Education, 15 November 1983.

United States Department of Education. *The Nation Responds: Recent Efforts to Improve Education.* Washington, D.C.: U.S. Government Printing Office, May 1984.

Wayson, William W. "The Politics of Violence in School: Doublespeak and Disruptions in Public Confidence." *Phi Delta Kappan* 67 (October 1985): 127-32.

Wayson, William W.; Achilles, Charles; Pinnell, Gay Su; Cunningham, Luvern; Carol, Lila; and Lintz, Nan. *Handbook for Developing Public Confidence in Education.* Bloomington, Ind.: Phi Delta Kappa Educational Foundation, forthcoming.

"Year of the Reports: Responses from the Educational Community." *Harvard Educational Review* 54 (February 1984).

Young, Gayle. "Good and Getting Better." *School Administrator* 41 (January 1984): 20-21, 47.

CHAPTER EIGHT

What Do Excellent Schools Do?

After . . . visiting schools in a large portion of the States of our Union, I went abroad. In European schools I saw many things, good, bad, and indifferent. The good I attempted to describe for imitation, and the bad for warning. . . . [N]o particular teacher, or town, or class of schools, was designated for special approval or disapproval. I left the good sense of the community to make the application. Before that tribunal all good schools and good teachers would be safe; nay, would obtain commendation.

—Horace Mann, 1845

As we began this study, we were interested in how a series of reform recommendations and a heavy dose of political hoopla and publicity were affecting local schools and districts. As the study progressed and the glitter of the movement began to fade, more important questions surfaced (as they have a tendency to do whenever passions yield to the cold light of morning).

Essential questions about excellence in education impelled us to look more closely at what individual school principals and teachers were doing to fulfill their professional and civic responsibilities to their communities and their nation. So, over the course of the study, our purpose shifted from describing how a political movement was affecting schools and communities to one of describing and celebrating what imaginative, capable, and

149

dedicated school personnel were doing that benefited students and communities, even when the "hot" public issues of the moment had cooled. Thus, while we gathered information to see what excellent schools were doing about the reform reports, we found that this information also might serve as a guide for other schools to develop successful practices.

In the course of the study, we reviewed questionnaires completed by more than 250 respondents, who described in detail what their schools were doing that had earned them reputations for being excellent. We visited and talked with teachers and administrators in more than 60 regional seminars, and we visited two dozen schools in as many parts of the country. We surveyed the literature for three years to examine articles, evaluations, and fugitive reports about specific school programs. We attended several state and national conferences at which exemplary school programs were featured, and we participated in a number of research meetings devoted to the impact of the Excellence Movement. In this chapter we report what we found that "excellent" schools do.

Some General Findings

1. Most of the programs in schools that were nominated as being "excellent" had begun before 1983. Yet these were the same schools selected by local and state officials to show what was being done in response to the reform reports. We attempted to categorize their programs to determine which of them might have been stimulated by the reform recommendations, but we found such an analysis unproductive; most of the programs could not be categorized in any way that was consistent with recommendations from the Excellence Movement.

2. Very few school personnel in schools identified as "excellent" mentioned any of the reform recommendations as an incentive or stimulus for their actions. In fact, many of their programs and practices went well beyond the recommendations, were different from the recommendations, or were directly opposed to the recommendations. So we abandoned any attempt to relate school programs and practices directly to the recommendations and let the data speak for themselves.

3. Among the few that did respond to the reform recommendations, the most frequently reported actions were adding requirements for high school graduation, monitoring students' achievement more closely (in elementary schools), reducing interruptions to classroom instruction, adding computer experiences in elementary schools, and initiating more tracking for high school students. Many of those changes were in response to state mandates or incentives, and some of them deterred or deflected these educators from

their central purposes (see Chapter Seven). When reporting practices that contributed most to reputations for excellence, the respondents did not mention reducing electives, changing bilingual education, or lengthening the school year.

4. One observable influence of the Excellence Movement was the adoption of new language or terminology to describe activities or to give new priority to activities that already were under way. Words such as "monitoring" have become very popular. Schools that give frequent quizzes and tests to check pupil progress now use the term to good advantage. "Excellent," not used widely before the movement, now is found attached to every possible noun; and "excellence" has become cliché in the literature and in school public relations copy. "Effective" and "orderly" are sprinkled through the writings and speeches of educators and politicians, who earlier would have used such phrases as "good achievement" and "well-disciplined students." The terms "basics" and "accountability," although old favorites, have come back with greater intensity. Astute educators now use these terms associated with the movement whenever they report to the state or to the community, and especially if they are applying for a grant or competing for an award.

State education departments and school districts were pushed to show that they had "something going." So they identified any program or school that had a reputation for being good and showcased it, even though such programs did not result directly from the movement. Nevertheless, identifying these programs and schools served to stimulate the movement by offering models for less successful schools and districts to emulate. And as models, they can be used as a point of comparison against which the impact of the movement can be assessed.

In this chapter, then, our purpose is not to assess the Excellence Movement but to look beyond it and to report practices found in schools reputed to be excellent so that they can be disseminated to other schools.

"Excellent" School Practices Related to the Curriculum

In our questionnaire we asked respondents from our sample of "excellent" schools to describe their most successful or promising curriculum practices that could be used in other schools. These responses were supplemented by as many interviews and observations as we could make. The practices we found in these schools provide a composite of what occurs in schools that causes them to be identified as excellent.

1. Excellent schools lay a firm foundation for learning by teaching basic math and communication skills; and they teach them by engaging students in experiences that require them to use the skills in real-life situations.

The Glendale Landmark School in Glendale, Arizona, offers an alternative program that emphasizes relationships between math and science and all other facets of the curriculum. Each year the program focuses on a current problem with implications for the future, such as nuclear energy and water conservation. More is included than just basic instruction; problem solving, thinking skills, and creative solutions are taught through daily hands-on applications both inside and outside the classroom. The program, initiated primarily to improve racial balance in the district schools, also serves as a model program for mathematics, science, and futures forecasting.

At Elizabethtown Area Middle School in Elizabethtown, Pennsylvania, students engage in academic studies in social studies, science, reading, math, and language arts each day. However, the schedule is designed to allow for varying abilities through enrichment and both on-grade and below-grade sectioning. All students also study specific areas in art, music, home economics, and industrial arts each year.

In keeping with the current emphasis on science and technology, these schools utilize structured and sequential math programs.

In the Comprehensive School Mathematics Program (developed by CEMREL, Inc., a regional educational laboratory) used at Way Elementary School in Bloomfield Hills, Michigan, students are achieving in traditional mathematics skills as well as gaining understanding of a broader range of important mathematics concepts and a higher level of skills in problem solving.

Clemens Crossing Elementary School in Columbia, Maryland, reports an effective math program in which 99% of the students in K-5 attained grade level. Program components include a facilitation model, differentiated groupings, units of sequenced objectives, laboratory experiences, computer practice and enrichment, acceleration, team-assisted instruction, nightly homework, and morning problem solving.

Many of these schools have created comprehensive programs for teaching children to communicate through written compositions. Several reported unusually productive writing programs that taught students the whole process of producing written works.

At Ganado Primary School in Ganado, Arizona, a K-3 writing program has published 36 volumes of student writing and a monthly newspaper, complete with literary supplement. Students are provided opportunities to write in many forms and for many purposes and audiences. Books written by individual classes, by grade levels, and by individuals in schoolwide writing competitions are published regularly. Writing seminars are held twice monthly and have replaced the traditional teachers' meeting.

Hardwick (Vermont) Elementary School uses a step-by-step approach to achieve a writing product. This process approach is used in all curriculum areas. The steps are:

1. Prewriting: helping the writer to find a subject; this might involve brainstorming, list making, class discussion, looking at journals and pictures, reviewing previous writing.
2. First draft: discovering what you know about the subject by getting the story down quickly, with little concern for mechanics.
3. Conferencing: talking your writing over with another person, one-on-one, or in small groups.
4. Second draft: revising the writing as a result of the conferences.
5. Conferencing: discussing the writing again to see if the writer's meaning is clear.
6. Final draft: writing the piece in its best form with as few errors as possible in usage and mechanics.
7. Editing: finding all errors in mechanics and usage.
8. Publishing: putting the piece before an audience other than the teacher; mounting on bulletin board, reading aloud in class, printing pieces in class booklet.

The process approach to writing has been described in detail by Graves (1983), Calkins (1983), and DeFord (1984). By following the steps in the process, children learn how to produce a good piece of writing. As children work through the process, they come to realize that writing takes careful thought and a lot of work. Evaluation and feedback are provided at each step in the process, not just after the final product has been submitted. A major feature of the process approach is that it makes children aware of the need to adjust their writing style in order to communicate with different audiences. The prospect of publication serves as an incentive to get the mechanics right. Teachers generally need well-designed and continuing in-service training to implement the process approach to writing.

Perry Meridian High School in Indianapolis, Indiana, has a non-graded writing lab, which provides individualized help over and above what is provided in classroom instruction. On referral from an English teacher, the student brings a checked diagnostic sheet to the writing lab, where an instructor gives one-on-one help in the areas checked on the diagnostic sheet. Or the student comes to the lab with a writing assignment, the rough draft of a writing assignment, or a piece of writing needing revision. The atmosphere in the lab is supportive and nonthreatening; the student can return to the lab as often as necessary. The lab is open to students who require help with basic skills and also to accomplished students seeking assistance in polishing their writing. A reaction from one English teacher in the school was: "It's wonderful! At first students avoided it for fear of being labeled; now, everybody wants to use it. It has become the thing to do."

Mullan (Idaho) School District is implementing a K-12 writing program that spans the entire curriculum. It enables students to become competent writers in various genres. This holistic approach to teaching writing includes: developing and organizing ideas; creating an individual style; and using appropriate words and phrases, grammar and sentence structure, punctuation, spelling, and manuscript form. An essential element of the program is student involvement in the process of writing and rewriting.

Some of the "excellent" schools encourage students to use the full range of reading skills. Many build their approach around recognized literary works.

Seventh-grade advanced reading students at L.J. Schultz Middle School in Cape Girardeau, Missouri, take a special course that emphasizes understanding and appreciating good literature, which reflects the values and cultural heritage of contemporary society. The course is designed to foster higher-level comprehension skills, writing, and language analysis.

Staff at Holderness Central School in Plymouth, New Hampshire, have replaced the basal textbook in the upper elementary grades with both contemporary and classic literature. Vocabulary exercises, comprehension checks, and analysis/evaluation skill worksheets are developed for each book. While students develop skills, they also are being exposed to good literature.

2. "Excellent" schools have various ways to help children who are not achieving. These schools' reputations are not based on the skills and abilities their students bring from home. They do not foster excellence by rejecting or retaining reluctant or slow students. They reach them and they teach them. A characteristic of many of the schools we studied was their effort to serve *all* students.

The Academic Intervention Program at Kenai Junior High School in Kenai, Alaska, targets students in the regular program who are not achieving at the minimum level. A formal process has been set up for students, parents, and teachers to meet and find ways to help students achieve academic success, and in the process develop a more positive self-image.

Quincy High School in Quincy, Massachusetts, has a "Grade Nine Team Program," a transitional program for students who have demonstrated a need in grade eight for a supportive alternative environment. Students selected for the program are those identified as having such problems as poor attendance, failing grades, poor attitude, poor conduct, or little parental support. The team is staffed with teachers of English, mathematics, science, and social studies, who work together to create a warm supportive environment that promotes a positive attitude toward school. Students enrolled in the program pursue the same course of study as all grade nine students.

The Reading Skills Center at John D. Pierce Middle School in Grosse Pointe Park, Michigan, provides remedial support in language arts and also helps students who do not quite qualify for advanced English classes. Instruction is individualized with class size of no more than 14 students. The students have won many writing awards, and some materials for the school's literary magazine are written at the center.

At Air Academy High School at United States Air Force Academy in Colorado Springs, Colorado, students are able to call or come to the campus in the evening for help from certified staff, library personnel, and counselors.

3. Many of these "excellent" schools create support networks to give students personal assistance in meeting academic expectations. These schools recognize that students learn as much or more from one another as they learn in their classes. They also know that learners, especially reluctant learners, learn best from those with whom they have developed relationships marked by trust and mutual respect. No student becomes a cipher in these schools.

Desert-Hills Middle School in Kennewick, Washington, has an informal networking system based on the premise that students with problems naturally seek out those they trust for advice, assistance, and support. They might be other students, teachers, or other staff. Called the "Natural Helpers" program, it trains the helping students and adults in communication and decision-making skills, provides information on major problems facing students and use of local resources, and develops an awareness of their limits as helpers.

Kelly Walsh High School in Casper, Wyoming, has an advisor-advisee program. Each teacher and administrator is assigned from 10 to 15 student advisees. The role of the advisor is to assess student interests and abilities in order to match their experiences in the school with their future goals and career intentions. U-32 High School in Montpelier, Vermont, has a similar program in which every adult has a dozen advisees for whom he or she acts as "parent surrogate" to offer help when needed and to protect students from any unfair treatment in the school.

4. "Excellent" schools provide special programs for academically talented students. In carrying out their commitment to serve all students, these schools challenge their brightest students to develop their special talents to the fullest.

At Oak Ridge (Tennessee) High School, more than 50% of the students participate in the advanced courses, which include 13 courses in 10 academic disciplines. In addition to the educational benefits of these courses, the students earned 900 hours of college credit in the 1982-83 school year, which represents an annual savings of more than $200,000 in tuition costs.

At Lulu M. Ross Elementary School in Milford, Delaware, academic awards are given monthly and quarterly. Each month, the student in each classroom who masters the highest number of reading and math objectives is named "Scholar of the Month" and has his or her photograph displayed in the lobby. Quarterly awards, such as ice cream, certificates, special films, and school pencils, are given to students who earn As or Bs in reading and math.

The Milford, Delaware, Rotary Club sponsors the Milford Middle School Academic Achievement Program. Students who make A/B Honor roll are awarded a free field trip. The Rotary Club provides a free lunch for all students when they are on a trip.

5. Some of the "excellent" schools provide students with experiences specifically designed to teach critical thinking and creative problem solving.

The staff at Robertsville Junior High School in Oak Ridge, Tennessee, has developed programs that present subject matter in ways that help students develop higher-level cognitive skills. Lesson plans offer a variety of group and individual activities suitable for all ability and skill levels and provide opportunities for those who are ready to move to the analysis, synthesis, and evaluation domains of thinking. A matrix planning model is used to plan learning experiences for students.

The Creative and Academic Thinking Skills program at Hamilton Park Elementary School in Dallas, Texas, teaches thinking-process lessons to all students on a weekly or bi-weekly basis. All lessons contain follow-up thinking activities, and learning centers are placed in classrooms on a rotating basis. A varied curriculum provides practice in problem solving, creative thinking, research, divergent thinking, and logic. New teachers are trained to use higher-level thinking processes and strategies in the content areas by observing experienced teachers in the program.

6. These "excellent" schools tend to broaden and enrich the curriculum with special in-depth courses, field trips, and independent study options. Most of the schools reported a variety of programs designed for many types of learners.

Princeton (West Virginia) High School has added a science electives program to the curriculum, providing a variety of science-related experiences for all students, not just the college-bound. The science department recently

156

received a mini-grant for developing student knowledge and appreciation of the wildflowers of Mercer County. The grant was used to photograph flowers and produce color slides for use in biology, photography, and gifted classes and in various clubs. Among the elective offerings are: human physiology, genetics, consumer chemistry, environmental science, photography, geology, and household physics.

Southport Elementary School in Southport, Indiana, offers a smorgasbord of experiences to enrich the curriculum. In a study of Elizabethan England, students learned to play recorders, wore Elizabethan costumes, and produced a madrigal dinner. For a "Back Home Again in Indiana" experience, students dressed up and paraded as famous Hoosiers, listened to a pioneer, husked corn, square danced, learned about clog dancing, and built a cornstalk teepee for storytelling hours.

7. Rather than responding to the latest fads, these "excellent" schools engage in curriculum planning and evaluation on a systematic basis, which enables them to solve problems before they become matters of public policy. Many of the schools use future-oriented approaches to curriculum development based on problem-solving strategies and studies of future trends.

In Bloomfield Hills (Michigan) School District, each curriculum area undergoes a five-year rotation process of review and revision. Teachers and administrators examine each curriculum area in five stages, each accomplished over the course of a year: 1) review; 2) identification of needs, potential problems, objectives, and instructional materials; 3) field testing of new courses, objectives, and materials; 4) implementation with all subject area teachers; and 5) monitoring and review.

In Mullan, Idaho, students participate in a districtwide survey, which provides a research base to guide curriculum revision. Also, students participate in the implementation and ongoing evaluation of the curriculum.

8. These "excellent" schools have an overall curriculum design with carefully conceived goals and objectives and a planned sequence of experiences. In this regard, these schools are consistent with recommendations of the Excellence Movement; but their efforts to meet individual differences give the curriculum a much wider scope than envisioned in those recommendations. Involving staff, students, and community representatives in developing curriculum goals contributes to a shared sense of purpose or mission for the school.

Consolidated School in Kennebunkport, Maine, reports a broad-based curriculum involving sequential learning and individualization. The principal reports that they "avoid radical pendulum shifts" in the academic program.

At Hazen Union School in Hardwick, Vermont, each grade level is scheduled for math at the same time. With this form of scheduling, each math teacher can teach grades 7 through 12, and students can be grouped according to their ability or achievement levels. Beginning at grade seven, students enter the core math program, which could last from one to five years depending on rate of achievement. On successful completion of the core math program, students advance to algebra or other math application courses.

9. Some of these "excellent" schools create new curricular structures by integrating traditional disciplines. Several schools reported interdisciplinary approaches using broad fields of study or topical combinations of subject matter and skills.

At Topeka West High School in Topeka, Kansas, a one-semester interdisciplinary humanities course is offered for 10th-, 11th-, and 12th-grade students. The course uses team teaching and is designed around the Socratic concept of "know thyself" and the Kierkegaardian dictum of "choose thyself." The course uses a "post hole" method for examining the historical periods of greatest significance in Western civilization: the Periclean Era in Greece, the Italian Renaissance, the nineteenth century Industrial Revolution, and the twentieth century Global World. Instructional methods used include discovery learning and high-level analysis and synthesis rather than memorization.

At Centennial High School in Ellicott City, Maryland, a pilot humanities course combines world cultures, history, and literature. Student assignments involve reading, writing, speaking, and group discussion. Critical thinking is combined with creative activities to produce research papers, films, and original plays.

10. These "excellent" schools acknowledge that time on task is important but recognize that time alone will not ensure more student learning. Curriculum planners in these schools emphasize interesting instructional activities, while also making sure that students have ample "chunks" of concentrated time for in-depth learning.

Clemens Crossing Elementary School in Columbia, Maryland, reports that time on task is an essential component of its mathematics program, in which 99% of the students attain grade level. "However," they point out, "the program is not a rigid, lock-step one. It includes differentiated grouping, laboratory experiences, computer practice, and enrichment."

Several schools reported that they started out paying more attention to "time on task" but found they needed to pay more attention to the "nature of the task" as well.

11. Some of these "excellent" schools find ways to extend learning time for students without adding time to the school day or year.

Neely Elementary School in Gilbert, Arizona, runs a "summer academic maintenance program" by mailing students appropriately selected worksheets weekly during the summer. Worksheets are from an inventory of those used during the school year. The school staff also encloses communications and answer keys for parents. Parents provide the school with 10 self-addressed envelopes. The children enjoy getting personally addressed mail from the school and carry out their assignments under the supervision of their parents.

Air Academy High School in Colorado allows students (and their parents) to take physical education classes in the evening. In this way students can take an extra class during the regular school day.

12. Some of the "excellent" schools have created a "weighted" grading scale for students taking more difficult courses. The purpose is to discourage academically talented students from taking only easier courses in order to maintain their grade-point averages.

Geyer Middle School in Fort Wayne, Indiana, uses a separate grading scale for courses requiring higher academic standards. Mt. Lebanon High School near Pittsburgh, Pennsylvania, offers incentives to encourage students to take more challenging courses. Courses have designated levels called Advanced, Honors, Regular, and Modified. Students enrolled in courses at the various levels are assigned weighted points when graded.

13. These "excellent" schools maintain extensive extracurricular programs for students.

Elizabethtown (Pennsylvania) Area Middle School reports an extensive activity program involving clubs, tutoring, and special sign-up activities.

Port Chester (New York) High School has an outstanding music and drama program. The marching band has been invited to many national and international festivals. The drama program offers many students an opportunity to participate in the arts. The extracurricular program is extensive and ever-changing. Students even have established their own radio show on a local station.

"Excellent" School Practices Related to Teacher Status

1. Teachers in "excellent" schools work together in instruction, in planning curriculum, in solving school problems, and in improving school organization. These cooperative working relationships clearly set these schools apart from the average schools. A recent survey of American high schools showed that one in five used problem-solving processes for resolving school

issues (Cawelti and Adkisson 1986), but at least three in four of the "excellent" schools we studied use continuous problem-solving processes to identify problems and seek solutions. Furthermore, they involve their staff members more intensively than do most schools. The impression we get from our sample and from others (Phi Delta Kappa Commission on Discipline 1982; Wayson et al. forthcoming; Frymier et al. 1984; Corcoran and Wilson 1986) is that staff cohesiveness and continuing attention to problem solving are the most readily identifiable features of good schools.

The staff at Marsalis Elementary School in Dallas, Texas, works in grade-level teams to plan achievement goals for the year, to develop common lesson plans, to assess progress, to identify problem areas, to devise ways to reach difficult learners, and to develop ways for improving the school climate (see Chapter Nine).

The faculty at Dixon Junior High School in Provo, Utah, is involved in Quality Circles. The group identifies problems, collects information, establishes priorities, communicates to the administration and faculty, and assists in implementation.

2. Excellent schools initiate and often carry out their own high quality staff development programs geared to identified problems and program needs.

At Ganado Primary School in Ganado, Arizona, teachers participate in twice-monthly writing seminars, which have replaced traditional teachers' meetings. Teachers and administrators share responsibility for presentations. A classroom support network emphasizes collaboration through hands-on demonstrations and interclassroom visits by teachers. A professional library has been established.

At Brook Park Memorial School in Brook Park, Ohio, curriculum planning includes a staff development component that is integrated with the curriculum goals. Staff at Aurora (Ohio) High School participate in the Model High School Project associated with Kent State University, which involves summer staff development to plan for the "new basics." At Calloway High School in Jackson, Mississippi, the Action Plan for an Effective School emphasizes building-level staff development.

3. "Excellent" schools use teacher evaluation systems to help teachers improve their skills.

The Charlotte-Mecklenburg (North Carolina) School District has devised a nationally recognized process for staff evaluation and development (see Schlechty et al. 1984-85).

The Toledo (Ohio) Public School system has joined with the Toledo Federation of Teachers to develop a peer supervisory program that has the acceptance of both staff and administration (see Waters and Wyatt 1985).

At Moyer Elementary School in Fort Thomas, Kentucky, teachers and administrators have developed a formative evaluation of professional performance designed to increase awareness and use of the elements of effective teaching. Administrators have worked to increase their supervisory skills in the areas of student motivation, reinforcement and practice theory, good lesson design, and effective conferencing techniques.

4. Teachers in "excellent" schools tend to develop their own instructional materials rather than purchase commercial packages.

At Apache Junction Junior High School in Apache Junction, Arizona, two teachers have written the textbook used in the six-level math program. At Holderness Central School in Plymouth, New Hampshire, teachers use both contemporary books and classics instead of a basal textbook for their reading program. To develop skills, they have created vocabulary exercises, comprehension checks, and analysis/evaluation skill worksheets for each book.

The faculty of Woodrow Wilson Junior High School in Roanoke, Virginia, worked during the summer to develop a weekly Teacher Resource Book of suggested group activities. This faculty "think tank" meets weekly to update staff needs before weekly activities are undertaken. Topics in the resource book include: Study Skills, Great Expectations, Self-Knowledge, Drugs/Alcohol, College Information/Career Planning, and Decision-Making Skills.

"Excellent" School Practices Related to an Orderly School Climate

1. "Excellent" schools have programs that help students meet their individual needs.

"We Make the Difference" is the theme of the Home-Based Guidance/Sharing and Caring Program at Woodrow Wilson Junior High School in Roanoke, Virginia. The advisor/advisee program involves weekly meetings of 36 groups of 16 to 17 students. Each group selects its own advisor. In addition, students with special problems often meet in preventative group counseling sessions with the principal, assistant principal, and guidance counselors. Between 1983 and 1985, attendance in the school increased from 88% to 93%. The dropout rate decreased from 4% to 1.4%, and the failure rate decreased. School suspensions were reduced 90%.

Windsor-Forest High School in Savannah, Georgia, has a teacher advisement program for academic, personal/social, and career counseling. Each teacher-advisor, aided by a grade-level counselor, works with individual students to select a program of studies appropriate for the students' personal and career goals.

161

2. The staff in "excellent" schools create a positive climate that communicates to students that they are wanted and can succeed.

Kickapoo High School in Springfield, Missouri, reports that its positive climate is the result of high expectations and an unusual level of cooperation by faculty and students. An atmosphere of mutual respect dominates Kickapoo's halls. This climate was not created by some master plan but has evolved over a period of years through excellent staff leadership, a cooperative student body, and strong community support.

At Wooster Intermediate School in Stratford, Connecticut, the administration, faculty, students, and parents have worked to create a climate of high expectations for academic achievement, personal growth, open communications, mutual respect, and self-discipline. The school instills this standard of excellence in each year's incoming class in order to maintain a collective sense of pride in the school. To encourage this school climate, Wooster instituted an awards program that recognizes a student each month who best typifies the school's standards of excellence.

3. Staff in "excellent" schools create ways to involve students in the life of the school.

At North East Elementary School in Kearney, Nebraska, students work as teacher aides, thus giving teachers more time to work with individual students. Student aides do a variety of jobs, such as preparing bulletin boards, checking papers, and working with students who need extra help.

"Aguilar Pride — Wildcat Spirit" is the motto of Aguilar School in Tempe, Arizona. This school has an organized program to build and maintain school spirit. Staff members say that it promotes community/parent involvement, enhances student learning, and stimulates student attendance and achievement. The program was the 1983-84 recipient of the Arizona School Boards Association Golden Bell Award, the first K-6 program in Arizona to be so honored. Other school mottoes appearing on Aguilar's letterhead are "Striving for Excellence" and "Best in the West."

Assemblies on American Heritage are components of the program for excellence at Crest Hill Elementary School in Casper, Wyoming. Its motto is "Only the Rarest Kind of Best is Good Enough for Our Crest Hill Children."

At Pinedale Elementary School in Rapid City, South Dakota, student "partners" from Pinedale and a nearby junior high school serve as library and classroom assistants and provide other services to the school.

4. Some of these "excellent" schools provide career counseling services to help students make informed decisions about their programs in terms of future career directions.

Windsor-Forest High School in Savannah, Georgia, provides career exploration to students through a computer-assisted/needle-sort program called Georgia Career Information Systems. Data regarding each student's academic, personal/social, and career choices are kept in advisement folders with the teacher-advisor and in the guidance office. The school developed a book of advisement activities using information from the Georgia Career Information Systems and from other sources.

"Excellent" School Practices Related to Testing and Evaluating Students

1. "Excellent" schools closely examine their testing programs to ensure that they are testing what is being taught in the school. These schools want their curriculum to govern their testing program, not to have the curriculum be test-driven.

At Pooler Elementary School in Pooler, Georgia, the staff undertook a curriculum alignment study to ensure that the content tested was the content taught. At the outset of the study, specific curriculum goals and objectives were identified so that they would be clear to both staff and the community. The school provided inservice programs to help staff develop skills and materials for diagnostic teaching. Staff also learned how to select teaching materials, design instructional activities, and use effective grouping techniques. The rationale underlying the curriculum alignment study was the strong belief that all children can and will learn if the instructional environment meets their needs. After the new approaches were implemented, most students were achieving at grade level or above.

Staff in the SHAL program in St. Louis, Missouri, are taking steps to ensure that students are learning higher-level skills, not just test-taking skills (see Chapter Nine). They have succeeded in raising achievement above grade level for a majority of the students.

2. "Excellent" schools devise ways to diagnose student learning and to evaluate both individual student progress and instructional effectiveness on a continuing basis.

Mullan Junior/Senior High School in Mullan, Idaho, uses teacher-made tests as well as competency-based testing. Students participate in an ongoing evaluation of their own progress and of the program's effectiveness.

At Marsalis Elementary School in Dallas, Texas, the staff make frequent use of teacher-made tests to monitor student progress and to identify instructional areas that need more attention. Teachers can tell very early whether their instruction is working and whether particular students need extra help (see Chapter Nine).

At Apache Junction Junior High School in Apache Junction, Arizona, students are pre-tested in math and placed in an appropriate instructional level. Students must score 80% or above on a math test before moving on to the next level. Teachers have written their own textbook.

"Excellent" School Practices Related to Involvement of Parents and Community

1. "Excellent" schools establish volunteer programs, which extend resources for the curriculum and increase support for the schools. Staff in these schools enlist the support of parents and the community to supplement what the district provides and to provide what the district cannot or does not provide.

"Partnerships in Education" is the theme of the "excellence" program at Pinedale Elementary School in Rapid City, South Dakota. The partners include community people, students at Pinedale and a nearby junior high school, and the school staff. Dozens of parent partners serve as classroom, library, and computer aides. Parents also make mini-lab presentations, act as mentors to students, coach drama productions, and engage in a variety of fund-raising activities.

At Green Run Elementary School in Virginia Beach, Virginia, parents serve as tutors for students in grades two and three. Before beginning to tutor, parents attend a training session; additional inservice sessions are scheduled as needed. Using lesson plans prepared for individual students by the reading teacher and instructional aide, a parent works one-on-one with a child for 20 minutes once or twice weekly. Almost all students who participated in the tutoring program have met or exceeded grade-level standards.

Without parent volunteers, Linden School in Oak Ridge, Tennessee, would not have a computer lab program. The PTA purchased a computer for the school, and a parent volunteered to train the staff. Through school publications and personal contacts, parents were recruited to supervise computer-assisted instruction in grades 3-6. The computer lab now has 10 computers; and with the help of a dedicated group of parent volunteers, the program has expanded to serve grades K-6.

2. Personnel in "excellent" schools use a variety of ways to communicate to parents about the school's programs, and they provide parents with information about their children.

At Hudson Elementary School in Topeka, Kansas, the principal receives a monthly report on all students, and every month parents are sent a bar graph showing their child's progress. The updated report each month shows academic progress, attendance, and progress toward the district's goals.

At Sam Hughes Elementary School in Tuscon, Arizona, parents are in classrooms on a daily basis and thus know firsthand about the quality of the program in the school.

3. "Excellent" schools provide services to parents and the community, thereby becoming a vital part of the community.

Air Academy High School at the U.S. Air Force Academy in Colorado Springs, Colorado, offers an evening community lecture series open to parents and other community members.

Students at Plantation High School in Plantation, Florida, often volunteer at nursing homes and senior citizen centers. Community service is a major function of Plantation's student service clubs.

All school buildings in Morris Central School District in Morris, New York, are open to children and adults seven days a week, year round, for any and all activities. Students are allowed to use the facilities with minimum supervision.

"Excellent" School Practices Related to Creating Effective Schools

Some of these schools in our sample had adopted one of the well-publicized approaches to instructional improvement. For example, about one in six of the "excellent" schools and districts had formally adopted some form of the Effective Schools Model (see Edmonds 1979). These schools tended to be in larger cities, but some were in smaller cities and suburbs. Typically, these schools conducted workshops for administrators to make them aware of the principles of the Effective Schools Model and of the need for instructional leadership at the school building level. Where the workshop training was comprehensive and was used as a basis for genuine problem-solving at the local level, the outcomes seemed to be positive.

The Callaway Action Plan for an Effective School (CAPES) at Callaway High School in Jackson, Mississippi, is a three-year plan designed to implement the Effective Schools Model characteristics as outlined by Edmonds. CAPES emphasizes protecting instructional time from interruptions, building-level staff development, a schoolwide homework policy, recognition of outstanding student achievement, a discipline code, mastery learning techniques, and a basic skills standardized testing program to determine the "entry" and "exit" characteristics of students.

At Lakewood High School in Lakewood, Ohio, the staff undertook a major study to look at the concept of excellence and self-improvement. A steering committee of about 15 staff members makes recommendations concerning broad areas that have been studied, such as time on task, curriculum articulation, recognition of talented students, and administration. The steering committee provides leadership by suggesting activities that will improve areas identified as needing improvement, and it establishes procedures for evaluating these activities.

At Perkins Middle School in Akron, Ohio, teachers, administrators, and parents have agreed on school goals; and they are communicated daily. The staff believe that they can instruct all students and that all students can learn. Further, they believe that setting high performance expectations in both academic and extracurricular programs will counteract apathy and negative attitudes. The staff is consistent in enforcing rules. One measure of Perkins' success is that, in a student body that is 78% minority, the average daily attendance is 94% and teacher attendance is 98%.

In many cases the Effective Schools workshops attended by administrators were supplemented with training in the Madeline Hunter instruction model. Again, where administrators elicited staff support and followed with intensive staff development at the local level, the results seemed to be helpful.

At Sunset High School in Beaverton, Oregon, teachers have made a strong commitment to using the Madeline Hunter instruction model. This school implemented the model with the assistance of a highly qualified staff development specialist and department chairs who are skilled in clinical supervision. The staff development experiences have stimulated general interest in school improvement research as well as improvements in the science, physical education, and English curricula.

At Moyer Elementary School in Fort Thomas, Kentucky, administrators who worked with Madeline Hunter learned about such instructional components as motivation, reinforcement and practice theory, good lesson design, and effective conferencing techniques. Evaluators working with teachers say the teachers have become more aware of the contributions these components make to good teaching and to student learning.

The Effective Schools and Madeline Hunter models were frequently reported responses in our sample because:

- Many school districts had already worked with them before the reform reports were issued,
- They were well known and widely publicized in the education community,
- Their training programs were packaged and ready for dissemination at reasonable prices,
- They were based on principles that fit well with many of the recommendations for top-down dissemination and highly controlled accountability systems,
- They claimed to have research bases, and

166

- Prominent state and national political and educational figures advocated or endorsed them.

Identification of the Effective Schools Model as a response to the reform reports calling for excellence needs to be put in perspective. In the first place, the Effective Schools movement began long before the reform reports were issued. Its advocates claim that the genesis of the movement began shortly after the release of the Coleman Report in 1965, which concluded that schools were doing little to help children who came from homes that did not provide a supportive environment for education. This conclusion was commonly misinterpreted to mean that schools could do little or nothing to change what socioeconomic and home factors had determined. Some education researchers and practitioners resented this interpretation and set about to determine what some schools serving lower-socioeconomic students were doing to effect greater educational outcomes than would normally be expected. Of course, they found many schools in which students were achieving better than expected, especially in the basic skills areas where they were conscientiously trying to improve achievement. Those schools came to be called "effective" schools. And their characteristics, once identified, were heralded as the basis for effective schools everywhere (see MacKenzie 1983).

The Search for an Effective Schools Formula

In 1979 the late Ron Edmonds piloted school improvement programs in 10 schools in New York City. Drawing from other studies as well as his own, he attributed success in these schools to characteristics that he reduced to five basic principles (Clark and McCarthy 1983). Energetic, committed, and charismatic, Edmonds inspired school personnel, policy makers, and funding agencies to implement his ideas in a number of cities. He insisted that schools could teach poor children if they made the effort. His criterion for an effective school was that poor and minority children's scores on standardized achievement tests were in proportions equal to those attained by children from the dominant culture. He asserted that schools could meet that criterion if they had these characteristics:

1. A strong principal dedicated to improving achievement.
2. Teachers who set high expectations that no child will fall below minimum levels of achievement and who believe that children can learn what they are trying to teach.
3. An orderly environment in which teaching and learning can take place.
4. School policies that give acquisition of basic and higher-order academic skills precedence over all other activity.

5. The staff (usually the principal) monitors instruction and student progress, provides feedback to staff and students, and guides and directs efforts to correct any shortcomings that appear.

Edmonds' Effective Schools Model spread quite rapidly, primarily because it promised success where others saw little hope; it was expressed in five simple principles that seemed to make common sense; it was interpreted by some administrators and school boards as a way to educate black children without desegregating schools; and it was promoted by a charismatic and articulate educator whose credentials and demeanor inspired school personnel and posed little threat to school board members. Educators, particularly in large cities, embraced the principles of the Effective Schools Model as a way to improve test scores in schools serving children from educationally deprived home environments. The Effective Schools Model became a minor movement in education. A number of researchers, program developers, and entrepreneurs joined the movement, many to give technical assistance to school personnel as they attempted to implement the principles of the model.

Criticism of the Effective Schools Model

The Effective Schools movement has been criticized on several grounds. The criticisms are informative to those who are trying to create excellent schools, because they point out some of the pitfalls to be avoided when developing any good school.

1. The Effective Schools formula is too simplistic. Defining effective schools by a brief list of general characteristics obscures what it really takes to make a good school. Such reductionism often leads to slapdash attempts to install piecemeal and poorly understood "innovations" that help children very little and tend to undermine both staff and community commitment to make real improvements.

2. The research base of the Effective Schools Model is not as solid as is claimed. A common overstatement is, "Research now shows what needs to be done to create effective schools." In fact, the research is spotty and claims of success and miracle cures have not been substantiated. Experience does not always support the claim that there is a direct relationship between any one of the Effective Schools characteristics and improved achievement. What is supported from experience is that creating excellent schools results from complex interactions between people, places, and resources combined with commitment, caring, knowledge, energy – and some serendipity.

3. The Effective Schools movement has been overpromoted with the promise of quick results. Many entrepreneurs have climbed aboard the band-

wagon to sell services or products that promise to create effective schools overnight. Many school personnel with only the experience of a weekend workshop are raising the banner of Effective Schools without having worked through the complex processes and long-range planning that it takes to create excellent schools.

4. The Effective Schools program has been tried mostly in elementary schools in large city systems with a large number of disadvantaged students, where it has been considered as an appealing alternative to busing students in order to desegregate schools. No doubt the basic characteristics of the Effective Schools Model can be implemented more easily in elementary schools because their structure is less complex and because of the emphasis on basic skills at this level. However, many educators believe that the same characteristics would improve learning in secondary schools as well. In fact, some school districts have begun pilot programs in junior high or middle schools and high schools.

5. The educational outcomes of Effective Schools programs are too narrow. By focusing primarily on improving standardized achievement test scores, the curriculum is restricted and teachers' creativity and initiative are diminished. Instruction becomes inflexible; curriculum materials are unexciting. Sometimes the drive to improve achievement scores results in punitive practices with children.

6. The Effective Schools programs call for a controlling form of supervision. The Effective Schools characteristic of "a strong principal dedicated to improving achievement" can be interpreted by a naive or insensitive administrator to mean heavy-handed, top-down control over both teachers and students. Such an authoritarian view of supervision is contrary to a participative leadership role in which an administrator works cooperatively with staff to help them develop the commitment and gain the skills needed to help children improve achievement.

7. The Effective Schools program, with its stress on improving achievment test scores, could lead to manipulating test data to show quick results. Such pressure, when combined with competition among schools in a district to improve scores, creates conditions that encourage cheating in both subtle and blatant ways. The use of authoritarian controls to improve test scores can lead to practices that do little to benefit students. A rich and vital curriculum cannot be judged solely on the basis of achievement test scores.

8. In implementing the Effective Schools Model, some administrators confuse standards with expectations. Expectations come from the teacher's belief that every child can learn. If a child is not learning, then the teacher

diagnoses the reasons for failure and devises more effective instructional techniques to help the child learn. Standards, as commonly used in schools, impose the responsibility for achievement on students and punish them when they fail, even though they might not have had effective instruction.

Several of the "excellent" schools in our sample (see cases in Chapter Nine) were using variations of the Effective Schools Model. These schools had principals who clearly were effective instructional leaders. But when we interviewed them to learn what made their schools outstanding, we could discern some reasons for the criticism of the Effective Schools Model. The Effective Schools lingo they used to describe their school simply did not convey all the dynamics — even their own behavior — that had made their school successful. Their eagerness to use the "in" terminology of the Effective Schools movement to describe their school failed to capture what was really going on. If another principal were to attempt to implement the Effective Schools Model on the basis of such a cursory description, the consequences could be harmful. We saw such negative consequences in a number of cities where the Effective Schools Model had been mechanically implemented with little attention given to the personal and organizational dynamics that characterize truly effective schools:

> Our principal went to one of the School Improvement workshops and came back feeling that she had to "monitor" the program. Well, she monitors. We have to be on page so-and-so, and we are so tied up with recording and reporting results that we have no time to achieve anything. Most of us on this staff do the silly stuff and hope to get 20 minutes a day for good solid instruction that will keep the kids interested when we are not being monitored.
>
> — teacher, Midwestern city

> Some of that gang of so-called "supervisors" went into a classroom in our building. Most haven't taught more than a year or two, but they are disciples and true believers and they will do whatever they are told to do. They don't really understand, though, what they are doing. The program that the superintendent bought says that a good teacher will "refocus the lesson frequently"; so, one team of these fools marked a first-grade teacher down for not saying the word "focus" frequently enough. Now the union is circulating a list of words to say when a team is in your room. The kids aren't getting anything out of that, and most of us in the building are thinking of early retirement. It just is no fun teaching anymore.
>
> — teacher, Southern city

Such misinterpretations of the Effective Schools Model are too common, and misapplications of the model can be disastrous for students and staff members as well as for the program itself.

Some Closer Looks at Effective Schools

Other researchers and program developers have formulated variations or expanded versions of Edmonds' five characteristics of effective schools (see *Educational Leadership*, December 1982, entire issue; also Stedman 1985, and Murphy 1985). For example, the Ohio Department of Education uses seven characteristics of effective schools to guide pilot projects based on the Effective Schools Model:

- Sense of mission;
- Strong building leadership;
- High expectations for all students and staff;
- Frequent monitoring of student progress;
- A positive, orderly learning climate;
- Sufficient opportunity for learning; and
- Parent/community involvement (Ohio Department of Education 1981).

Despite Effective Schools advocates' claims, research findings on the effect of these characteristics are insufficient to explain why some schools are more productive or effective than others. For example, the characteristic that seems to support a tightly structured, hierarchical system of curriculum and instructional control over teachers and students is often associated with poor achievement rather than with success (Astuto and Clark 1985). Stedman's (1985) review of the literature found Edmonds' five characteristics too simplistic to explain what makes a school truly effective.

All of the researchers contend that no set of characteristics guarantees effectiveness. However, one does not find effective schools that do not exhibit many of the characteristics listed in the model. For that reason alone, they are worthy of emulating. The effective schools characteristics listed below owe much to Murphy (1985), with additions from Stedman (1985), McCormack-Larkin and Kritek (1982), and our own interviews and observations:

I. Curriculum and Instruction Factors

A. Opportunity to learn
1. More time spent on academic subjects.
2. Students actively engaged in the subject matter.
3. Class time protected from interruptions.
4. Students work more and cover more content.
5. Planning and monitoring ensures fuller coverage of content.
6. Flexible teaching styles used.

7. Work ensures students a high rate of success.
8. Personal attention to students through tutoring, extra helpers, smaller classes, fluid ability groups, or extra help after class.
9. Provisions for bilingual students.

B. Coordinated curriculum
1. Specific objectives, particularly in reading, math, and language.
2. Instruction linked to objectives.
3. Assessment linked to objectives and instruction.
4. All auxiliary services linked with classroom objectives, expectations, and practices.

C. Active teaching
1. Teacher active in instruction.
2. Teacher uses methods appropriate for learning objective.
3. Multiple opportunities for students to practice new skills.
4. Teacher monitors and provides feedback to students.
5. Teacher plans for more than one year's growth.
6. Capable teachers assigned to key instructional roles.

D. Clear academic mission and focus
1. Basic goal is to improve achievement.
2. Mission is reaffirmed by actions.
3. Mission is framed in measurable terms.
4. Mission is established with timelines and target dates.
5. Mission is communicated in many ways to parents, students, and staff.

E. Instructional leadership (Principal's key role diminishes as staff gains skill.)
1. Principal believes students can learn.
2. Principal emphasizes instructional skills.
3. Principal leads staff in setting goals and monitors them.
4. Principal promotes improved instruction through staff development.
5. Principal structures school to reinforce academic mission and promotes staff planning and problem solving.
6. Principal has faith in staff's abilities.
7. Principal enlists staff leadership and participation in developing and implementing program.
8. Principal demonstrates sound judgment in selection and assignment of staff.

F. Structured staff development
1. Staff development is an integral part of school's mission.
2. Systematic plan exists to upgrade staff skills related to school objectives.
3. Principal and non-teaching staff participate in staff development.
4. Staff volunteers to participate in staff development.
5. Staff exchanges practical classroom techniques.
6. Staff is involved in planning and carrying out staff development.

G. Frequent monitoring of program
1. Tests and quizzes are taken seriously.
2. Test-taking skills are taught when needed.
3. Monitoring procedures are related to objectives and mission.
4. Achievement results are shared with parents, staff, and students.
5. Achievement results are used to adapt instruction.

II. School Climate Factors

A. High standards and expectations
1. Staff believes all students can learn.
2. Staff feels accountable for student learning.
3. Staff sets expectation for high quality work.
4. Staff enforces rigorous grading and promotion requirements.
5. Staff provides personal attention to individual students.

B. Safe and orderly environment
1. Fair rules of conduct are established and consistently enforced.
2. Rules and consequences for violating them are clearly communicated to parents, students, and staff.
3. Consequences for violating rules vary according to the seriousness of the violation.
4. Discipline atmosphere of the school is derived more from a cooperative school spirit than from rules or external controls.
5. Systematic plan exists for tracking student offenses.
6. All adults in school accept responsibility for conduct of all students.
7. Principal works to maintain school climate that fosters self-discipline.
8. Central office policy supports school's discipline efforts.

C. Widespread use of recognition and awards
1. Awards are an integral part of the school's mission.
2. Awards are given for many types of contribution.

3. Academic awards have a high priority.
4. Awards are presented with appropriate ceremony.
5. High percentage of students receive some kind of award.
6. Curriculum promotes racial and ethnic identity.

D. Student participation and responsibility
1. Many students are involved in many facets of school life, including governance and problem solving.
2. Students are taught skills of democratic participation.
3. School demonstrates respect for racial and ethnic diversity.

E. Home-school cooperation and support
1. School welcomes parents and invites them to participate.
2. Parents offer strong support for school's attendance, discipline, and homework policies.
3. School communicates regularly with parents about program, student progress, and student problems.
4. Parents are represented on policy-development and problem-solving committees or task forces.
5. Parents use effective political action techniques to gain support for the school.

F. Collaborative organization processes
1. Open communication exists within and across groups.
2. Shared decision making is practiced.
3. Staff engage in collegial planning and problem solving.

G. Staff and student cohesiveness
1. Sense of community prevails.
2. Problems and possible solutions are discussed openly.
3. School displays symbols (banners, posters, T-shirts, etc.) to build loyalty and unity.
4. Widespread participation builds commitment to school's mission.
5. Interaction between teachers and students fosters mutual respect and support.

The above list includes school characteristics similar to those reported by the Phi Delta Kappa Commission on Discipline (1982), and they support the contention that good schools are structured and operated in ways that foster participation and involvement from staff and students. Through involvement, staff, students, and parents develop a sense of ownership and commitment to the school's purposes. When these qualities exist in schools, student learning improves, good discipline prevails, staff morale is higher, and public confidence in the schools increases.

Although no formula exists for guaranteeing effective schools, we can state with assurance that truly excellent schools exhibit more of these characteristics than do other schools. Further, we feel strongly that no school will become excellent until it begins actively to cultivate these characteristics.

Characteristics of the Secretary of Education's Models for Excellence

We looked at the exemplary high schools selected in 1983 by the U.S. Secretary of Education to see if they differed in any way from the "excellent" schools we had identified in our sample or from the effective schools identified in other studies. We found no essential differences. The Secretary's criteria for excellence did not differ from what our respondents told us or from what has been said by others who have done intensive studies of effective schools over the past decade.

In 1985 Research for Better Schools conducted a study for the Secretary of Education to determine the common characteristics of the 571 schools that had been honored by the Department of Education between 1982 and 1985 (Corcoran and Wilson 1986). Their findings corroborate our own impressions: good schools reflect a broader mission than simply the transmission of academic subject matter. They have achieved excellence because their staff and students share common purposes; they work together in both formal and informal ways to accomplish those purposes. These schools are human, not mechanical, enterprises.

Some Observations About Excellence in Alternative Schools

The proportion of alternative schools among schools identified as being "excellent" is much greater than the proportion of these schools in the normal school distribution. Why is this so? It behooves school administrators and education policy makers to identify the factors that have enabled these schools to become such productive educational settings. They are likely to find that the staffs of these alternative schools operate in settings free from policy restrictions imposed on other schools, so they are able to create the kinds of learning environment we have identified in good schools. Also, these alternative schools generally have a voluntary constituency that is more likely to hold them accountable for achieving the purposes they advertise. In return, this constituency protects them from restrictive mandates that come from higher authority. Above all, these schools have a powerful sense of mission that causes them to exert unusual energy to live up to their reputation and to maintain the success that has given them so much personal satisfaction and community recognition.

Postscript

These "excellent" schools we have described are more like the ones that Goodlad, Sizer, and Boyer have depicted as excellent. They are not the tightly controlled, lock-step institutions that many spokespersons of the Excellence Movement seem to advocate. They have many of the same characteristics found in schools with good discipline, achieving students, high staff morale, and public confidence. Administrators who want to have excellent schools will have to work with their staffs, their students, and their communities to implement these characteristics. Simply responding to federal, state, or even district mandates will result in little excellence for any significant number of American students.

References

"A + Schools." *Instructor and Teacher* 95 (May 1986): 24-26.

"A + Schools." *Instructor and Teacher* 95 (March 1985): 26-28.

"A + Schools." *Instructor and Teacher* 95 (February 1986): 26-28.

"A + Schools." *Instructor and Teacher* 95 (September 1985): 22-23.

"A + Schools: Portraits of Schools that Work." *Instructor and Teacher* 94 (September 1984): 20-22.

"A + Schools." *Instructor and Teacher* 93 (April 1984): 20-22.

Aldrich, J. "Literacy: A Personal View of a Language Program." *Delta Kappa Gamma* 51 (Winter/Spring 1985): 15-18.

Anton, Roger, and Binkley, Mike. "Creating a Positive School Environment." *Thrust* 13 (April 1984): 27-30.

Astuto, Terry A., and Clark, David L. "Strength of Organizational Coupling in the Instructionally Effective School." *Urban Education* 19 (January 1985): 331-56.

Austin, Gilbert R. "Exemplary Schools and the Search for Effectiveness." *Educational Leadership* 37 (October 1979): 10-14.

Black, Steve, and Welsh, John J. "This 'Step System' of Discipline Helps Kids Improve Their Behavior." *American School Board Journal* 172 (1985): 43-44.

Brookover, Wilbur B. "Distortion and Overgeneralization Are No Substitutes for Sound Research." *Phi Delta Kappan* 69 (November 1987): 225-27.

Brookover, Wilbur B., and Lezotte, Lawrence W. *Changes in School Characteristics Coincident with Changes in Student Achievement.* East Lansing: Institute for Research on Teaching, Michigan University, 1979.

Butterfield, John. "Excellence Comes First." *Columbus Monthly* (May 1986): 13-19.

Calkins, Lucy M. *Lessons from a Child: On the Teaching and Learning of Writing.* Exeter, N.H.: Heinemann, 1983.

Cawelti, Gordon, and Adkisson, Janice. "ASCD Study Documents Changes Needed in High School Curriculum." *Curriculum Update* (August 1986): 1-10.

Clark, Terry A., and McCarthy, Dennis P. "School Improvement in New York City: The Evolution of a Project." *Educational Researcher* 12 (April 1983): 17-24.

Corcoran, Thomas B., and Wilson, Bruce L. *The Search for Successful Secondary Schools: The First Three Years of the Secondary School Recognition Program.* Philadelphia: Research for Better Schools, 1986.

Cuban, Larry. "Transforming the Frog into a Prince: Effective Schools Research, Policy, and Practice at the District Level." *Harvard Educational Review* 54 (1984): 129-51.

DeFord, Diane E. "Classrom Contexts for Literacy Learning." In *The Contexts of School-Based Literacy,* edited by Taffy E. Raphael. New York: Random House, 1984.

Donohue, John W. "One School's Secret." *America* 148 (2 April 1983): 254-58.

Douds, Barbara, and Savidge, David. "Turning the School Around: Getting the Most Out of Least." *NASSP Bulletin* 67 (February 1983): 118.

Edmonds, Ronald. "Effective Schools for the Urban Poor." *Educational Leadership* 37 (October 1979): 15-24.

Educational Leadership 40 (December 1982). Entire issue.

Farrar, Eleanor; Miles, Matthew B.; and Neufeld, Barbara. *Review of Effective Schools Programs: The Extent of Adoption of Effective Schools Program.* Vol. 2. Cambridge, Mass.: Huron Institute, 1983.

Fibkins, William L. "What Makes a Middle School Excellent?" *Principal* 64 (March 1985): 50-51.

Finn, Chester E., Jr. "Toward Strategic Independence: Nine Commandments for Enhancing School Effectiveness." *Phi Delta Kappan* 65 (April 1984): 518-24.

Fischer, Bill, ed. "America's Schools: A Panorama of Excellence." *Today's Education* (1984-85 Annual): 3-36.

Frymier, Jack; Cornbleth, Catherine; Bonmoyer, Robert; Gansneder, Bruce; Jeter, Jan; Klein, Frances; Schwab, Marian; and Alexander, William. *One Hundred Good Schools.* West Lafayette, Ind.: Kappa Delta Pi, 1984.

Gallup, Alec M. "The 18th Annual Gallup Poll of the Public's Attitudes Toward the Public Schools." *Phi Delta Kappan* 68 (September 1986): 43-59.

Graves, Donald. *Writing: Teachers and Students at Work.* Exeter, N.H.: Heinemann, 1983.

Gray, Peter, and Chanoff, David. "Democratic Schooling: What Happens to Young People Who Have Charge of Their Own Education?" *American Journal of Education* 94 (February 1986): 182-213.

Greenleaf, Warren T. "A 'Turnaround' Principal: Baltimore's Evelyn Beasley." *Principal* 63 (September 1983): 6-11.

Harrington, Theresa. "Annehurst School for Tomorrow." *Theory Into Practice* 13, no. 2 (1974): 71-74.

Hawkinson, Howard. "Hatch School: Not at Risk." *Phi Delta Kappan* 66 (November 1984): 181-82.

Krajewski, Robert J. "The Principal as Catalyst: An Interview with Troy Mills." *Theory Into Practice* 18 (February 1979): 21-27.

MacKenzie, Donald E. "Research on School Improvement: An Appraisal of Some Recent Trends." *Educational Researcher* 12 (April 1983): 5-16.

McCormack-Larkin, Maureen, and Kritek, William J. "Milwaukee's Project RISE." *Educational Leadership* 40 (December 1982): 16-21.

Murphy, Joseph F. "Effective Schools: What the Research Reveals." *APEX Case Report* 1 (February 1985). APEX Center, 1310 S. Sixth Street, Champaign, IL 61820.

Murphy, Joseph F., and Hallinger, P. "Effective High Schools: What Are the Common Characteristics?" *NASSP Bulletin* 69, no. 1 (1985): 18-22.

Phi Delta Kappa Commission on Discipline. *Handbook for Developing Schools with Good Discipline*. Bloomington, Ind.: Phi Delta Kappa, 1982.

Ravitch, Diane. "A Good School." *The American Scholar* 53 (1984): 481-93.

Raywid, Mary Ann, and Shaheen, J. "Diversity: Surviving and Thriving." *Early Years* 14, no. 2 (1983): 28-31.

Rowan, Brian; Bossert, Steven T.; and Dwyer, David C. "Research on Effective Schools: A Cautionary Note." *Educational Researcher* 12 (April 1983): 24-31.

Sarason, Seymour. *The Creation of Settings and the Future Societies*. San Francisco: Jossey-Bass, 1972.

Schlechty, Phillip C., et al. "The Charlotteville-Mecklenburg Teacher Career Development Program." *Educational Leadership* 42 (December-January 1984-85): 4-8.

Scott, Ralph, and Wahlberg, Herbert J. "Schools Alone Are Insufficient: A Response to Edmonds." *Educational Leadership* 37 (October 1979): 24-28.

Solorzano, Lucia. "High School '82: You Know You Have to Work Hard." *U.S. News and World Report*, 28 June 1982, p. 47.

Stedman, Lawrence C. "It's Time We Changed the Effective Schools Formula." *Phi Delta Kappan* 69 (November 1987): 215-24.

Stedman, Lawrence C. "A New Look at the Effective Schools Literature." *Urban Education* 20 (October 1985): 295-326.

Stoddard, Lynn. "The Great Brain Project." *Principal* 64 (March 1985): 48.

Thomas, Donald M., and Sorensen, LaVar. "South High School: An Effective Inner-City School." *NASSP Bulletin* 67 (November 1983): 36-39.

Waters, Cheryl M., and Wyatt, Terry L. "Toledo's Internship: The Teacher's Role in Excellence." *Phi Delta Kappan* 66 (January 1985): 365-67.

Wayson, William W., Achilles, Charles; Pinnell, Gay Su; Cunningham, Luvern; Carol, Lila; and Lintz, Nan. *Handbook for Developing Public Confidence in Education*. Bloomington, Ind.: Phi Delta Kappa Educational Foundation, forthcoming.

Wexler, Henrietta. "An Outstanding High School Breaks the Logjam of Mediocrity." *American Education* 20 (June 1984): 25-26.

Whittaker, Douglas, and Lutz, Jay P. "Excellence by the Book." *Principal* 65 (January 1986): 34-37.

CHAPTER NINE
A Closer Look at Excellence

You can only write so many national reports and pass so many acts by the legislature. Eventually you have to go back and ask what is happening in individual schools.

— Ernest Boyer

This study undertaken for Phi Delta Kappa enabled us to see how staffs in a number of schools attained outcomes that caused them to be identified as "excellent." Improved educational outcomes occur in individual schools as a result of actions taken by dedicated and competent staff members, often against great odds and sometimes without adequate support from state education agencies and local districts. Moreover, those who are most successful in achieving excellence in their schools sometimes arouse strong opposition from their fellow educators.

The outstanding schools we visited uniformly demonstrated energy and confidence. They revive one's faith in the power of public education. They demonstrate that what many believe to be impossible can be done. They violate many of the normal operating procedures we see in mediocre schools; and they belie the standard myths in the form of excuses that keep so many from performing well. In these schools both staff and students — and sometimes whole communities — are inspired to higher levels of personal commitment in the pursuit of common purposes.

179

Although these schools often seem to result from fortuitous confluence of good people, adequate resources, and a positive learning environment, they really did not come about by accident. The elements that make these schools excellent can be replicated; they are not secrets waiting to be discovered. Ordinary teachers and administrators are capable of developing the types of excellent schools we saw during our study.

The Excellence Movement and many of the federal and state policies it has spawned often seem oblivious to what it takes to attain educational outcomes we saw in good schools. The top-down, controlling, and exclusionary policies and practices that characterize some aspects of the Excellence Movement are not found in good schools. The good schools we saw are not laissez-faire operations, nor are they anarchies. They have order, but the control is neither authoritarian nor hierarchical; it comes from a commitment to purposes that transcend personal convenience or individual aggrandizement. These schools are communities that care for everyone's welfare, that enlist everyone's participation, and that display deep commitment and abiding loyalty. In these schools all participants are learners.

In this chapter we present four case studies of schools that, in our judgment, exemplify good education. They include: an elementary school where children are achieving well above expectations, a middle school that was turned around, an unusual high school serving unusual students in unusual ways, and a school-university inservice project in reading that challenges traditional approaches to remediate reading failure. We make no claim that these exemplary schools are perfect, but they do serve as models of what most could be and what many more must be if we are to achieve excellence in our public schools.

A Dandy in Dallas

Five years ago the achievement test scores at Marsalis Elementary School in Dallas, Texas, were among the lowest in the city. Today they are near the top and shooting for first place. By 1985, 95% of the students tested above the national average on the Iowa Test of Basic Skills and on the Texas Basic Skills. After a visit to the school, Francis Chase, former chairman of the University of Chicago Department of Education, noted:

> I spent last Friday at Marsalis Elementary School in South Dallas. After attending an enthusiastic teachers' meeting, which featured a pep talk by the principal, Sherwin Allen, I visited classrooms at all levels in order to form an impression about teacher and student morale and about the effectiveness of instruction. During the early morning hours,

Iowa Tests were being administered. Later, I observed instruction in language arts and mathematics in a sampling of classrooms at each level.

At the end of the day, I was in a sixth-grade classroom when Principal Allen announced over the loud speaker the preliminary results of test scores. The students listened with rapt attention and applauded enthusiastically as Allen reported that 90% to 100% of the students were scoring at or above grade level on both language usage and mathematics computation.

Of the many hundreds of schools I have visited, I have observed very few in which teacher and student morale appeared to be so high, or in which the expectation of high achievement for all was so apparent. In this school the enthusiasm usually reserved for athletics and other extracurricular activities was bestowed liberally on academic achievement. And all the students exhibited confidence in their own capabilities and in those of their fellow students.

Is there a secret to the Marsalis success? Not really. Perhaps the quality of the teachers and their teaching provides the best explanation for excellence at Marsalis. The staff has high morale, and for the best of reasons: teachers have done their job well and they know it. They readily admit that five years ago they did not think it could be done. When asked in a teachers' meeting what factors contributed to such a high level of productivity and satisfaction, a teacher stood up and said emphatically: "We won't let any teacher teach in this school who does not believe that these children can learn!" The teachers consider all children as their collective responsibility, and they cooperate to meet the academic expectations they have set.

Most members of the staff and some parents take their annual spring break together. They have gone to Las Vegas, New York City, Atlantic City, Lake Tahoe, and San Francisco. Planning these trips generates immense enthusiasm among the staff and, at the same time, develops cohesiveness and commitment to the school's philosophy and purpose.

Most students are just as enthusiastic and single-minded in their purpose as the teachers are. They resent intrusions into their instructional and learning time. They interact easily and respectfully with staff and with visitors. They welcome their homework assignments and seem determined to improve their performance with each new assignment.

The principal assigns teachers to grade-level teams to determine new goals for the year, to develop ways to reach the goals, and to diagnose learning problems of students who are not achieving. The teams also plan instructional strategies for their grade level. Planning sessions involve much teacher interaction; but once decisions are made, all team members are expected to comply with the instructional strategies agreed on, which include — but are not limited to — following the same lesson plans, doing the same class-work and homework, and taking the same tests.

Team members feel a responsibility to the whole team and all the children it serves. While we were visiting in one classroom, a teacher stuck her head in the door and said, "I have a free period and I'm working with any children who need help in math. Do you have anyone in here who needs help?" One child volunteered, and the regular teacher pointed out two others. The three quickly gathered up their math textbooks and notebooks and followed the voluntary tutor out the door. It was all too natural to have been staged for our benefit.

We asked whether a teacher on the team would feel threatened if the public discussion of achievement results showed that his or her class failed to meet the goal when all other members of the team surpassed it. A teacher with 15-years of experience in the building replied, "We would not see it as his or her failure but as the team's failure. No one needs to take the blame if we all missed the shot. We would all feel responsible and we would get busy to make it better the next time around."

Students are randomly assigned so that each classroom has an even distribution of children whose test scores were above and below national norms for the grade. Thus each teacher has roughly the same mix of students. This method of class assignment eliminates the usual excuses given for one teacher's classes achieving at higher levels than others. The staff operates on the premise that differences in achievement among classrooms are due to the teacher and the school, not students' mental abilities or home life. Because of the the similarity among classes, comparisons are fairer and more palatable to the staff, and there is a common incentive for improvement.

The PTA gives $100 for instructional materials to each teacher whose class reaches or exceeds the team's goal for the year. Each team that exceeds the goal gets another $100 for materials, which is divided equally among the teachers on the team. In 1985 the PTA spent $2,400 on this incentive program. The two classes that do the best get to take a trip. There is no jealousy; the teachers whose classes do not get to go are motivated to try harder next year.

The principal, Sherwin Allen, also has a "kitty," which is funded by one money-raising event. Principal Allen says, "I permit only one sale a year because I won't have the kids always out there selling things when they should be learning." The "kitty" is used to support teachers' proposals for school improvement. The staff feels that anyone who has a good idea should get financial support for trying it out.

182

Principal Allen is a young man who was employed from outside the system. Both staff and parents say the improvements in the school began with his arrival on the scene. He brought a strong sense of mission to the school, won respect and allegiance from the staff, insisted on improvement in student achievement, and organized the school so that problems could be solved and improvements could be planned and carried out. He attributes the success of the program to the staff's willingness to believe all students can learn and to do whatever needs to be done to get them to learn. Allen comments on his first year at Marsalis:

> Student achievement was low, staff morale was fading, and parents were hostile. I treaded water the first year because I had to gain the confidence of the parents, teachers, and students. We spent a lot of time formulating how we wanted our program to be structured. Through it all, I applied a simple philosophy: Kids do what teachers expect, just as teachers do what principals expect. Five years ago, we had very little direction, but today we have a highly structured program from the first day of school to the last. Now everybody knows what has to be done.

Principal Allen devotes much of his time to improving instruction; and achievement test scores do drive the process. He regularly plots the scores for every child in the school and for every classroom. His office walls are lined with charts of achievement scores, class by class, student by student, teacher by teacher, team by team. Those charts are used publicly to provide tangible evidence to stimulate progress, to identify needs, and to reward success. According to Allen:

> The profile charts on the wall are indicators of student, teacher, and team strengths and weaknesses in identified skill areas. The profiles come from ongoing in-house testing that we do for ourselves. These data help us with more effective planning and instructional delivery.

When one witnesses the natural rapport between teachers and students and among the staff, it is clear that something more is going on at Marsalis than simply raising the test scores to record on the principal's profile charts. This school exhibits all of the characteristics we found in schools with exemplary discipline and high levels of public confidence (Phi Delta Kappa Commission on Discipline 1982; Wayson et al. forthcoming). One sees here all the signs of humane educational programs as well as high achievement. Another indicator that real learning is occurring is that the students score higher on word-problem tests requiring mathematical reasoning than they do on straight computation, the reverse of what one sees in many American schools, particularly in those that spend considerable time on work-book drill exercises in a vain attempt to improve achievement scores.

When teachers were asked what made the turnaround at Marsalis possi-ble, their first response was, "We are free to do whatever we want." Al-though, obviously, such a response is not totally true, it is significant that it was the first response the teachers offered. It no doubt reflects the atti-tude of Principal Allen, who trusts his teachers to do the work he demands of them. They, in turn, trust him to support their efforts and to protect them from edicts emanating from the school board and central office. He finds resources for his teachers beyond what the district provides, and he rewards their efforts and successes. He expects commitment and competence, and most of the staff appreciate the results. Some few find the pace too demand-ing and a few may feel burned out, but the majority obviously are ener-gized and proud of what they have accomplished.

When Principal Allen describes why Marsalis has improved, his ideas sound similar to those advocated by proponents of the Effective Schools movement (see discussion in Chapter Eight). Certainly, Allen is a strong principal with a mission of improving achievement; he and his teachers close-ly monitor student progress; and the curriculum appears to be test-driven. But these Effective Schools characteristics do not explain the success of Marsalis in a way that another principal in another setting could implement them with the same success. These characteristics are not what Marsalis is all about. What Marsalis is all about is the far more subtle interaction of a principal and staff working together to ensure that every child learns. It is this element that needs to be examined when we try to understand what makes good schools work.*

A Sensation in St. Louis

Stowe Middle School in St. Louis is in the heart of an urban poverty area, where 90% to 95% of its students receive a free school lunch. The neigh-borhood is run-down and shows every sign of urban decay. The graffiti-covered school doors are locked and bear scars from past kicks and thrown stones. However, once inside, the visitor experiences an entirely different world. The halls are clean and well-lighted. Students pass through them in orderly fashion, but they smile and greet visitors with visible pride in themselves and their school. The principal is a seasoned administrator, who might be expected to display the cynicism that comes from years of frus-

---

*Sherwin Allen was transferred to another school in summer 1986.

trating work in an inner-city school. He admits that five years ago he did not believe that Stowe Middle School could change so dramatically.

Displays posted near the main office highlight the school's success in raising achievement test scores. All average scores are up over last year's scores. The percentage of eighth-grade students passing the Missouri Basic Essential Skills Test (BEST) in reading and language arts in 1986 was 97.6%, up from 72.5% in 1981. Just over 90% passed the math portion compared to 42% five years before, and the 15% who passed all three parts of the test in 1981 had risen to 87%. Grade equivalent scores on the California Achievement Test (CAT) for the eighth month of the eighth grade in 1986 were 10.0 in reading (up from 7.7 in 1981), 10.7 in language arts (up from 8.0 in 1981), and 9.2 in math (up from 8.0 in 1981).

While it may seem that the most important goal at Stowe is raising the average achievement to the national norm on the California Achievement Test, the morale and healthy rapport among students and teachers indicate that much more is being stressed than test scores. In 1986 the staff initiated steps to ensure that the students were not just raising test scores by becoming more "test wise" but by being genuinely better educated.

A group of visiting teachers, principals, and professors made the following comments about what they saw, and felt, in the school:

> The general philosophy was that they would not try to do anything about those things they could not change, but they would do everything possible to change those things the school could change. That meant that the school could not do anything about the child's home life or the community, but it could do something about his or her achievement and sense of personal worth. The motto for the school is: "Every child can and will learn." Both staff and students act as though they believe it.
>
> — visiting principal

> The first thing we noticed in the school was the enthusiasm of nearly all of the students as they sought to answer questions put to them by the teachers. The hands in the air made every room look like a group of skygrabbers. And they weren't just waving to fool anyone; they knew the answer when called upon or they made a good stab at it. No one seemed bored, none slept. Neither they nor the teachers were thrown off by having adult visitors in the room. Although they made us feel very welcome, they went on with the lessons as though we were not there.
>
> — visiting rural teacher

185

The quality of the work was apparent in every corner of the school. Posters were superior. Students' work on the bulletin boards was very good and did not come from only a select few.

— visiting high school teacher

The dioramas in the science room were remarkable. They were done with care and they reflected a lot of study. Each student was given three plastic dinosaurs, each from a different era, and they had to make a diorama that reflected what the terrain was like for each of the different types of dinosaurs. They learned a lot and they loved it. There was a lot of good-natured competition to see who could do the best one.

The coats of arms displayed in the art room showed the same meticulous care and the same kinds of concomitant learnings. Each student had to research heraldry, then had to choose emblems appropriate for the coat of arms he or she wished to have. Each wrote an explanation for the final product.

— visiting professor

Staff morale was exceptionally high. They were running their own staff development on the Friday evening and Saturday morning we were there. I've never worked with a staff that would work on Friday night without pay! In fact, I've never known teachers to run their own inservice program. They worked hard during the work sessions scheduled until 10:00 that Friday evening and from 8:30 till noon on Saturday. They played hard after the sessions. We were impressed that they had planned their own staff development, that they had volunteered to participate, and that they worked so hard.

—visiting teacher

The topics selected for the inservice showed that it is not a wasted enterprise with them; it was serious business carefully designed to solve some of the problems in instruction and to increase achievement. They were teaching themselves how to teach reading in the subject areas, how to use writing in the subject areas, and how to promote student team-learning. They bragged a lot about an earlier staff development activity in which they had taught themselves how to listen for a student answer after they have asked a question in class. They had discovered that they, like most teachers, did not wait long enough for answers from the students, particularly if the student was one of the slower learners. Since significant gains in average achievement scores depend on raising scores in the lower quartile, they concluded they needed to wait longer for answers from slower students, and these students would realize that they were expected to have answers.

— visiting teacher

186

Stowe Middle School was part of a program called Project SHAL, which also included three elementary schools (Hempstead, Arlington, and LaClede). The acronym SHAL was derived from the first letter of each school. Since these three elementary schools had made the same level of achievement gains we saw in Stowe, we asked the principals what they thought made the difference. One of them commented:

> It was a lot of things. Mostly Rufus [Area Superintendent Rufus Young] hammering at us that it could be done, I guess. He kept us going when we thought it couldn't be done. We had some workshops, but they really didn't turn us on a lot. I think the one significant thing was a workshop that showed us how to take criticism from teachers. I didn't like taking criticism, wasn't even sure that a principal should permit them to criticize. But I tried it. What happened seemed to be that when I took criticism from them, they would accept it from me.

The driving force behind Project SHAL was Area Superintendent Rufus Young, who set out to find ways to improve the schools under his jurisdiction, schools characterized by urban pathology typical in segregated, low-income areas found in most large American cities. Such characteristics include:

- A large percentage of students moving frequently from one school to another.
- Many teachers being transferred from school to school, resulting in instability in the instructional environment.
- Staff reductions resulting in loss of leaders who had previously directed staff development.
- Many students performing far below national averages.

One of the staff spoke about these problems and the frustrations they caused.

> Although the kids come from differing degrees of impoverished backgrounds, we believed they could achieve if properly motivated and taught. Some of the school staff were frustrated; although their efforts and output were great, the resulting student achievement was neither satisfactory nor up to standard. We knew it could be done if we could convince staff that change was needed and that success was possible. The majority was receptive, but, needless to say, there were skeptics.

Young had heard Ron Edmonds speak at a conference and was inspired to establish in Stowe and its feeder schools a pilot program organized around Edmond's Effective Schools Model. He enlisted staff and parents to help identify the problems in St. Louis schools and then began to plan a sys-

187

tematic program for improvement. Because no district resources were available, Young persuaded the Danforth Foundation to fund some staff development for the principals and staff in the schools. At later stages in the project, Young received small grants from the Parsons Blewett Memorial Fund and from the school district's desegregation funds.

As former Director of Personnel in the district, Young had contact with most of the building staffs and knew their capabilities. He enlisted the support of the principals in the three elementary schools and Stowe Middle School and invited them to participate in the project. The staff in the area superintendent's office also were strong supporters of the project. Because of their years of experience working in urban schools, they were able to provide competent leadership for many aspects of the project. However, they saw their primary role as serving the building principals and their staffs. They give full credit to the school staff for the success of the program.

Young was able to use both formal and informal channels to garner support for the project. In his official position as area superintendent, he had access to resources; but equally important were his informal relationships and personal allegiances developed over many years in the district, which allowed him to buffer the participating schools from bureaucratic entanglements.

In 1982-83 the project added 12 new schools, and in 1983-84 three more schools joined the project. By 1985 Young was promoted to assistant superintendent with the charge to extend the project throughout the city. Evaluation of the project indicates that, as more schools are added and as the leadership is spread thinner to cover more schools, achievement of the project's goals may not reach expected levels.

The original intervention was a three-year plan to accomplish two goals: 1) to increase the average student achievement level to the national norm, and 2) to develop a change model that could be replicated in other schools. The project has been continuously evaluated. Although the goals were not reached fully or equally in all of the original schools, remarkable progress has been made (Achilles and Young 1985). The evaluation indicates that the student achievement goals can be met, but achievement scores do not begin to show an increase until after about three years. The evaluation also indicates that, although the principal's role is key in the beginning, the teachers' role becomes more important after they have a better understanding of the project and become committed to its goals.

Further, the evaluation indicates that the processes developed in the change model can be replicated, or at least approximated, by other school personnel if they are: 1) committed to improving student achievement, 2) willing

188

to move beyond existing roles and practices, 3) able to adapt the model to the local school situation, 4) able to assemble a stable and effective mix of human resources and weld them into a cohesive team, and 5) able to protect their efforts from bureaucratic interference that may be well-intended but is disruptive to the project's goals.

A High School with High Expectations

High schools have been the primary focus of the Excellence Movement. Since they are the immediate providers of the labor force for many of the industries experiencing severe competition in the international marketplace, there is the implication that they are somehow responsible for the economic woes of the nation. Since they prepare students for college entrance, they have come under attack for failing to maintain academic standards. In truth, the American high school has been in an unresolved identity crisis for nearly three decades. Many of the reform reports have faulted high schools for being dreary, dull, and cheerless places.

Despite the prevailing negative image of the American high school, there are many that are exemplary. Lightfoot (1981) identified a number of them and recommended guidelines for duplicating their successes. The U.S. Department of Education has honored several hundred exemplary high schools in the past few years (see discussion in Chapter Eight). International comparisons indicate that the top graduates of U.S. high schools compare favorably with the top high school students in other developed countries of the world. Let us look at one such exemplary high school.

The North Carolina School of Science and Mathematics is an exciting and innovative approach to public secondary education. It is by no means a typical high school, but some of the elements of this publicly supported residential school could serve as a model for educators who are committed to excellence in secondary education.

This school for gifted students in science and mathematics was established by the North Carolina legislature in 1978 at the behest of then Governor James Hunt. The principles guiding the operation of the school were initially formulated by legislation and then refined by the faculty recruited to develop the program. The principles are:

- The student body should be representative of all the state's population.
- The curriculum will emphasize math and science but also will provide a broad general education.
- Teachers are encouraged to be experimental.
- Comprehensive learning will be provided both in the classroom and outside.

- Students must have a total commitment to learning; no automobiles and no off-campus living is allowed.
- The school will teach responsibility by requiring community service in the school and outside.
- The school will share its resources with other schools in the state.
- Efforts will be made to accommodate individual student needs as long as doing so violates no policy.

The school opened in 1980 with 150 juniors selected from across the state. The first graduating class in 1982 earned 38 National Merit Certificates, 9 National Achievement Certificates for Outstanding Negro Students, and 20 National Merit Letters of Commendation. Graduates were offered more than $325,000 in scholarships. In 1986 three students were among the five winners from a five-state region in a competition for designing experiments for the space shuttle. An indication of the breadth of its educational program is that its students won national essay contests, Presidential Scholar awards, art design competitions, and state moot court trials. Given the select population the school serves, it is not surprising that its students receive so many honors. They would probably do so even if they were not in residence 24 hours a day, seven days a week. However, more central to our interests were the elements of the school's program and climate that could be replicated in more typical high schools.

Students of both sexes are selected primarily on the basis of "curiosity, initiative, and character and a track record for productivity and performance." They come from all socioeconomic levels and from rural and urban communities. About 25% are from minority groups. Although they are the intellectual elite, any feelings of superiority are tempered when they are with others who have similar or greater ability. Some students reported that they had been treated like "freaks" in their home schools but felt more comfortable now with peers who were similarly academically oriented.

The school offers a rigorous set of courses and other learning experiences in science and math, but the goal is to develop well-rounded students. The school also offers equally rigorous study in foreign languages, literature, social sciences, art, and music, as well as a program in sports and physical education. To graduate, students must complete 4 years in science and math, 4 in English, 2 in social science, 2 or 3 in a foreign language, 1½ in physical education, and 3½ in electives. Many students also take internships in businesses and industries in a nearby research and development complex.

Students are required to work eight hours a week in the residence halls where they live and must participate in some type of community service.

190

The following comments from students and faculty provide a flavor of what these kinds of experiences contribute to their education:

> I work in a nursing home for the elderly. It has helped me very much; I now know that I can contribute. I feel I am doing important work, and I have gained a lot of respect for older people. I've learned a lot. It is a valuable part of the program.
>
> — student

> The work in the cafeteria has taught me a lot about people: they complain until they have to solve the problem. I appreciate more what people have to do to make a living. I don't like the work, but I can see that it has to be done, and I feel like a part of the action this way. At home, my parents did everything, and I had no idea what went into it.
>
> — student

> These students have to work eight hours a week in this residential school. It is hard to feel superior when you have to carry garbage or clean toilets.
>
> — faculty member

The staff is a carefully selected and talented group of individuals, whose greatest problem is overcoming their personal need for autonomy in order to work in collegial relationships. They have worked together to build the school's program from the ground up. The school's mission also includes helping other schools in the state to upgrade their science and math programs. Although that mission is not so clearly developed or operational as is its own academic program, the school secured funds from the Ford Foundation in 1985 to begin a Mathematics Council, which provides workshops and instructional improvement activities for mathematics teachers in its region. In 1986 IBM funded 16 faculty and students to develop new ways of using microcomputers.

The school has aggressively solicited outside funding and enjoys much support from both North Carolina and national corporations. Contributions in 1986 totaled more than $500,000 to fund the general program, more than $125,000 to promote teaching excellence, and additional funds to establish a photography laboratory. Parents contributed almost $90,000 in 1985-86 to fund the recreational, cultural, and athletic activities at the school.

The North Carolina School of Science and Mathematics is atypical because of its highly selective faculty and student body, its outside financial support from business and industry, and its opportunities to work with corporations and other community institutions. Yet, the school shares a dilemma that faces most American high schools: How do you get a staff of diverse subject matter specialists to work together in the pursuit of common academic objectives such as developing competency in writing and higher-order thinking skills?

After visiting the school and examining its program, we learned that even though the legislature and the governor provided the financial support to establish this unique school, no top-down mandates can guarantee the creation of a school devoted to excellence. This can happen only when the administration and faculty work cooperatively to develop policies, procedures, and programs that are appropriate for adolescent learners. This did happen at the North Carolina School for Science and Mathematics, where both academic excellence and civic responsibility are nurtured. The staff of this school had the benefit of developing its programs without the restraints imposed by the bureaucratic and community forces found in most school systems. Nevertheless, its programs demonstrate what creative educators can do when they design both the formal and informal curriculum to create a vital learning community for what is admittedly a highly selective group of adolescents. What this school accomplishes or fails to accomplish should provide valuable lessons for any school striving toward excellence.

A School-University Project in Reading Success

The Ohio Reading Recovery Project is a collaborative effort of the Ohio Department of Education, Ohio State University, and school districts in Ohio that elect to participate. The project, imported to the United States from New Zealand where it has had remarkable success, is an early intervention effort to reduce reading failure by providing young children with daily individual lessons in reading and writing. According to research in New Zealand, after an average of 12 to 14 weeks of intervention, first-grade non-readers learned to read; and they continued to read at grade level with regular classroom instruction with no further remediation. Three years later, those children retained their gains and continued to progress with their peers (Clay 1979, 1982).

Clay's research shows that young children who fail to learn to read are those who develop poor reading strategies at the very beginning. The longer they use those strategies, the harder remediation becomes. In effect, poor readers practice failure, which affects all future learning that relies on reading. This cycle of failure usually results in loss of confidence and poor self-esteem. Reading Recovery calls for intervention before poor reading strategies are established and the cycle of failure begins. Through individual instruction, the child learns the system of reading operations that all good readers use. The reading operations can be taught regardless of the child's socioeconomic or language group and they "work" with almost any basal series or other choice of materials (Clay 1982).

The Columbus Public School District was the first district to pilot this intensive program for the lowest readers in first grade. Its success led the Ohio legislature to fund a statewide pilot program in 1985-86. More than 100 districts participated, with most of them using their Chapter I program personnel to staff the project. The state considers the program a legitimate Chapter I intervention. Many districts also have invested general budget funds in the program.

The results of the pilot Reading Recovery project during its first three years in Ohio are promising, even impressive. Reading Recovery students, all of whom attend schools serving low-income areas, were substantially higher than a matched group in measures of reading and writing ability (Huck and Pinnell 1985; Pinnell et al. 1986; DeFord et al. 1987). Two-thirds of the previously failing students achieved average or above average levels in reading and writing after 12 to 15 weeks of instruction. Even three years after instruction, the Columbus children maintained their gains and continued to make good progress (Pinnell et al. 1986; DeFord et al. 1987). Teachers' stories about their pupils, who when selected were the lowest readers in their classes, convey the excitement that this program arouses:

> Lakisha managed 24 books — Lakisha, who we thought would never do anything! I don't know what's going to happen next because she comes in saying, "How many can I read today?" And I'll say, "Oh, how about seven?" And she picks out seven. She is correcting herself now and I can hardly believe it.
>
> — teacher, Columbus Public Schools

> Tim says, "It's so neat to be able to read." He said, "I like these books. You can pile them in my box." He said, "I like to flip through them and look at the pictures. I can read the name at the top. I know what the name of the book is." He says to me, "It's really neat to read, isn't it?"
>
> — teacher, Columbus Public Schools

> I think they have integrated their strategies and now they are just ready to move on. They need very little introduction — just time to look through a text and read it. They're independent, and I'm ready to release them.
>
> — teacher, Columbus Public Schools

Children of all types seem to benefit from the instruction. Teachers benefited as well. They reported that they gained confidence in themselves with their new skills in teaching reading. And they changed their attitudes about teaching reading to children who had a history of reading failure.

I always sensed that children approached reading in very individual ways, and I knew there were strategies they learned. But I don't know if I could have articulated these things before participating in this program. I'm not sure I could have said what kind of strategies I was looking at, what kind of cues I was expecting children to be able to use, or what I meant by independence or self-correction. My theory is better defined now.

— teacher, Columbus Public Schools

I no longer feel so vulnerable to the demands of the system, because I know how children learn and I can justify what I'm doing.

— teacher, Columbus Public Schools

When I started teaching, I followed the teacher's manual verbatim: no books in the children's hands until January — just letters and sounds. Now I put books in children's hands immediately, and they start writing immediately.

— teacher, Columbus Public Schools

Each child receives 30 minutes of daily instruction devoted to learning the strategies for making sense out of the written word. Each lesson includes the reading of many books and composing and writing a story. Writing helps the child understand how written language carries messages. During the writing, the teacher helps children hear the sounds in words they use and shows them how to monitor their own reading. Every day the child is introduced to a new book, which is expected to be read without help the next day.

The emphasis is always on what students *can do* rather than on what they have not yet learned. They work with what they know, experiencing success while "recovering" attitudes and skills needed for independent reading. The goal is to become an independent reader. A child is released from the program after becoming proficient enough to function in regular classroom work without extra help. Then the teacher works with another child who needs extra help. Three years later, almost all children released from the program have continued their progress (DeFord et al. 1987).

Teachers keep daily notes on how the child reads and writes. This running record shows the level of books read, reading accuracy and types of errors made, words the child can write, and writing behavior. This information helps teachers to understand the reading and writing behavior of each child in great detail, and they use this information to guide future instruction.

The key to the Reading Recovery approach is not materials (any age-appropriate materials can be used) or even its procedures. Rather, the key is the teacher who understands the reading process, knows how children learn, and knows each child in great detail. This level of professional expertise requires a year of intensive staff development during which teachers conduct reading lessons with children and observe other teachers doing the same kind of instruction.

> Reading Recovery does not have a pre-packaged program. There are procedures for teaching parts of the lesson, but what goes into those parts is tailor-made for the individual child. Sometimes people ask how they can buy the "package" for Reading Recovery. The answer is that there is no package. It's in the teacher's head and in the decisions the teacher makes. It's the inservice education needed to make this approach work that the school system has to buy.
> — Director of Reading, Columbus Public Schools

Those who are trained in the Reading Recovery approach are all experienced teachers. They meet weekly to learn diagnosis and intervention strategies, to discuss their children's progress, and to observe each other teaching. They take turns conducting a lesson with a child while their colleagues observe from behind a one-way glass partition. While the teaching is in progress, the teacher observers describe and analyze the child's reading and the teacher's responses. Observers discuss what they see occurring and consider possible alternative strategies the teacher might have used. After the lesson, the observers discuss what they saw with the demonstrating teacher.

> It's scary when you first do it. You think you have to do everything perfect. Then, you know everybody has to do it, and we're all in this together. The main thing is to help each other observe the child and find the best way to help him.
> — teacher, Marion Public Schools

> We've developed a strong support group. We can talk about anything we feel like; we can criticize each other constructively without bad feelings. That is an incredible thing! When I watch my staff now and hear them respond to each other and how defensive they are about their techniques, I realize how far we've come in the project.
> — teacher, Columbus Public Schools

This teaching of a reading lesson in front of one's peers and getting immediate feedback forces teachers to think about reading processes and their own instructional practices. The process they go through amounts to a group coaching session. As a result, they become much more competent teachers and often end up knowing more about teaching reading than most reading specialists, who often are wedded to a particular basal series or a pet theory of reading instruction.

> In Reading Recovery, teachers gained a new level of skill. They gained a new confidence in their own instructional decisions. One teacher told me, "I now know I really can teach any child to read. I never would have thought Mary would learn to read. If you can help kids like her learn to read, you can teach them all."
>
> — teacher, Columbus Public Schools

> Teachers learned to observe children; they learned to make instructional decisions; they learned about the reading process; they learned about young children and how they learn to read and write. I think that there were benefits that carried over into other areas of their classroom teaching. They incorporated more writing into the curriculum. One teacher said, "I've got two groups of children who are writing — the top group and the Reading Recovery children. I think I better get the middle group writing."
>
> — teacher, Columbus Public Schools

The changes required to implement a program like Reading Recovery put demands on the individuals involved. The program requires them to redefine their teaching roles. And it requires adaptations in the organizational structure of the school system. Initially, many of the experienced teachers who volunteered to participate were skeptical of the program. They had seen many programs come and go. Even after experiencing success, they were not confident that "the system" could accommodate Reading Recovery.

> I don't know where I'll be at the end of the year or what effect all this is going to have on my teaching in general. I guess this sort of thing makes me feel uneasy because I feel myself changing more than I would have. It's sort of like going through a divorce.
>
> — teacher, Columbus Public Schools

> Well, I was very depressed last week. Here we are learning these different approaches to teaching reading and next year the school system is going to say, "Well, that was enough of Reading Recovery. It was a nice experiment. Now you guys go back to doing what you were doing."
>
> — teacher, Columbus Public Schools

> I'm afraid the powers that be don't realize what it entails. It's not something you do half-heartedly, and it's not something you can put into a system overnight. I never have worked so hard in my life in 25 years of teaching. I wish I had 25 more years.
>
> — teacher, Columbus Public Schools

Teachers are justified in being apprehensive. Reading Recovery, like other excellent programs, challenges belief systems and organizational structures that have been in place for many years. For example, the procedures and materials are different from traditional remedial reading programs; the length of an individual child's program may vary; the program prohibits "blaming" the child or family for failure and requires the school to accept responsibility for teaching all children to read. These differences and many others can create uneasiness and controversy, which thwarts innovation (see Chapter Two).

Despite the apprehensions, the benefits of the Reading Recovery program to children and to teachers justify the changes demanded. As Mary Fried, Coordinator of Reading Recovery for Columbus Public Schools, says:

> The child who cannot read will have low self-esteem and will continue to have academic difficulties in all areas of school. We've tried retention; we've tried traditional remediation and support. We've had improvement, but we've never had the success of children catching up. Reading Recovery gives that failing child the second chance that he needs. Part of the reason it is effective is that it comes early enough so children can sort out the confusion before practicing it the wrong way for years.
>
> You can see the impact of this program by looking at Mary's performance. She was a child who was classified as low/normal by a standardized test and was not making progress even with good classroom instruction. She was destined to be in the low track and to fail in first grade, but with Reading Recovery she was able to reach average level. She was not a failure. She went on to second grade, where she still made good progress, and is going on to third grade.
>
> We had lots of interaction with parents because the children were making such noticeable gains. One little boy's mother decided she would move to Cleveland when spring break came, but because he got into Reading Recovery and started making some progress, his mother said, "I'm not going to move. I'm going to wait until the summer. And if he can be in Reading Recovery next year, I won't even go then." We have story after story like that.

Testimony from other school districts indicates that the Reading Recovery program has had a profound effect on groups of children who have been too often neglected or undereducated in many schools.

> There was an attitude change in the staff toward low-achieving children. This has always been a problem in our district; we just didn't think Appalachian or black kids could do it. They now became a challenge for the staff. They were ready for them; they wanted to really work with them.
>
> — principal, Columbus Public Schools

We were thrilled this year that 27 of the 35 children who had been designated LD's [learning disabled] when they came into the program learned to read well enough, after an average of 87 days, to test out of the LD classification and to perform at average or above levels in regular classes.

— staff member, Reading Recovery Project, Ohio State University

One unanticipated benefit from the program was that a Japanese child and five other non-English-speaking children from the Dublin, Ohio, School District not only made remarkable reading progress, but they also learned to speak, read, and write English in the short time they were in the program.

The Reading Recovery Project illustrates what can be accomplished when a state department, a university, and local school districts combine their resources to implement a program that allows teachers to learn and to apply a new set of skills so that every child can learn and succeed. One Ohio superintendent summed it up well:

This school system has a new understanding of what it takes to bring about change in learning. We are now looking at long-term inservice for our teachers. Our administrators are now very skeptical of the so-called "teacher proof" materials or "quick fix" programs. We realize that if you are going to make some changes that have an impact on learning, it takes some investment. It takes time. Reading Recovery has been the key that brought that about.

A Postscript to Excellence

From Dallas to St. Louis, from North Carolina to Columbus, Ohio, we witnessed administrators, teachers, and students working together in the pursuit of excellence. The basic lesson we learned from these excursions is that there is no one "best" way to to produce quality. In fact, we are uneasy about the overload of prescriptive practices that characterizes the Excellence Movement in general. Simply put, we should study the history of school reform in order to understand the dynamics of effective change before we invest time and resources in ill-considered reforms that exacerbate, rather than solve, persistent problems in our schools.

Whatever reforms are proposed by the federal government, state legislatures, colleges of education, or the central office, the inescapable fact is that their successful implementation depends on what happens in individual schools. Only as we understand the processes involved in releasing the talent and creativity of individual school staffs can we expect to achieve excellence in education.

198

References

Achilles, Charles M., and Young, Rufus, Jr. "Replication/Implementation Model Field Test: Project SHAL." Evaluation Report for the St. Louis Board of Education. Mimeographed. June 1985.

Astuto, Terry A., and Clark, David L. "Strength of Organizational Coupling in the Instructionally Effective School." *Urban Education* 19 (January 1985): 331-56.

Brieschke, Patricia A.; Crowson, Robert L.; and McPherson, R. Bruce. "Marjorie Stallings: A Walk Through a Mine Field." *Urban Education* 21 (April 1986): 62-85.

Clay, Marie M. *Observing Young Readers.* Auckland, New Zealand: Heinemann, 1982.

Clay, Marie M. *Reading: The Patterning of Complex Behavior.* Auckland, New Zealand: Heinemann, 1979.

Coleman, James S.; Hoffer, T.; and Kilgore, S. *High School Achievement.* New York: Basic Books, 1982.

Crim, Alonzo A. "A Community of Believers." *Daedalus* 110 (Fall 1981): 145-62.

DeFord, Diane E.; Pinnell, Gay Su; Lyons, Carol A.; and Young, Philip. *Follow-up Studies of the Reading Recovery Program.* Columbus: Ohio State University Department of Educational Theory and Practice, 1987.

Educational Research Service. "Polling the Principals." *Principal* 64 (March 1985): 54-63.

Educational Research Service. *Effective Schools: A Summary of Research.* Arlington, Va., 1983.

Frymier, Jack; Cornbleth, Catherine; Donmoyer, Robert; Gansneder, Bruce; Jeter, Jan; Klein, Frances; Schwab, Marian; and Alexander, William. *One Hundred Good Schools.* West Lafayette, Ind.: Kappa Delta Pi, 1984.

Huck, Charlotte S., and Pinnell, Gay Su. *The Ohio Reading Recovery Project: Pilot Study, 1984-85.* Columbus: Ohio State University Department of Educational Theory and Practice, 1985.

Justiz, Manuel J. "How Principals Can Produce Change." *Principal* 64 (March 1985): 38.

Lightfoot, Sarah. "Portraits of Exemplary Secondary Schools." *Daedalus* 110 (Fall 1981): 17-38, 59-80, 97-116.

Lodish, Richard. "A School Alive." *Principal* 64 (January 1985): 28-31.

McCurdy, Jack. *The Role of the Principal in Effective Schools: Problems and Solutions.* Sacramento, Calif.: American Association of School Administrators, 1984.

McKee, Patricia; Wilson, Bruce L.; and Corcoran, Thomas, B. "A Salute to Success: The Elementary School Recognition Program." *Principal* 66 (September 1986): 14-19.

National Commission on Excellence in Education. *The Excellence Report: Using It to Improve Your Schools.* Arlington, Va.: Communications Department, American Association of School Administrators, 1983.

Nolan, Fred, and Richardson, Marjorie. "Vistas Unlimited: A Success Story for Rural Principals." *Principal* 64 (March 1985): 34-36.

Phi Delta Kappa Commission on Discipline. *Handbook for Developing Schools with Good Discipline.* Bloomington, Ind.: Phi Delta Kappa, 1982.

Pinnell, Gay Su; Short, Kathy; Lyons, Carol A.; and Young, Philip. *The Reading Recovery Project in Columbus, Ohio: Vol. III, 1985-86.* Columbus: Ohio State University Department of Educational Theory and Practice, 1986.

Roueche, John E., and Baker, George A., III. *Profiling Excellence in America's Schools.* Sacramento, Calif.: American Association of School Administrators, 1983.

Sergiovanni, Thomas. "Rational, Bureaucratic, Collegial, and Political Views of the Principal's Role." *Theory Into Practice* 18 (February 1979): 12-19.

Walberg, Herbert J., and Shanahan, Timothy. "High School Effects on Individual Students." *Educational Researcher* 12 (August/September 1983): 4-9.

Wayson, William W.; Achilles, Charles; Pinnell, Gay Su; Cunningham, Luvern; Carol, Lila; and Lintz, Nan. *Handbook for Developing Public Confidence in Education.* Bloomington, Ind.: Phi Delta Kappa Educational Foundation, forthcoming.

Wilson, Bruce L., and Rossman, Gretchen B. "Collaborative Links with the Community: Lessons from Exemplary Secondary Schools." *Phi Delta Kappan* 67 (June 1986): 708-11.

CHAPTER TEN

Guidelines for Achieving True Excellence

There is one experiment which has never yet been tried. It is an experiment which, even before its inception, offers the highest authority for its ultimate success. Its formula is intelligible to all; and it is as legible as though written in starry letters on an azure sky . . . Education has never been brought to bear with one hundredth part of its potential force upon the natures of children, and through them, upon the character of men, and of the race.

— Horace Mann
12th Annual Report, 1848

Excellence is what American education is all about. Any educator is not worthy of the name when he or she gives up the pursuit of excellence for all students. Educators cannot default to any group the right to to define excellence — particularly any group that defines it in ways that exacerbate social-class tension and systematically deny opportunity to children from disadvantaged backgrounds. Our schools will never know excellence if the term becomes a political slogan for institutionalizing punitive and elitist practices.

Excellence cannot be attained by repeating the mistakes of the past. The Excellence Movement is foundering because it has failed to understand what it takes to achieve it. Business as usual is not enough. Excellence cannot be attained if educators ignore enduring public concerns about our schools.

201

Denying endemic problems will lead to epidemic problems. Attributes that characterize the *best* schools today must become the accepted standard for *most* schools tomorrow.

Attaining excellence is difficult within the current governance structure of public schools. Yet the existence of so many excellent schools in so many different settings proves that excellence is possible. The excellent schools are not models that can be duplicated and mass produced, but the factors that make them excellent provide useful guidelines for others striving for excellence. Even if they were models, something in the American grain causes us to reshape models into something uniquely our own. That, too, seems to be a part of excellence.

No formula exists to guarantee excellence; it is born of a persisting commitment to do well and to do well by others; it develops from a blend of inspired leadership, committed personnel, and adequate resources; it occurs as a result of initiative, perseverance, faith, and pluck. Excellent educators are confident of the past, undaunted by the present, and eager to shape the future.

A Warning About Striving for Perfection

Holding up excellent schools as models of perfection is fraught with dangers. We need a more realistic way to view effective schools and effective teachers. We usually take characteristics from schools and teachers judged as excellent and try to put them together into a composite model. Then we feel we have to copy every one of those characteristics as we try to create an effective school. As we try to create this composite model, let us remember that no school exhibits all of the characteristics of excellence. Each of the schools from which we create the composite has some faults, some unresolved dilemmas, and some less-than-desirable practices. Similarly, no teacher exhibits all the virtues gleaned from a study of many effective teachers; each has some shortcomings, some faults, or some less-than-desirable pedagogical practices.

What distinguishes good teachers from poor ones is that, on balance, their personal virtues and their professional competence far outweigh any shortcomings they might have. If a teacher leaves a lasting impression on students by bending rules when circumstances call for it or by stimulating students' curiosity and imagination enough in a history or literature class to displace their worries about Saturday's date or their bad complexion, then that teacher may be forgiven an occasional day of grumpiness or a sarcastic remark to the class clown. Similarly, a school may be in poor physical condition, but this can be overlooked as long as quality instruc-

tion is going on in the building. Our point is simply that the pursuit of per- ·
fection can hamper efforts to improve.

Characteristics of an Excellent School

Neither the nation nor its children are at risk in schools that are truly
excellent. We have seen schools that are exciting and productive places for
learning, where children are succeeding on many measures of achievement.
These schools, in our opinion, are models of what every child deserves
and what the nation needs to ensure its prosperity, to compete in the international marketplace, and to preserve its freedoms. The staff in the good
schools we have described in Chapters Eight and Nine reflect commitment,
professionalism, creativity, and energy.

The model is incomplete and cannot be die-cut to fit every situation. But
good schools exhibit some common characteristics that can guide people
who want to advance educational outcomes for students and for society:

- They are not rigid; they are flexible and relaxed.
- They are not punitive; they accentuate the positive.
- They are not elitist; they welcome and encourage all students.
- They do not have a narrow curriculum limited to the basics; they of-
  fer a varied curriculum that is flexible and adapted to students' needs.
- They are not test-driven; their students do achieve well because they
  teach higher-order thinking processes.
- They do not rely on packaged programs; they do rely on their staffs'
  commitment and creativity.
- They do not have authoritarian principals; rather, they have principals
  who have a vision of what the school should be and the determination
  to accomplish that mission.
- They recruit and keep staff members on the basis of merit and have
  procedures for removing those who do not contribute to the school's
  mission.
- They have intensive staff development.
- They know what they are trying to accomplish and have ways for assessing how well they are doing and for correcting any shortcomings
  they detect.
- They believe in themselves and their students and hold themselves
  responsible for instructing all children.
- They put student welfare above all other concerns.
- They have structures that foster decision making and problem solving by staff members as groups, not as individuals.

- They have a "cheerleader" who generates staff enthusiasm and participation and who solicits support from outsiders.
- They celebrate their successes and give recognition to staff and students for their achievements.
- They are loose (flexible) about means and tight (demanding) about ends.

Guidelines for Creating Excellent Schools

From our study of "excellent" schools, we have come up with 23 guidelines that we believe will lead to the creation of more effective schools. While following these guidelines cannot guarantee more effective schools, we feel confident that a school cannot be effective if any of these guidelines is ignored.

Guideline 1. At every level of policy making in the system, a vision of excellence must be communicated and accepted throughout the system.

Ideally, a policy of excellence should emanate from a set of coordinated decisions made at each level of the system to produce desirable outcomes among students. While policy decisions may be made at any level of the system, their implementation rests with teachers who work directly with learners. Therefore, policies that do not enlist and involve staff in individual buildings and teachers in individual classrooms likely will result in only cosmetic changes rather than real improvement. If policy decisions are to make a difference in student outcomes, there must be communication at all levels to clarify purposes, to enhance understanding, and to enlist commitment.

Guideline 2. Programs to foster excellence in education should focus on the individual school building.

The state, the school board, and the central office are too distant to have a direct impact on learning. Students learn in classrooms. It is there that policy decisions are translated into action. It is there that individual learning problems are diagnosed and remediated. Mandates from higher levels in the system have little likelihood of being implemented without the full involvment of staff at the building level.

Guideline 3. Given the political realities of American public school systems, it is essential that someone in line authority is a strong supporter of the programs to develop excellent schools.

An effective program needs both a committed individual (usually the principal, but not always) with a vision and enough lasting power to get something going and to keep it going and line authorities (usually administrators in some central office position) who are supportive of what is happening or who do not get in the way or do things to undermine it.

Truly excellent programs often are vulnerable in many districts. By accident or design, a superintendent or other central office personnel may withdraw resources or change staff, thereby undermining or destroying an effective program. Or the teachers' union may negotiate contract clauses that hinder a school staff's freedom to pursue excellence. Or special interest groups in the community may mount a campaign to abolish an effective program because they do not agree with its philosophy. In such instances, a program needs a friend in high places, someone who can run interference when a program is threatened.

Some excellent programs do exist without such protection and support, but they seldom continue for long. The wear and tear on the principal and staff to sustain the program eventually takes its toll. Many effective programs have been scuttled by transferring the principal or key staff members, by unfair evaluations, or by withholding resources.

Guideline 4. School system policies and practices on personnel, curriculum, and resource allocation must support programs at the building level if excellence is expected.

Every personnel function from recruitment and assignment through orientation, supervision, and staff development must support the goals agreed on for the program at a particular school. This does not mean that a staff must be so harmonious that no disagreement exists. To the contrary, no program can be excellent without constructive tension. But if disagreements are so irreconcilable that the program is compromised, then personnel changes will be necessary. Inappropriate staffing decisions probably do more harm to quality education than any other single administrative action.

Policies for allocating resources should ensure that each school staff has what it needs to accomplish the goals it has set for itself. While school staffs can — and often do — find or create their own resources, the central administration should be responsible for supplying most of the curriculum resources needed for the program.

Guideline 5. Policy decisions at the central office level may specify the ends or outcomes, but the means should be left to those closest to the students.

The central office may specify the outcomes expected in the program, but decisions about the instructional practices to achieve the outcomes should be left to the school building staff who are working with students. If the outcomes are not achieved, then the school staff should be responsible for devising more appropriate ways to achieve the outcomes. However, the building staff should be free to request training or technical assistance from the central office when it feels the need for outside help.

Policy makers and administrators usually get what they ask for. But if they insist on dictating the means in the form of specific methods and materials to be used, then the staff may come to feel that the requirements are fulfilled when those means have been used, whether or not the children have achieved the learning outcomes. If the desired outcomes do not occur, the staff is likely to blame the methods and materials that were mandated and the policy makers who mandated them and will not accept responsibility for producing better results.

Guideline 6. Any efforts to standardize practices must be examined carefully to determine their effect on program success.

While some degree of standardization is essential for efficiency, stability, and predictability, a school system can sacrifice productivity by slavish devotion to standardized practices. Up to a point, standardization seems an efficient way to get things done; but past that point it hampers creative teachers from achieving the desired outcomes in ways that are best for them and their students.

Guideline 7. Most schools already have the resources they need to produce excellence if they use communication and problem-solving processes that take advantage of those resources.

This broad assertion is not intended to mean that legislatures and school boards do not have responsibility for providing schools with adequate resources to carry out new mandates. However, personnel in good schools do not wait for others to act, nor are they deterred from solving their problems and improving their programs until some higher authority makes resources available. They use what they have or they use their contacts to get what they need.

Most school improvement programs require changes in attitude more than they require material resources. When a school staff feels the need to improve (an attitude change), it tends to find ways to do it. If they need resources from the central office, they try to persuade central office to supply them. If the the central office is not persuaded, they create their own resources, or they revamp their plans and use available resources. These staffs make do with what they have; they use existing personnel, space, and materials more creatively and more flexibly than other schools do; they draw more from outside sources than other schools do; they know how to get more from the system; and they stretch themselves further than staffs do in less effective schools. Their greatest resource is their own pooled intelligence; they work together productively, drawing on their own resourcefulness and creativity to solve problems and to develop effective programs.

Unfortunately, staff in good schools sometimes do more than any school system should ask its personnel to do. They burn themselves out. The pursuit of excellence need not require such extraordinary sacrifices, and this guideline is not intended to call for efforts beyond human endurance. What the guideline asserts is that good school staffs use what they have more efficiently and generate more resources from pooling their talents than other schools do.

Guideline 8. In good schools the staff, students, and parents share a vision of excellence; and they make that vision a reality in their everyday encounters.

The vision of excellence is attained when everyone is working toward a common purpose that is tangible enough to guide decisions, to motivate behavior, and to serve as the basis for evaluation. In good schools a sense of common purpose does not inhibit freedom and independent decision making. Rather, it provides a tangible benchmark against which to measure success and fosters a greater feeling of professionalism and autonomy than one finds in less effective schools.

Guideline 9. Almost without exception, excellent schools are led by principals with a vision of what an excellent school should be and with the ability to communicate that vision and to enlist the support of their staffs in carrying out that vision.

The principal is not the only person who makes a school excellent, and no principal can do it alone; however, the evidence is overwhelming that a strong principal's leadership is indispensable to school improvement and that under weak principals progress is all but impossible. School districts committed to excellence should appoint principals who are instructional leaders and should provide the support and training to prepare principal candidates for instructional leadership.

Guideline 10. The staff of a school engaged in the pursuit of excellence must believe that they and their students are capable of excellence.

Perhaps the most stringent of all the guidelines, this one calls for the best from the staff and the best from the students. One cannot elicit learning from a student who is presumed unable to profit from instruction. For too long we have accepted excuses for students' failure to learn, and these excuses have become self-fulfilling prophecies. Educators must communicate by word and deed that they believe all children can learn. Similarly, teachers must believe they can achieve outcomes with students that others have not achieved in the past.

Guideline 11. Evaluation criteria used for assessing programs must be directly related to the outcomes sought.

Unfortunately, too many evaluation systems in education are based on the dictum, "What is inspected is what is respected." To ensure that specific outcomes are "respected," they should be included in all evaluation criteria used in assessing a program.

Guideline 12. Some of what students learn in school can be measured by achievement tests, but such kinds of assessment are not enough to save them or the nation from risk.

Achievement testing of cognitive outcomes is a necessary but inadequate measure of educational purpose. Excessive and exclusive focus on achievement test scores as the measure of school outcomes ignores all the other qualities the school is trying to nurture, such as ethical behavior and responsible citizenship. Moreover, the cognitive outcomes measured by achievement tests cannot be achieved without attending to the attitudes and interests of students that motivate them to learn academic subject matter.

Raising test scores can give a school staff a goal to strive for. Improved scores can show a staff visible evidence of progress, and poor scores can stimulate a staff to revise instructional strategies in order to improve the scores. But achievement scores will not do any of those things unless the staff believes that all students can learn and accepts responsibility for doing whatever is necessary for ensuring that they do. In the absence of professional responsibility, test scores are likely to become instruments of pedagogical tyranny.

Guideline 13. Standards must not be confused with expectations.

The experience of excellent schools clearly demonstrates that holding high expectations for students produces good results. By setting high expectations, a staff disciplines itself to find ways to meet those expectations. If the expectations are realistic and the staff believes that students can learn, then the staff feels a professional obligation to find ways to meet the expectations.

Standards, on the other hand, impose discipline on the student. If the standards are not met, the student is blamed. Standards may seem to raise test scores by eliminating students from taking the test through retention, discouragement, or dropping out. Average test scores will rise, but children will not be learning more. Excellence is a mockery if failure is its most important product.

Guideline 14. If achievement scores or other measures of excellence are to improve, the lower quartile of students must be helped to achieve at higher levels.

Average achievement can be raised in two ways: 1) eliminate the less academically able students' test scores when computing the average or 2) raise the achievement level of the slower students. If no students are eliminated, the average cannot be raised much by concentrating on the top students; they already are achieving near the top of the scale. The greatest room for growth, of course, is among those students who are in the lowest quartile of the distribution. The average achievement rises when these students achieve at or near the old average. Enough schools have increased achievement among the lower quartile of students to prove that the goal is not foolhardy.

Guideline 15. The teacher must be given a central role in the planning and decision making involved in all facets of the school's operation.

We must hold teachers in greater respect than they are now accorded in most school systems. Even most negotiated teacher union contracts accord little respect to individual teachers, preferring to place the general welfare of the group above the welfare of the individual.

In good schools, teachers and other staff members make many more decisions about the operation of their schools than is customary in less effective schools. And they make them about facets of school life that are commonly thought to be outside their realm. They may design curriculum and select instructional materials; they may decide how to organize the schedule; they may decide about student placement; and they may have a strong voice in selecting new teachers. In some schools, they decide on the rules and their enforcement; in others, they design their own staff development; and in a few they participate in selecting their principals. Good schools confer respect by having faith in their teachers' professional competency, and their administrators know that sharing decision-making responsibilities builds allegiance to the school's program.

Guideline 16. School staffs must be organized in ways that facilitate problem solving and foster practices that result in excellence.

Good schools encourage collegial decision making. It is the nature of groups to generate more and better ideas than any one individual can. So, many of the good schools find ways to organize teachers and other staff members into teams; to find time for these teams to meet and interact about school problems, curriculum planning, or staff development; and to foster greater staff participation in making decisions about how to increase learning productivity. The amount and quality of staff participation increases as group-process skills mature.

Guideline 17. Staff in schools that pursue excellence must reject the excuses commonly given for why students fail to learn.

It may start with one individual or a small group, but eventually most of the staff reach a consensus that no excuses traditionally used to "explain" why students do not achieve will be accepted. No matter what the child's background, the socioeconomic level of the community, or the physical conditions of the school plant, these staffs expend extraordinary effort in finding ways to overcome obstacles to learning.

Guideline 18. Every school building that pursues excellence must become a teacher training institution.

Good schools do not assume that academic degrees guarantee competence. Schools of education provide the credentials to enter the teaching profession, but their products are unfinished. Good schools regard themselves as continuing education institutions, and everyone on the staff is viewed as a learner. Continuing training is seen as necessary for the entire staff because it is endeavoring to do what few staffs do and for which few have been trained. Everyone shares in decisions, and everyone is a learner. Beyond the demands of the broader roles that staffs of good schools play, they also see the need for continuing study in order to improve student learning.

Many schools have instituted such practices as lunch-time seminars where staff share the results of research on instruction and learning. In some of these good schools, the staffs conduct informal "studies" in their own classrooms and with their own students. Teachers in these schools often design their own staff development around problems they have identified. They use either the expertise of their own staff or they call in persons in whose expertise they have confidence. They are protective of their time and do not want it wasted on "dog-and-pony" shows or on topics not directly related to the problems they know exist in their classrooms or in their school. They often volunteer to participate in staff development outside the regular school day, and they expect results they can use. They are intolerant of "canned" solutions to instructional problems; they are more likely to come up with their own solutions.

The staffs in good schools are stimulated to search for better solutions because they get constructive feedback about their own performance from people they trust and whose expertise they respect. The feedback provided differs in purpose, tone, and outcome from traditional evaluation approaches.

Guideline 19. Staff who undertake new programs in the pursuit of excellence must be able to communicate to parents, other community

210

members, fellow teachers, and administrators about what they are doing and why they are doing it.

In a business-as-usual school, teachers do not need to explain or defend
what they are doing. They are doing what people expect teachers to do.
However, if the program is changed or if its purposes seem different from
what parents and others have come to expect, adults in the school system
and in the community may be confused, uneasy, or feel threatened and even
hostile about what is happening. The risks of being misunderstood or of
having one's motives challenged are too great to let them go unattended.
More programs fail because of misunderstanding or misinterpretation than
because of any intrinsic weaknesses in the programs. The way to avoid such
problems is to teach the skeptics just as carefully and as patiently as one
teaches children. However, there is a difference: the staff must have the
skills for dealing successfully with adults.

**Guideline 20. A staff that wants its program to continue must work
actively to build a constituency in the school, the school system, and
in the community.**

Good school programs are constantly at risk. They are fragile and can
easily be destroyed or regress to mediocrity. Their survival depends on political support when a threat arises, and that support cannot be built overnight or at the time of crisis. When a program is threatened, the best security
is a constituency who will defend the program and support it when others
are abandoning ship. Such a constituency includes people who understand
and can interpret the program and defend it when attacked. It also includes
those who benefit from the program. Time spent cultivating a constituency
among parents and others in the community is a wise investment.

**Guideline 21. Nearly all schools that achieve excellence have a "cheer-
leader" who conveys enthusiasm and commitment and enlists support
and participation from staff and others.**

Good schools have a person (often the principal, but sometimes another
staff member) who is best described as a "cheerleader." They have bound-
less energy that, when combined with a strong belief in what the school
is doing, enables them to enlist the support of other staff members. Some
of these "cheerleaders" spend much time on the phone at night enlisting
support, encouraging colleagues, and reminding others of tasks that have
to be done. Others exercise management skills, laying out schedules or organizational schemes to promote the school's purposes. Others use community contacts or political skills to secure resources for the school. Others
plan staff development, serve as trainers of others, hold both professional

and social meetings in their homes, or act as informal supervisors and confidants to improve instruction in their teams.

If the "cheerleader" is not the principal, he or she must have the principal's trust and at least tacit support. Without such support, the "cheerleader" is likely to become disenchanted and give up, leave, or start in-school revolutions. Astute principals realize how important it is to align themselves with staff members who have taken on the "cheerleader" role.

Guideline 22. Good schools are based on established norms, which require at least minimal levels of stability in the school.

Good schools cannot survive if there are constant changes in leadership, staff, and procedures. Such instability is exacerbated if the children in the school come from unstable homes and communities. Stability comes from the hundreds of norms or ways of doing things, which make people comfortable in the setting they are in. These norms are learned, of course; but in an unstable school they have to be learned over and over again, each time consuming time and energy that should be devoted to learning.

Guideline 23. Every effort must be made to reduce depersonalization of staff and students in schools, particularly for traditionally neglected students.

Depersonalization fosters alienation, and alienation undermines the will to achieve. Both staff and students need to feel accepted and valued if they are to contribute to efforts needed to achieve excellence in a school.

The Real Mandate for Excellence

The Excellence reformers' basic shortcoming is that they have substituted means for ends. Their purpose was not, we should hope, to have every graduate show 21 Carnegie units rather than 18 on a high school transcript; they surely wanted every graduate to have a broad knowledge in a range of subjects. Their goal was not that every student should have a certain score on a minimum competency test; certainly they wanted students to know much more than the minimum. They did not care whether teachers took a specified number of liberal arts courses; they wanted children to have broadly educated teachers. They did not care whether teachers took a competency exam; they wanted teachers who can spell, write clear sentences, and show proficiency in an academic area. Most educators would agree with these goals and would gladly join the reformers in efforts to achieve them. But when the reformers focus all their energy on the *means* for solving problems before clarifying and getting agreement on what the problems are, then the reform efforts are likely to fail and the problems will continue to fester.

Reformers are caught in a dilemma: unless they make specific recommendations for action, educators will say they have no solutions to offer. But any solution can be proven deficient (see Chapter Two). Nevertheless, reformers should invest more effort on demonstrating that a problem exists and getting agreement that a problem exists before devising political strategies to install predetermined solutions. Reformers must be good teachers; they must define, describe, and discuss all facets of a problem in order to persuade others to take action. But they must allow maximum flexibility to the appropriate jurisdictions to develop ways to solve problems and achieve desired goals.

The greatest shortcoming of the criticism embodied in the reform reports is that it is too sweeping to apply to a social institution as diverse as the public schools. Criticism from national commission reports tends to contaminate all schools and all educators; it generates public anxiety and provides fodder for those who oppose increased support for public education. Meanwhile, the real problems in education are obscured, and the reform movement is drowned in its own rhetoric. This has happened to the Excellence Movement. Its criticisms of American education do not apply to all school districts or to all teachers. As we have shown, there are enough good schools and good teachers to prove the criticisms unfounded.

Educators and reformers may not agree on every point about what good schools should be, but there are large areas of agreement in which they can find common cause. Focusing on these common areas would be politically advantageous for both parties. But educators must take the lead if they wish to maintain control over their professional prerogatives. Following are several points on which educators and reformers can agree:

- They want all children to achieve, but some children do fail.
- They do not want children to learn only low-level academic skills unrelated to life problems, but far too many children are learning only that.
- They do not want anyone to be functionally illiterate, but many citizens are functionally illiterate.
- They do not want teachers to be poorly educated, to write poorly, to be unable to articulate a rationale for the methods they use, or to be unable to engage in professional problem solving; but too many teachers fit these descriptions.
- They do not want America to fall behind other nations in productive capacity, but we have fallen behind in areas we formerly dominated and will continue to do so if we do not educate more of our children well.

On these points, and others, educators and reformers can agree. How foolish it is, then, for reformers to exaggerate problems to make it appear that all schools and educators are failing. And how foolish it is for educators to become overly defensive about criticism, when such defensiveness makes it appear that they are ignorant of social and economic conditions, do not care about failing students, or do not feel any responsibility for improving their own institutions. Understandably, educators become defensive when they feel criticism is unfair. Their usual response is to point out the many schools that are exceptions to the criticisms and to overpower the opposition by rallying the support of individuals in those schools to whom the criticism does not apply. But what these educators fail to acknowledge is that there are *some* schools and *some* teachers that are not measuring up to the professional standards that a community has a right to expect.

Where deficiencies exist, educators have a responsibility to correct them. When a child is not learning, when a student drops out, when a high school graduate is ill-prepared for life, when a teacher is inadequately prepared to handle individual differences in the classroom, or when societal changes dictate the need for change in the system, educators have a responsibility to take action to solve the problem.

While educators as a group must be responsible, individuals also must take responsibility, because achieving excellence ultimately depends on an individual's willingness to take action – often in the face of adversity and with little outside support. In our opinion, the central issue in education today is reaffirming the social contract that guarantees every child a comprehensive education, which will enable him or her to achieve personal fulfillment and to contribute to a productive and peaceful society. Any nation that is serious about excellence will give its children the best that it can. Any educator worthy of the title will see to it that every child learns. The window of opportunity is always open.

References

American Association of School Administrators. *Effective Teaching: Observations from Research.* Arlington, Va., 1986.
American Association of School Administrators. *Staff Development: Problems and Solutions.* Arlington, Va., 1986.
Andrew, Loyd D.; Parks, David J.; Nelson, Lynda A.; and the Phi Delta Kappa Commission on Teacher/Faculty Morale. *Administrator's Handbook for Improving Faculty Morale.* Bloomington, Ind.: Phi Delta Kappa, 1985.
Berliner, David C. "In Pursuit of the Expert Pedagogue." *Educational Researcher* 15, no. 7 (September 1986): 5-13.

Berman, Paul, and McLaughlin, Milbray. *Federal Programs Supporting Educational Change, Vol. III: Implementing and Sustaining Innovations.* Santa Monica, California: Rand Corporation, 1978.

Bogue, E. Grady. *The Enemies of Leadership: Lessons for Leaders in Education.* Bloomington, Ind.: Phi Delta Kappa Educational Foundation, 1985.

Corbett, H. Dickson, and D'Amico, Joseph J. "No More Heroes: Creating Systems to Support Change." *Educational Leadership* 44 (September 1986): 70-72.

Croghan, John H., and Lake, Dale G. *Competencies of Effective Principals and Strategies for Implementation.* Southeastern Regional Council for Educational Improvement Occasional Paper No. 410. Research Triangle Park, N.C., November 1984.

Joyce, Bruce R.; Hersh, Richard H.; and McKibbin, Michael. *The Structure of School Improvement.* New York: Longman, 1983.

Louis, Karen Seashore. "Reforming Secondary Schools: A Critique and an Agenda for Administrators." *Educational Leadership* 44 (September 1986): 33-37.

Mangieri, John N., ed. *Excellence in Education.* Fort Worth: Texas Christian University Press, 1985.

"The Mission to Ensure Equity and Excellence in the Minneapolis Public Schools." Adopted by the Minneapolis Board of Education, 8 June 1982.

Peters, T.J., and Waterman, R.H. *In Search of Excellence: Lessons from America's Best-Run Companies.* New York: Harper & Row, 1982.

Phi Delta Kappa Commission on Discipline. *Handbook for Developing Schools with Good Discipline.* Bloomington, Ind.: Phi Delta Kappa, 1982.

St. Louis Public Schools. "Project SHAL: An Effective School Implementation/Replication Model." Mimeographed. St. Louis Board of Education, undated.

Spady, William G., and Marx, Gary. *Excellence in Our Schools: Making It Happen.* Arlington, Va.: American Association of School Administrators, Far West Laboratory for Educational Research and Development, 1984.

Stephens, Gail M., and Herman, Jerry J. "Using the Instructional Audit for Policy and Program Improvement." *Educational Leadership* 42 (May 1985): 70-75.

Wayson, William W.; Achilles, Charles; Pinnell, Gay Su; Cunningham, Luvern; Carol, Lila; and Lintz, Nan. *Handbook for Developing Public Confidence in Education.* Bloomington, Ind.: Phi Delta Kappa Educational Foundation, forthcoming.